The Russian Far East in Transition

The Russian Far East in Transition

Opportunities for Regional Economic Cooperation

EDITED BY

Mark J. Valencia

Westview Press

BOULDER • SAN FRANCISCO • OXFORD

Copyright © 1995 by Westview Press, Inc., except for Chapter 7, which is copyright Booz Allen and Hamilton, Inc., and Appendix 1, which is copyright World Bank

Published in 1995 in the United States of America by Westview Press, Inc., 5500 Central Avenue, Boulder, Colorado 80301-2877, and in the United Kingdom by Westview Press, 12 Hid's Copse Road, Cumnor Hill, Oxford OX2 9JJ

Library of Congress Cataloging-in-Publication Data
The Russian Far East in transition : opportunities for regional economic
    cooperation / Mark J. Valencia, editor.
        p.   cm.
    Includes bibliographical references and index.
    ISBN 0-8133-8890-2
    1. Russian Far East (Russia)—Foreign economic relations.
    2. Russian Far East (Russia)—Commerce.   I. Valencia, Mark J.
    HF1558.2.Z5F377   1995
    337.57'7—dc20   95-822
                                                                                       CIP

Printed and bound in the United States of America

The paper used in this publication meets the requirements
(∞) of the American National Standard for Permanence of Paper
for Printed Library Materials Z39.48-1984.

10   9   8   7   6   5   4   3   2   1

This book is dedicated to Burnham (Burnie) Campbell (1926–1994). Burnie was a visionary for Northeast Asian cooperation in economic development, a mentor of many Northeast Asians, an intellectual inspiration—and a friend.

Contents

Acknowledgments

This book is based on a two-year joint project between the University of Hawaii's Center for Russia in Asia (CeRA) and the Program on International Economics and Politics (IEP) of the East-West Center. It was supported by a grant from the University of Hawaii/East-West Center Joint Research Fund. I wish to acknowledge the assistance of colleagues Patricia Polansky and Robert Valliant of CeRA in the organization and successful implementation of the project and its associated workshops. I also wish to recognize the support of Charles Morrison, Director, IEP. John Thomas edited the manuscript. He also guided it through the publication process from acceptance to production. Carolyn Eguchi provided valuable assistance in fiscal matters. Kelly Kanetani provided logistical support. The manuscript was word processed by Ann Takayesu in her usual highly efficient manner.

Mark J. Valencia
Honolulu

Contributors

Pamy J.S. Arora, Principal, Booz Allen & Hamilton, Inc., McLean, Virginia

Burnham O. Campbell, Consultant, Program on Population, East-West Center, Honolulu, Hawaii

James P. Dorian, Fellow, Program on Resources, East-West Center, Honolulu, Hawaii

David Fridley, Manager, Business Development, Caltex China, Ltd., Hong Kong

Douglas M. Johnston, Chair in Asia-Pacific Legal Relations, Centre for Asia-Pacific Initiatives, University of Victoria, Victoria, British Columbia

Won Bae Kim, Fellow, Program on Population, East-West Center, Honolulu, Hawaii

Robert B. Krueger, Lewis, D'Amato, Brisbois & Bisgaard, San Diego, California

Pavel A. Minakir, Director, Economic Research Institute, Far Eastern Branch, Russian Academy of Sciences, Khabarovsk

William T. Onorato, Principal Counsel, Energy and Mining, International Finance Corporation, The World Bank, Washington, D.C.

Leon A. Polott, Lewis, D'Amato, Brisbois & Bisgaard, San Diego, California

Kristin Tressler, Department of International Affairs, Columbia University, New York

Mark J. Valencia, Senior Fellow, Program on International Economics and Politics, East-West Center, Honolulu, Hawaii

Allen S. Whiting, Regents Professor and Director, Center for East Asian Studies, University of Arizona, Tucson

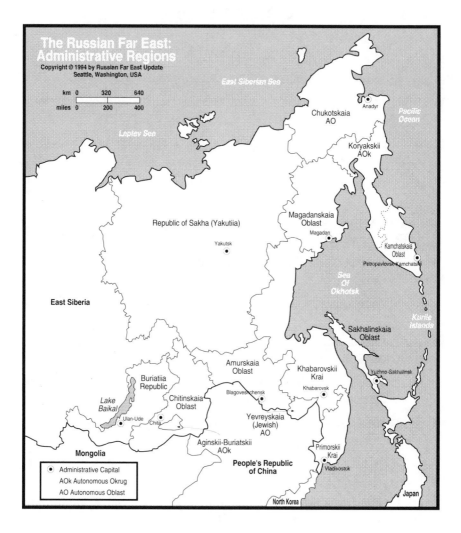

The Russian Far East: Administrative Regions

Copyright © 1994 by Russian Far East Update
Seattle, Washington, USA

| km | 0 | 320 | 640 |
| miles | 0 | 200 | 400 |

East Siberian Sea

Laptev Sea

Pacific Ocean

Anadyr

Chukotskaia AO

Koryakskii AOk

Republic of Sakha (Yakutiia)

Magadanskaia Oblast

Magadan

Yakutsk

Kamchatskaia Oblast

Petropavlovsk-Kamchatski

East Siberia

Sea Of Okhotsk

Kurile Islands

Sakhalinskaia Oblast

Amurskaia Oblast

Khabarovskii Krai

Yuzhno-Sakhalinsk

Buriatiia Republic

Blagoveshchensk

Khabarovsk

Lake Baikal

Chitinskaia Oblast

Yevreyskaia (Jewish) AO

Ulan-Ude

Chita

Aginskii-Buriatskii AOk

Primorskii Krai

Mongolia

People's Republic of China

Vladivostok

- ⊙ Administrative Capital
- AOk Autonomous Okrug
- AO Autonomous Oblast

North Korea

Japan

1

Introduction

Mark J. Valencia

This book examines the opportunities for multilateral economic cooperation between the Russian Far East (RFE) and Northeast Asia—Northeast China, Mongolia, North Korea, South Korea, Taiwan, and Japan. Such cooperation will depend on the general political and economic setting. During the Cold War, international relations there were heavily influenced by the Soviet–United States dynamic and thus were almost indistinguishable from the global system. But the future central dynamic of this system is likely to depend more on relations among the Northeast Asian countries themselves. In the past century these relations have been characterized by revolving patterns of amity and enmity, frequent tension between the strongest powers in the region, and resultant attempts to forge alliances with the lesser powers. Moreover, Northeast Asian countries have tended to operate on the basis of "worst case" scenarios: for the large powers, of being isolated by the other powers; for the lesser powers, of having the two strongest join in a hegemonic alliance. Conflict in this region has generally been along the weaker boundaries between the major powers—the Korean peninsula, Taiwan, Manchuria, Mongolia, and Sakhalin/the Kuriles—and the seas between them were a dangerous frontier.

Indeed, of the major geographical regions of the world, the North Pacific (Northeast Asia and Northwest North America) is striking for the virtual absence of institutionalized regional cooperative arrangements in the Cold War period, reflecting the strong political tensions in a region that includes divided states and competing large powers. In the Gorbachev era, the divisions among the larger powers were considerably ameliorated: increasing elements of cooperation characterized U.S.–Soviet relations; Sino–Soviet relations were normalized; Soviet–South Korean relations were established; and Soviet-Japanese relations improved after Gorbachev's April 1991 visit to Tokyo, despite the continuation of the territorial dispute over the "northern territories." Although relations among the two Korean parties remain the most difficult problem within the re-

1

gion, high-level talks have been initiated, and both nations have joined the United Nations.

Indeed, we are now witnessing a transformation of the political system in the region. Most Northeast Asian governments are more motivated toward maximizing wealth than controlling territory, and their increasing economic interdependence makes outright conflict too costly. With the development of political multipolarity and the abandonment of Stalinist economic models, economic relationships have begun to develop a more "natural" pattern. These economic relations have tended to concentrate in boundary areas where adjacent regions have obvious economic complementarities—"natural economic territories" (NETs)[1]—for example, southern China, the Yellow Sea Rim, the Tumen River area, and the Sea of Japan Rim.

The trans-Pacific economic axis, so prominent in the Cold War era, is being gradually modified by more multidirectional intra-Asian relationships. This multidirectional pattern implies a more diversified set of cooperative and conflictual economic relations in much of the North Pacific, creating a need for rules, codes of conduct, and harmonization of domestic practices that affect international economic relations—that is, regional institutions. Indeed, economic interaction across ideological and political boundaries is already creating a "soft" regionalism in Northeast Asia— regionalism that lacks organizational structure but is accepted and even encouraged by governments. Notwithstanding these efforts, the region remains characterized by lackluster cooperation and insufficient mechanisms to facilitate trade, technology transfers, or bilateral investment. Cross-border economic exchange and the emergence of NETs raise questions of jurisdiction and control and impinge on national sovereignty. Nationalism is being rekindled and is competing with internationalism and regionalism in the formulation and implementation of national policies. Indeed, the interplay between localism, nationalism, and internationalism is likely to be a major theme of political relations between the Russian Far East and Northeast Asia for several decades to come.

Whither the Russian Far East

The Russian Far East is clearly at a political and economic crossroads. Its alternative political and economic futures run the gamut from colonial subjugation by the "center" or Asian neighbors, to virtual anarchy, to full independence, all with varying degrees of economic intertwining with Northeast Asian states.

If Russia maintains its integrity as a nation, and if the past is any indication of the future, national security concerns and dependence on the region's mineral and energy resource wealth will dictate the maintenance of some central political control. Strong central political and economic control could mean a return to the pattern of the past in which the RFE is treated virtually as a colony of the European portion of the country.

However, reemergence of authoritarian central control does not necessarily rule out economic openness. The RFE could yet come to be viewed by Moscow as its "window on Asia" rather than as a bulwark against it. In this scenario, an NET would emerge: RFE resources could be developed by Chinese and North Korean labor, with capital, technology, and management expertise provided by Japan, South Korea, and perhaps the United States. But would this lead to economic colonialism by Russia's neighbors, or to a more equal partnership?

A few years ago, the focus of most discussions of the RFE was Russia's military role in Northeast Asia. Today, the central question is whether Russia, despite its considerable remaining military forces, is so politically weak that its huge Far Eastern territory and resources may present themselves as opportunities for competitive exploitation by powerful Asian neighbors. In the pessimistic scenario, raw materials would be extracted by *foreign* labor, employed by *foreign*-owned and -managed companies, and exported for processing outside the RFE. Profits would accrue to the investor, and revenues to the central government. The natural resources—minerals, gas and oil, fish, timber, scenic beauty—would be exhausted (probably sooner rather than later), and the region would be left with no economic base, a polluted and despoiled landscape, a significant immigrant Asian population, and little in the way of revenues, upgraded technology, or management knowledge.

In a more optimistic scenario, that of equal partners, the central government and local leaders would insist on the RFE being an equal partner in its transformation to a modern industrial state. Resources would be extracted, to be sure, but with the best available technology, stringent environmental controls, and the full participation of the local populace at all levels. Processing would be undertaken locally, adding value to the product prior to export. Requirements for technology transfer, training, and involvement of locals in management would be mandatory. Land would be leased, not owned, and labor would be imported under temporary permits and strictly controlled.

Another possibility that must be considered is the total disintegration of Russia and full political and economic independence for the RFE. Although this is a dream of some intellectuals in the region, it is a nightmare for Moscow and other countries' defense planners. It is a nightmare because the Russian Pacific fleet, with its nuclear weapons, would make the RFE an instant nuclear power—another Ukraine. But the likely result for the RFE would be a domino-like effect of autonomy for each of the provinces, and anarchy for the region as a whole. Certainly, if the foreign currency reserves were to be based on the gold and diamond output mainly from the northeast of the region, issues of indigenous peoples' rights and equitable distribution of revenues would arise. Further, separate exchange rate regulations, trade barriers, and custom levies for this region are difficult to imagine. In addition, given the remote entry points, massive black marketeering and bribery would be expected. Demagogues could come to the fore, and the provinces could wind up competing and even conflicting in an unseemly scramble for foreign investment. There might be little cooperation or coordination between the provinces on such vital matters as defense, transportation, and communication systems, or on policies on foreign investment. Thus this collection of autonomous provinces could be economically and politically defenseless against potential predators and dependent on the rest of Russia or Asia for most of their consumer products.

Another possibility is eventual, partial integration of the RFE economy with its neighbors, perhaps initially with China. China has a surplus of labor, which could be used to develop Russian resources. Chinese entrepreneurship and management could be combined with Russian science and high technology to forge joint ventures that would manufacture competitive products from Russian resources for the enormous Chinese market. China has much *light* industrial production and has a demand for *heavy* industrial production, which could come from converted Russian military industries. One specific example might be the harnessing of the Amur River to produce hydroelectric power for northeast China and the RFE.

Perhaps the best possible future for the RFE is increased political and economic autonomy within the Russian nation. In the ideal, the center would protect the region from political or economic domination by neighbors, but at the same time it would refrain from such domination itself. The region's economic development would then be oriented toward creating strong and deep economic ties with the nations of the Asia-Pacific region, not only in terms of commodity trade but also in the exchange of technologies and capital. The basis for a new financial system could be a Far Eastern Bank for Economic Development backed by the natural resources of the region, including reserves of minerals, particularly gold, as well as forestry and fishery resources and all furs.

But several factors stand in the way of economic independence for the RFE, at least as a unified whole. First, the region consists of ten separate political entities, and the institution necessary to coordinate autonomous regional economic development is not yet sufficiently robust to be effective. Second, the region depends on the central government for energy, and without foreign investment and aid, the RFE cannot develop energy self-sufficiency. Third, there is still a severe labor shortage in the region, and to use foreign labor as a stable and effective impetus to economic growth in the region, the immigration and labor market rules would have to be changed—everywhere in Russia. Fourth, agricultural production is insufficient to sustain even the eight million already there, and infrastructure is poor and sparse. Fifth, despite the momentous changes in the region, the RFE is still extremely important in terms of Russian security, and the influence of the Ministry of Defense will make it difficult for the region to convert to a fully open economy and society. Sixth, in lieu of foreign investment, the RFE must continue to depend on the center for the modernization and development of its extractive sector and for implementation of the enormous but necessary infrastructural investment. This would be a tall order even for a healthy national economy, let alone one that is bankrupt. And, last but not least, if a special development fund were established to finance infrastructural investments, other regions and republics would immediately demand the same.

The pessimistic view holds that, even if the RFE acquires much greater political and economic control over its destiny, it may have to lower its expectations. The RFE is peripheral to the booming Pacific economy today and may have to accept an economically peripheral role. Still, freedom from central control and open cross-border and barter trade will most likely result in small-scale, localized development that may marginally improve the lot of the population. And, in the long run, its undeveloped state, wide-open spaces, and still largely pristine environment may become its greatest assets.

Opportunities for Multilateral Cooperation with the RFE

It is a great irony that the crisis in Russia has created opportunities for multilateral cooperation in Asia. With the dramatic developments in the Soviet Union in August 1991, and the devolution of Russian power from the center to the provinces, the Soviet—now Russian—Far East has already become more autonomous in its domestic political and economic policies and in its relations with Northeast Asia. The changed international and Russian domestic political climate also makes possible the creation of new technically oriented regional institutions.

Although Russia and its eastern extension are not presently major political or economic factors in Asia, they may be—indeed, some predict they will be—in the not too distant future. If RFE autonomy increases, it will become a player in its own right. Although in the short term the future of the RFE is seemingly of less interest to its Asian neighbors than to others, it does have significant longer-term implications for North Pacific security and economic relations. Since the Asian political environment is largely benign but indifferent to the RFE, the task is to identify the potential benefits of regional economic cooperation. Accordingly, our objective in this book is to assess the current situation with a view to delineating and illuminating the sectors that present opportunities for multilateral cooperation and the issues that can be expected to surface.

The RFE could gain from regional cooperation that fosters greater international specialization, creates opportunities that generate demand for improvements in the physical, policy, and legal infrastructure, and gives sometimes needed rationalizations for difficult political changes. The RFE could also gain from regional cooperation that allows inputs to be combined more cheaply by accessing them throughout the region, that opens up economies of scale, and that provides opportunities to develop products and technology prior to entering world markets. The obstacles to economic cooperation between the RFE and the region are several: differences in the stage of economic reform between the countries; the undeveloped legal, social, and economic environment in Russia, including a lack of common standards; problems of regions versus the center; financial instability; policy and price distortions; minimal infrastructure; and needed structural adjustments. In Chapter 2, Burnham Campbell provides the regional economic context, delineates and analyzes the prospects for regional economic cooperation, and reviews the interests of Asian neighbors in each of these options.

Unfortunately, the economy of the RFE is in a state of crisis. GDP decreased 30 percent since 1991 because of withdrawal of subsidies, noncompetitiveness, reduced investment, and disintegration of the economic system. The basic ingredients of a market economy lacking in the RFE include entrepreneurship, the role and use of convertible currency, private ownership of land, and a labor market. Rays of hope include a beginning reorientation of the economy and some investment in transport infrastructure. Needed is a model of development for the RFE which accommodates an open mixed economy and attracts foreign capital. In Chapter 3, Pavel Minakir assesses the current political and economic malaise in Russia and the RFE, the reasons for it, its possible effects on RFE–North Pacific cooperation, and ways and means for stabilization. Because Dr. Minakir was deputy governor of Khabarovsk Krai and responsible for economic planning, his analysis indicates the level of understanding of market economics in the RFE and thus the difficulties of making the transition from a command economy to a market economy.

The RFE is a frontier region of vast expanses and few people. Ultimate control of such frontier regions in Northeast Asia in the past has generally been determined by population movement. Japan, for example, consolidated its control of Hokkaido, and China its claims to Manchuria, by the movement of Japanese and Chinese peoples into these regions. Russia has been wary of concentrations of such immigrants from neighboring countries, removing ethnic Koreans to central Asia and expelling Japanese from Sakhalin and the southern Kurile Islands.

However, development of the RFE will involve major demographic changes and bring enormous social change, with its attendant stresses. The RFE is labor-short. Industrial projects will require more labor and may eventually result in immigration—from the rest of the former Soviet Union, and perhaps from adjacent China and North Korea—at least on a contract basis. This will increase demands for improved housing, social welfare programs, health care, and education in a region where social infrastructure is already considered woefully inadequate. Ethnic tension, already evident in recent incidents between Russians and North Korean laborers, may increase. Moreover, indigenous groups are beginning to organize and may press claims for their share of the resources or the benefits to be derived from them. In Chapter 4, the first of this volume's sectoral analyses, Won Bae Kim analyzes the potential problems of labor migration and provides the rationale for a regional labor market.

The RFE has traditionally been considered one of the country's major sources of minerals. It is a leading producer of mercury, tin, tungsten, nickel, gold, and platinum. It has large reserves of nonferrous, rare, and noble metals and diamonds; substantial deposits of coal, iron, copper, lead, and cobalt have also been identified. Major deposits of coal are known, and a Japanese–Soviet joint venture for the development of Sakhalin's continental shelf oil and gas has existed since 1976.

The potential for regional resource development fascinates Japan and South Korea because their indigenous resources are so limited. U.S. firms are also interested in these resources. Political constraints have, however, stood in the way, and there remains much uncertainty about future Russian economic policy. Moreover, Russia regards the export of unprocessed minerals as undesirable for the long-term development of its Far East because it wants to upgrade its processing technology and capture the value processing will add. But this will require major foreign investment. James Dorian, David Fridley, and Kristin Tressler give an overview of Northeast Asia's mineral and petroleum potential in Chapter 5, review the region's past and present cooperative energy and mineral projects, and assess the remaining challenges to regional resource development.

As a specific case, Allen Whiting in Chapter 6 describes his vision of a natural gas pipeline from Yakutia through China, North Korea, and South Korea to Japan—perhaps under the auspices of a Northeast Asia Energy Consortium. He provides the rationale for the project as well as the formidable obstacles to be overcome.

Inadequate transportation systems are widely regarded as the major infrastructural obstacle to development of the RFE, both internally and in conjunction with neighboring regions. Domestic and international political factors have impeded efficient regional networks. RFE transportation infrastructure presently has adequate "new" capacity, but poor operating practices and bottlenecks in the landside systems significantly reduce the effective capacity. Higher costs and unreliable customer service are barriers to growth of the trans-Siberian landbridge. Improvements are required in operating and in management systems and practices, as are new investments in specialized cargo terminals, telecommunications systems, and traffic management systems. The air transportation system must be rehabilitated and modernized. Writing from the perspective of the private sector, Pamy Arora in Chapter 7 highlights the deficiencies of the transportation infrastructure in the RFE, and pinpoints the ways it can be upgraded to provide a sufficient basis for economic cooperation and development.

RFE fisheries are in bad shape: stocks are declining, the management system is disintegrating, and foreign fishing is increasing, sometimes with little regard for long-term sustainability of the stocks. A regional regime is necessary and desirable and could begin through networking—a consultative mechanism of government officials in their personal capacities. In Chapter 8, Douglas Johnston and Mark Valencia analyze the present situation pertaining in RFE fisheries and prescribe an outline for a regional regime that might benefit both the stocks and the RFE.

Several appendices supplement these chapters. William Onorato supplies a thorough list of oil and gas developments in Russia and reviews implications of recent World Bank internal policy decisions which may enable the Bank to serve as a catalyst and pump primer for oil and gas projects. James Dorian provides a table of regionwide cooperative mineral and energy projects. And Robert Krueger gives a detailed description and analysis of one of the most ambitious privatization projects to date—the plan for the economic development of South Primorie, Vladivostok.

Notes

1. This concept was first advanced by Robert Scalapino. For elaboration, see Scalapino, "The Post–Cold War Asia-Pacific Security Order: Conflict or Cooperation?" Paper presented at the Conference on Economic and Security Cooperation in the Asia-Pacific: Agenda for the 1990s, Canberra, 28–30 July 1993, p. 16.

2

Prospects for Trade and Regional Cooperation

Burnham O. Campbell

In this chapter I look at the prospects for regional cooperation in Northeast Asia, both in general terms and from the viewpoint of the advantages or disadvantages to the Russian Far East (RFE) and its neighbors. There is little such cooperation now, but there is much discussion and some ground breaking in the UNDP Tumen River Project.

Economic history shows that sustainable economic growth is achievable where domestic policies and incentives encourage competition and where production evolves, at least roughly, along the changing lines of international comparative advantage. Regional cooperation is not necessary for this to happen, but it can speed the process. It is safe to say that the major reason developing Northeast Asia is one of the poorer regions of the world is that its policies of domestic production and international exchange have not been right in the foregoing sense. However, if the current drive toward reform in Northeast China, the RFE, and Mongolia continues and a similar push begins in North Korea, the potential is great for sustainable growth at very high rates.

Briefly, developing Northeast Asia has abundant natural resources and a large labor force, including many skilled workers, almost all with at least a primary education. South Korea has growing capital and production know-how and has established brand name products, but it lacks natural resources and is increasingly short of labor. In moving ahead to more technology-based production, South Korea can use a nearby proving ground. Japan has even more capital, is a world leader in production and technology, has an unrivaled marketing network, and is very short of unskilled and semiskilled labor. These circumstances suggest that the regional complementarities and the incentives needed to achieve the exceptional growth potential of the region exist. Tables 2.1 and 2.2 provide

TABLE 2.1 Income and Population of Northeast Asia and Selected Regions, 1990

	GDP (US$ billion)	Popula-tion (million)	GDP/ Capita (US$)	Growth: GDP/ Capita, 1965-90 (%)	Area ('000 km²)	km²/ 1,000 Pop.
Northeast China[a]	38.2	99.9	382	—	956	9.6
North Korea	21.5	21.8	986	—	121	5.6
Russian Far East[b]	19.4	8.0	2,425	—	6,215	776.9
Mongolia	1.9	2.1	919	—	1,567	746.2
Developing NEA	81.0	131.8	615	—	8,859	67.2
South Korea	236.4	42.8	5,523	7.1	99	2.3
Japan	2,942.9	123.8	23,771	4.1	372	2.3
Northeast Asia	3,260.3	298.4	10,926	—	9,366	29.4
China (- Northeast China)	326.7	1,051.4	311	5.9	8,605	8.2
Hong Kong	59.7	5.8	10,293	6.2	1	0.2
1997 China (- NEA)	386.4	1,057.2	365	—	8,606	9.0
Indonesia	107.3	178.2	602	4.5	1,905	10.7
Malaysia	42.4	17.9	2,369	4.0	330	18.4
Philippines	43.9	61.5	714	1.3	300	4.9
Singapore	34.6	3.0	11,533	6.5	1	0.3
Thailand	80.2	55.8	1,437	4.4	513	9.2
ASEAN	308.4	316.4	975	—	3,049	9.6
United States (1990)	5,392.2	250.0	21,569	1.7	9,373	37.5
Canada (1990)	570.2	26.5	21,517	2.7	9,976	376.5
Mexico	237.8	86.2	2,759	2.8	1,958	22.7
NAFTA	6,200.2	362.7	17,095	—	21,307	58.7
EEC[c]	5,996.3	327.0	18,337		3,140	9.6
ex-USSR[d]	672.4	281.0	2,393	—	16,151	57.5

[a]Lioaning, Jilin, and Heilongjiang provinces.
[b]GDP is 2.8 percent of the old USSR GDP estimated as discussed in note (d).
[c]Germany includes the old Federal Republic only.
[d]GDP is estimated from 1985 base given in Kim and Campbell (1992), using estimates of annual growth rates from World Bank and news sources; population data are from World Bank (1992).
Sources: World Bank (1987, 1992); Chinese State Statistical Bureau (1988, 1991); Republic of China (1992); U.S. State Department (1989).

TABLE 2.2 Hechscher/Ohlin and Ricardo Resource Endowments

| | Capital/ Labor Ratio (US$ 000) 1983 | Labor Force (million) 1990 | Age Group (%) Enrolled at | | | Economies of Scale Index[d] 1985 | Arable Land (km²/1,000 Pop.[e] 1981-83 | Woodland (km²)/ 1,000 Pop. 1981-83 | Mineral Resource Index[f] 1987 | Coastline (km)/ 1,000 Pop. 1983 |
			Primary 1985	Secondary 1985	Tertiary 1985					
Developing NEA										
Northeast China	3.7[a]	53.7	≥ 100	> 39	> 2	22	> 3.8	> 1.3	159	< 13.6
North Korea	4.6[b]	9.6	100	96	16	5	1.1	4.4	0	128.7
Russian Far East[c]	8.6	4.3	106	99	21	2	< 21.8	> 33.1	335[g]	> 168.0
Mongolia	3.4	1.0	105	88	26	1	666.7	83.3	na	0.0
NEA NICs										
Taiwan	13.0	8.3	—	—	—	7	4.4	9.1	—	0.1
South Korea	11.1	16.9	96	94	32	13	0.6	1.6	0	59.3
Japan	48.4	60.8	102	96	30	100	0.5	2.1	100	114.1
China	2.6	609.6	124	39	2	230	3.8	1.3	600	13.6
ex-USSR	8.6	154.9	106	99	21	89	21.8	33.1	3,350	168.0
United States	64.0	121.6	101	99	57	272	18.5	11.8	1,247	83.8
World							9.7	8.6		—

[a]All China ratio times average Northeast China or provincial ratio of original cost fixed assets per household to the all China original cost fixed assets per household.

[b]Derived from partial data in Eberstadt and Banister (1990) and World Bank (1987).

[c]Assumes same as the USSR where other information is not available.

[d]Japan=100. Equals 3 times GDP index (Japan base) + Pop. Index (Japan) with sum ÷ by 4.

[e]Includes croplands, meadows, and pastures.

[f]Japan=100. Based on number of times in World Resource list of top 15 producers weighted by share in world output when listed.

[g]Assumes the Russian Far East has 10 percent of old USSR's mineral wealth and Northeast China has 25 percent of China's mineral wealth.

Sources: Capital stock estimates derived by summing real investment data from World Bank data tapes; labor supply estimates from the same source; fixed assets per household, etc., from Chinese State Statistical Bureau (1988); USSR, North Korea, and Mongolia estimated as described in Kim and Campbell (1992); Asian Development Bank (1992); World Bank (1987, 1992); World Resources Institute (1988).

background on Northeast Asia's basic economic performance and endowments.

Basically, the income differences shown in Table 2.1 would lead to a major relocation of the region's population if free movement of labor were possible. Since this is not now possible and is not likely to be possible in the foreseeable future, real per-capita incomes are not going to be equalized by labor migration. However, if the large existing differences in per-capita income truly represent differences in capital and technology per worker and not simply differences in the efficiency of use of capital, movements in capital and technology in response to profit incentives can equalize per-capita incomes upward. With substantive reforms, such movements of capital and technology into developing Northeast Asia from Japan and South Korea—and elsewhere—are likely.

The differences in economic achievement between developing and developed Northeast Asia reflect four major, related factors: differences in capital/labor ratios, differences in the level of technology applied, differences in the efficiency of resource utilization, and differences in the degree of international specialization. All are correctable and, increasingly, the developing region's countries are putting ideology aside and concentrating on economic growth and a pragmatic exploration of the steps necessary to begin catching up.

The Current Level and Composition
of Northeast Asian Trade

The export performances covered in Table 2.3, though severely limited by available data, show that the countries and parts of countries in Northeast Asia do indeed have wide differences in degree of international specialization and in approach to integration with outside markets. Taiwan and South Korea have by far the greatest export share in output, high exports per capita, and the highest recent growth rates in exports per capita. On any scale for a resource-poor, low-income, far-from-self-sufficient country, North Korea is way below optimum on all measures of international specialization. China and Northeast China also have a long way to go to achieve a respectable per-capita export effort. Northeast China is ahead of the Chinese average export effort but still far behind the more open economies. Russia lags far behind the United States and Japan in export effort, and the same is likely true for the Russian Far East. Though comparable data are not available, a reasonable guess is that the export share and effort are relatively low in Mongolia. These relative performances clearly show the scope for trade development in developing Northeast Asia and so the potential for regional cooperation that facilitates trade development.

TABLE 2.3 Export Performance of NEA and Selected Pacific Rim Regions

	Exports/GDP 1985 (%)	Exports/Pop. 1985 (%)	Exports/ Imports 1985 (%)	Relative Export Growth 1972/76 to 1987 (Thailand=1.00)
Developing NEA				
Northeast China	16.0	53	na[b]	< 1.07
North Korea	7.1	74	71	—
Russian Far East[a]	13.9	278	96	—
Mongolia	—	—	—	—
NEA NICs				
Taiwan	33.3	1,606	153	2.15
South Korea	35.1	737	97	2.37
Japan	13.2	1,456	135	1.23
China	10.3	26	64	1.07
ex-USSR	15.7	314	106	—
Southeast Asia				
Hong Kong	na	5,590	102	1.63
Indonesia	21.5	115	154	0.38
Malaysia	48.9	980	124	0.75
Philippines	14.2	85	85	0.23
Singapore	130.6	8,774	87	1.26
Thailand	18.6	137	77	1.00
NAFTA				
United States	7.0	891	59	0.51
Canada	27.0	3,445	107	0.79
Mexico	12.3	277	162	0.91

[a]Russian Far East exports estimated as 0.87 (from Jensen et al. 1983) times USSR export share times GDP.

[b]Totals do not include Northeast China since imports through other parts of China could not be measured.

Sources: GDP data—Table 1; World Bank (1987); China Resources Advertising Company (1988); U.S. State Department (1989); Republic of China (1992).

Northeast Asian Trade with the Developed World

Northeast Asia's trade with the European Community (now, European Union) (EC) is a useful illustration of the region's trade with other developed nations. As defined in Table 2.4, with China instead of Northeast China and Russia instead of the Russian Far East for lack of data, Northeast Asia has a surplus with the EC. This is solely a result of trade with China and South Korea, so there is a net capital outflow, unless services offset, from Northeast Asia to the EC. This is truly surprising with Russia included.

To be expected, given comparative advantage, the EC has a surplus in the food category with all but China. However, the EC has a deficit with

TABLE 2.4 EC Trade with China, North and South Korea, and Mongolia

	Regional Total			China		
	Exports (%)	Imports (%)	Balance (million ECU)	Exp. (%)	Imp. (%)	Balance (million ECU)
Food products	4.1	6.0	-845.7	4.2	8.0	-961.7
Minerals	0.4	1.3	-251.0	0.5	1.9	-256.4
Other resource-based	5.5	10.4	-1,690.1	2.6	11.6	-1,591.0
Chemicals	13.5	6.6	216.6	13.6	7.3	-327.8
Textiles and apparel	4.2	32.5	-6,917.5	3.9	35.0	-5,022.4
Metal manufacturing	7.4	2.2	449.5	6.8	2.0	83.2
Other manufacturing	55.2	40.2	-2,130.2	60.4	33.5	-1,617.3
Miscellaneous	0.9	0.4	20.4	0.6	0.4	-26.1
Unallocated	8.9	0.5	1,034.7	7.4	0.4	356.6
Total (million ECU)	12,844.8	22,920.2	-10,075.4	5,629.0	14,976.9	-9,347.9

Source: Based on UNDP (1992).

China large enough to more than offset the surpluses with the others, and that gives the EC a deficit in food trade with Northeast Asia and thus with the region in the food category. Generally food trade is a low share of total trade, with the largest share being the 8 percent of China's exports to the EC. China's net surplus in food runs counter to the comparative advantage of China.

Also as expected, minerals and other resource-based exports (hides, ceramics, forest products, etc.) contribute importantly to Northeast Asia's regional surplus with the EC. If based on the RFE instead of Russia, the EC deficit would likely be even greater, at least in relative terms. Together these resource-based categories account for over 20 percent of North Korean exports to the EC, over 10 percent of Chinese exports, and just under 10 percent for the exports of South Korea and Mongolia.

In labor-intensive production, based on the "textiles plus" category and the labor-intensive part of other manufacturing, the region has a large surplus with the EC. If industrialization follows the lines of regional comparative advantage, this is where industrialization would begin, and that is happening in Northeast Asia–EC trade. Of China's large exports to the EC, 35 percent are in the "textiles plus" category. Over half of North Korea's and three-fourths of Mongolia's exports are also here (but closer to the straight resource end of the category). Even 27 percent of South Korea's exports to the EC still remain in this low-tech category. Further, 31.9

North Korea			South Korea			Mongolia		
Exp. (%)	Imp. (%)	Balance (million ECU)	Exp. (%)	Imp. (%)	Balance (million ECU)	Exp. (%)	Imp. (%)	Balance (million ECU)
6.1	2.3	4.6	3.9	2.1	111.7	7.5	10.3	-0.3
0.5	10.5	-8.1	0.3	0.1	13.4	0.5	0	0.1
8.7	11.8	-0.5	7.7	8.2	-97.3	1.6	9.0	-1.3
13.6	1.6	13.1	13.4	5.4	526.3	22.7	0.1	5.0
3.9	59.2	-44.5	4.4	27.4	-1,837.0	2.6	76.0	-13.7
16.6	0.7	17.0	7.8	2.6	349.0	1.7	0	0.4
48.9	13.3	40.8	51.1	53.4	-566.0	55.7	0.2	12.3
0.5	0.6	0.0	1.1	0.4	46.6	0	0.4	-0.1
1.2	0.1	1.2	10.2	0.6	675.9	7.8	4.1	1.0
105.7	82.2	23.6	7,087.9	7,842.5	-754.6	22.2	18.7	3.4

percent of South Korea's and 26.5 percent of China's exports are found in relatively labor-intensive light manufacturing, including electronics.

In the more human and physical capital- and technology-intensive trade categories, the expected EC surpluses with Northeast Asia are found. This is true for chemicals and metal manufactures—basically heavy industry, although a fairly large deficit with China partly offsets the large surpluses elsewhere (especially with South Korea) in the chemicals sector. It is also true for heavy manufacturing, with this being a major component of EC sales to Northeast Asia. Heavy manufacturing is the only category in which South Korea is clearly distinguished from its neighbors, with 18.8 percent of its exports to the EC in this category.

In sum, continental Northeast Asian trade with the EC clearly now follows comparative advantage. Command economy distortions are not significant in terms of the composition of trade when the trading partner is driven by market considerations as is the EC; with greater openness, the amounts of trade would change but not the general shares. South Korea is evidence of this point, with a trade pattern much like China's despite its higher stage of development. There is, at the high degree of aggregation involved, some evidence of intraindustry trade developing (e.g., other manufacturing in China and South Korea).

Regional cooperation in Northeast Asia might lead to import substitution in the heavy industry category, as some fear, but it could just as well

TABLE 2.5 Northeast Asian Intraregional Trade (US$ million)

	Mongolia	CIS	China	North Korea	DNEA	% of DNEA	South Korea	Japan	NEA	% of NEA	World
Mongolia to		420	11	—	431	54.4	—	8	439	55.4	793
Mongolia from		642	30	—	672	55.9	—	10	682	56.7	1,202
balance		-222	-19	—	-241		—	-2	-243		-409
CIS to	642		2,140	446	3,228	6.5	577	3,356	7,161	14.5	49,390
CIS from	420		2,240	45	3,117	4.8	625	2,564	6,306	9.6	65,510
balance	222		-100	-11	111		-48	792	855		-16,120
China to	30	2,240		358	2,628	4.3	3,441	12,024	18,093	29.1	62,091
China from	11	2,140		124	2,275	4.3	1,003	6,131	9,409	17.6	53,345
balance	19	100		234	353		2,438	5,893	8,684		8,746
North Korea to	—	457	124		581	30.0	106	298	985	50.8	1,940
North Korea from	—	446	358		804	28.2	6	176	986	34.6	2,850
balance	—	11	-234		-223		100	122	-1		-910
Dev. NEA to	672	3,117	2,275	804	6,868	6.0	4,124	15,686	26,678	23.4	114,214
Dev. NEA from	431	3,228	2,628	581	6,868	5.6	1,634	8,881	17,383	14.1	122,907
balance	241	-111	-353	223			2,490	6,805	9,295		-8,693
South Korea to	—	625	1,003	6	1,634	2.3		12,356	13,990	19.5	71,870
South Korea from	—	577	3,441	106	4,124	5.1		21,120	25,244	31.0	81,525
balance	—	48	-2,438	-100	-2,490			-8,764	-11,254		-9,655
Japan to	10	2,564	6,131	176	8,881	3.1	21,120		30,001	10.5	287,040
Japan from	8	3,356	12,024	298	15,686	6.7	12,356		28,042	12.0	234,588
balance	2	-792	-5,893	-122	-6,805		8,764		1,959		52,452
NEA to	682	6,306	9,409	986	17,383	3.67	25,244	28,042	70,669	14.9	473,124
NEA from	439	7,161	18,093	985	26,678	6.08	13,990	30,001	70,669	16.1	439,020
balance	243	-855	-8,684	1	-9,295		11,254	-1,959			34,104

Source: Based on UNDP (1992).

lead to increased exports of resource-based manufactures and skilled labor-intensive manufactured goods in exchange for consumer goods and capital equipment, thus increasing trade. In the longer run, the present intraindustry trade with the EC would grow relatively, with Northeast Asia maintaining an advantage in resource-based goods.

Intraregional Trade in Northeast Asia

Quantitative information on trade within Northeast Asia is particularly incomplete. We must rely on overall data for China and the CIS to represent Northeast China and the Russian Far East. Further, most intraregional trade is barter trade. Pricing such trade is difficult, and there are undoubtedly considerable errors, compared to relative pricing at world prices, in the trade flows reported. Finally, in all the developing Northeast Asian countries and subregions, trade is carried out by provincial authorities, central government organizations, and private or quasi-private entities, each reporting to different authorities. There is no uniform compilation.

Export orientation and regional trade are low in Northeast Asia; as Table 2.5 shows, intraregional trade is 5–6 percent for developing Northeast Asia. This ratio might be somewhat higher if the RFE and Northeast China were included rather than the CIS and China. Still, it would not approach the 30 percent of ASEAN trade carried out within ASEAN. Since the underlying resource endowments are much more complementary and thus conducive to intraregional trade in developing Northeast Asia than in ASEAN, the development of such trade to date is woefully below its potential.

Only Mongolia and North Korea have a large part of their trade with regional partners. Both have regional deficits. The CIS is the largest regional partner (but there are no data on what part of this trade is with the RFE). Both China and the CIS have regional surpluses. If we define Northeast Asia to include Japan and South Korea, 23.4 percent of developing Northeast Asia's exports and 14.1 percent of its imports are regional, so broader regional dependence is larger, but still fairly low. Basically these data imply that there is much room for improvement in intraregional trade, especially given the inherent resource complementarities and the experience in other large regional markets like the European Union and North America. This is sufficient reason to be highly bullish about any changes, including regional cooperation, which would open and thus increase economically efficient intraregional trade.

Over half of Mongolia's large trade deficit is with developing Northeast Asia, mostly with the CIS. This probably cannot and will not continue. The CIS has approximate balance in developing Northeast Asia but a surplus with Northeast Asia (mostly with Mongolia and Japan) and a large world deficit. So the CIS needs Northeast Asia's trade to help cover its deficits elsewhere. China has a medium surplus (about 13 percent of exports) with Northeast Asia and a surplus with each part of Northeast Asia. China's largest surpluses are with Japan and South Korea, which could make some other countries, or at least the mercantilists in those countries, jealous. The size of China's Northeast Asian surplus is about the same as China's surplus with the world. This could mean that China is exchanging goods for funds from its neighbors to buy from the West, or it could be the result of barter trade mismatches; it is probably some of both. North Korea has an even larger deficit than Mongolia (35 percent of imports) but is essentially in balance with Northeast Asia; a deficit with developing Northeast Asia is just offset by its surpluses with South Korea and Japan. Again, this cannot continue, since there is no way to finance North Korea's overall deficit. Interestingly enough, developing Northeast Asia has a large surplus with Northeast Asia, although a deficit with the world. So, at present, the developing part of the region is using yen/won earnings to finance trade elsewhere. This is probably the only region in the world able to do that!

South Korea also has a world deficit, accounted for and then some by its deficit with Japan. South Korea also has a surplus with the CIS, a larger deficit with China, and so an overall deficit with developing Northeast Asia, which suggests a net capital flow in the "wrong" direction. South Korea's trade with the four countries included in developing Northeast Asia represented just 2.3 percent of total exports and 5.1 percent of total imports in 1991 (this ignores indirect trade with China via Hong Kong, including 6.6 percent of South Korea's exports). This is small—smaller than the 7.9 percent of exports going to Taiwan, Singapore, and Indonesia. Even though trade with China and the CIS is growing quickly, there is clearly lots of room to expand South Korea's trade in developing Northeast Asia.

Interregional Trade by Product Category

There is considerable partner trade data, thanks to the UNDP. Still, provincial data for Northeast China and the Russian Far East are suspect, because of the problems noted above affecting national data and because of the differences in provincial trade reporting for the different trade categories—each reported, if at all, to a different entity. For example, in China there are three types of trade: (1) national monopoly trading corporations headquartered in Beijing; this trade is largely but not exclusively barter, with accompanying valuation problems, and the exports involved are often limited by government degree; (2) border trade (direct trade in the

RFE)—really, the counterpart of the above with the exporters involved licensed at the provincial rather than the national level; and (3) individual trade, including the trade of producers without intermediaries.

The first category appears in national data but often not in the regional data for the region in which the exports originated or imports ended. Most subnational data refer to the second category, which is almost exclusively barter trade, again with all the problems this implies. There is little data on the third category, but anecdotal information indicated that it is growing rapidly. It is not possible to break exports into goods produced in the reporting regions and transit goods, though it has been roughly estimated (UNDP 1992) that 80 percent of goods exported from Heilongjiang and Jilin provinces represent goods produced in those provinces.

Most of the following data for Northeast China and the RFE refer to direct or border trade. For both Heilongjiang and Jilin, but especially for the RFE, this could give a significant downward bias to reported trade data.

Northeast China and the RFE. Provincial exports to neighboring countries are given in Table 2.6 for Heilongjiang and Jilin. Jilin's total exports in 1991 (covering all categories of trade, not just the direct trade shown in the table) were $1.027 billion, of which at most $163 million went to neighbors (CIS and North Korea). Jilin has a pronounced trade surplus and a below-average trade ratio. It exports food and textiles to Russia in exchange for resource-based goods, especially fertilizers and other chemicals, and resource-based products. Jilin has a large surplus with the RFE in this trade.

Heilongjiang Province, one of the most industrial in China, also has one of the largest oilfields and the largest timber reserve in China. Of its reported total trade of $1.9 billion in 1991, trade with the CIS was slightly more than one-third (direct trade was about half of this). Trade is growing dynamically along the Heilongjiang border—from almost nil to $1 billion, almost all barter, in the past few years. Seventy percent of all Russia–China trade passes this border.

Heilongjiang exports food and textiles to Russia, but the unallocated category (light consumer goods, and perhaps consumer electronics) is the largest. By product, Heilongjiang exchanges grains, canned meat, fruits, vegetables, potatoes, garments (jackets and coats especially), and electronic consumer equipment for fertilizers and other chemicals, heavy industry products, including military vans and heavy passenger cars, and a large unallocated share. Like Jilin, Heilongjiang also has a large surplus in its trade with Russia.

Northeast China's surpluses imply that barter is not balancing out and that Northeast Chinese exporters are sending capital into Russia in exchange for IOUs. This illustrates the problem of finding something from Russia/RFE to trade in exchange, a major constraint on present border trade along with the high export tax on many RFE products. One product

TABLE 2.6 Trade by Category between NEA Regions (%)

	Heilongjiang/Russia		Jilin/Russia		South Korea/Russia	
	Exp.	Imp.	Exp.	Imp.	Exp.	Imp.
Food	15.1	2.9	64.2	5.2	1.6	25.4
Other resource	1.7	1.2		14.3	0.2	10.9
Petroleum		2.7				
Chemicals	5.7	41.1	0.4	59.3	12	10.6
Textiles	26.1		21.0		17	5.7
Metals/HI	1.2	27.4	1.3	8.8	32.0	43.5
Other manuf.	2.4	1.0	5.8	3.1	28	0.5
Unallocated	47.8	23.4	6.7	8.4	8.2	2.9
Miscellaneous		0.2	0.6	0.8	0.7	0.4
Total (US$ 000)	292	210	97	44	625,080	577,293

	Heilongjiang/North Korea		Jilin/North Korea		South Korea/China	
	Exp.	Imp.	Exp.	Imp.	Exp.	Imp.
Food	4.3		47.3	53.8	0.3	23.2
Other resource	57.5		11.1	32.7	13.4	28.0
Petroleum						
Chemicals	20.4	99	7.1		19.4	6.5
Textiles	3.4		18.6		28.8	27.3
Metals/HI	6.3		2.4		22.0	11.9
Other manuf.	4.4		11.9		14.4	3.2
Unallocated	3.7	0.8	1.4	13.3	1.6	
Miscellaneous			0.2	0.2	0.1	
Total (US$ 000)	73	1	63	10	100,251	3,440,548

Source: Based on UNDP (1992).

the Chinese side would like, fertilizer, cannot be supplied in the amounts required, and there is no market to respond to the excess demand. There is clearly room for diversification and greater value added on the RFE side. This situation cannot be continued and suggests the possible urgency of financial and other reforms necessary to put trade on a monetary basis, though no one would feel too secure holding either country's currency. Also, there is no reason to believe that exchange rates based largely on what is happening in western Russia and coastal China will work to balance trade pressures and capital movements between the RFE and Northeast China.

In future, there is a possibility of the RFE importing more capital goods and technology for light industries and of a growing intraindustry trade in agricultural machinery. Possible growth sectors for joint ventures include forestry, where the RFE has the resources and Northeast China has the downstream industries. The RFE can also serve as a base for research and development in many of the product lines pursued by Northeast China. Regional cooperation could help in facilitating these developments and in working the region out of its barter trade dilemma. Within a relatively narrow focus, the UNDP Tumen Project is exploring all these possibilities.

Northeast China and North Korea. A wide variety of Northeast Chinese exports (coking coal, agricultural products, and to a lesser extent garments and textiles, chemical products, and tires) are made to North Korea. By province, Jilin has a huge surplus with North Korea, with food exports largest, followed by textiles, light manufactures, and resource-based goods. The small return imports are mostly food (perhaps primarily for Jilin's ethnic Koreans) and minerals and other resource-based goods. By product, Jilin's exports include automobiles, TVs, sewing machines, and other manufactured goods. It gets back timber, rice, seafood, and products transshipped through North Korea from third countries. Heilongjiang has essentially no imports from North Korea but exports to it leather, hides, glass, forest products, and chemicals. A big change not fully reflected in these data is China's conversion of trade with North Korea from barter to hard currency payments. In the absence of considerable reforms, probably only possible with international cooperation, either trade will shrink to the low levels of North Korean exports or untenable levels of Chinese financing of North Korea must occur.

North Korea and Russia/RFE. Trade between Russia and North Korea reflects the command economies of both and the high level of dependency of the latter. North Korea exports agricultural products, garments, other textiles, steel, metals, and non-staple foods to Russia and imports basic necessities such as crude oil and petroleum products, coking coal, ores, metal, transport equipment, and machinery. Since Russia has converted its trade with North Korea from barter to hard currency payments, that trade is rapidly dwindling. North Korea is concerned. It knows it must take steps to increase exports by improving its professional business capabilities and the availability of necessary information; by creating export industries based on local raw materials (processing industries based on comparative advantage and cheap labor); and by adopting an appropriate tariff structure. The difficulty is in finding a way to do these things but remaining consistent with an extremely centralized command system.

North Korea and South Korea. There are few details available on trade between the two Koreas, which is largely through third parties. Trade was not possible before 1988 and has expanded only slowly since then—at least the traceable portion. The major characteristic of this trade is the very large South Korean deficit. By 1992, South Korean exports to North Korea were only $11.2 million. Its imports from the North were, however, a much more substantial—but still low—$198.8 million. With integration, trade between the two Korea's would be in the billions of dollars, so the present level is essentially little different from zero. The existing deficit is a minor form of politically palatable foreign aid.

South Korea and China/Northeast China. Major exports of South Korea to China are textiles, iron and steel, heavy industry, chemicals, light manufactures, and other resource-based goods. South Korea's major imports from China are other resource-based goods, textiles, food, and metal manufactures. China exports raw materials and intermediate inputs for South Korea's textile and garment industry as well as mineral fuels, cement, and steel. More significant is the rapidly growing intraindustry trade in textiles, chemicals, steel, and electronics. This is a dynamic trade portrait— doing very well on a bilateral basis without any supporting regional trade agreement. However, there is no way to tell what portion of this trade involves Northeast China specifically; it may be that trade with Northeast China is still in its infancy and could gain from regional cooperation.

South Korea and Russia. Exports to Russia from South Korea are mostly manufactured goods: iron and steel, ships, transport vehicles, electronics, and other consumer goods. South Korea also sells textiles and chemicals. The largest category of imports from Russia covers heavy industry and metals manufacturing, including considerable intracategory trade at this level of aggregation. Next in line are food imports and then other resource-based and chemical imports. Generally this trade follows the expected pattern. Given their nature, it seems that most of these imports are not from the RFE.

Mongolia and the Others. Most of Mongolia's trade has been with the CIS; it involves raw materials and agricultural products going into Russia and consumer goods and some capital goods coming out. Thus, exports follow Mongolia's comparative advantage but because the trade is primarily barter, there is little room for growth. To get a larger share of the value added from the products involved, more of the processing has to take place in Mongolia. Trade with the CIS declined in 1991 to 50 percent of 1990 as adjustment to a cash basis got under way.

Regional Obstacles to Trade

To determine what regional cooperation might accomplish, it is useful to consider the proximate causes of the relatively low levels of trade and capital inflows in the region.

Command Economies. The planning mentality that characterizes the command economy has been first and foremost among the blocks to world trade. The plan turns inward and emphasizes specialization within the planning area, not internationally. This can lead to some division of labor between planned economies, if the political will is there, but mostly in developing Northeast Asia it has meant that the neighboring regions and countries have turned away from the Northeast Asia region. This approach, coupled with the ideology of extreme centralized control, has also precluded consistent, codified, and implemented "rules of the game" to guide traders or potential foreign investors. The result has often been a corrupt bureaucratic nightmare of trade administration, left in place by reforms largely directed toward production.

Although economic reforms in China have begun to break down the autarchical planning system, Northeast China, with its preponderance of planning-led state enterprises, has lagged behind the rest of the country in integrating into the world economy. Liaoning is furthest along, and there is growing border trade in Heilongjiang and Jilin. Change is also under way in the Russian Far East and Mongolia, but both have recently moved back from earlier liberalization policies. Moscow is still very much involved in eastern events, though the RFE has been trying to change this by unilaterally declaring itself a republic. Ex-planners have regained control of Mongolia. Change in North Korea so far is miniscule, though there has been much discussion and, if some of the actions promised under the UNDP's Tumen Project are actually taken, the process of liberalization will have finally begun.

For the region as a whole, directly relevant to trade, the command approach has given rise to an inefficient separation of production and marketing functions, with trade channeled through government-run trading organizations with few bottom-line responsibilities. To quote a UNDP report, "Despite announcements to the contrary, emphasis continues to be placed on the administration of trade rather than on the promotion of trade. The reason is simply that the parties concerned do not know what to do" (UNDP 1992). The managers of trade in the Russian and Chinese capitals often do not have adequate information about trade possibilities at the provincial level and do have interests that conflict with those of the provinces. In addition to the obvious benefits of any contribution regional cooperation could make to the regional implementation of more outward-looking, market-oriented policies, the RFE and Northeast China—and Northeast Asia—will also gain to the extent regional cooperation helps increase local autonomy in administering such policies.

Role of Barter Trade. As a heritage of the planning philosophy guiding economic activity in the past, most trade between the countries of Northeast Asia is barter trade. This is very inefficient and gives rise to large imbalances because of the difficulty of finding timely agreement or delivery on barter obligations. Such trade involves high transaction costs, especially for three-way deals. Finding the necessary coincidence of wants requires time and ingenuity. Often the product specifications are unclear, and it is difficult to get prices and quantities correctly set where barter is involved. Where local trading units are engaged in the negotiations, the goods contracted for exchange often turn out to be unavailable or ineligible for national export licenses. These problems are said to be major factors in constraining the exports of North Korea and Primorski Krai. In sum, as is well known, barter trade is simple to conclude and difficult to transact, as opposed to cash trade which is difficult to conclude and easy to transact.

Lack of Financial Infrastructure. A major constraint on growth of trade and development of any sort, not to mention effective reform, is the low to nonexistent level of banking and financial services. Mongolia, North Korea, and Russia are simply unable to accommodate the monetization of international trade. There is little availability of foreign exchange and no banking sector that can clear balances, finance production, or trade on a timely basis using internationally known (and marketable) financial instruments. It is not possible to make payments for goods, despite these countries' shortage of foreign exchange, with credit cards, foreign checks, even certified or travelers checks. Most of these conditions apply de facto in Northeast China as well.

This situation partly explains the prevalence of barter trade; with the rudimentary financial system in place on all sides of the border, barter is almost a necessity for any trade to take place. But with most trade in barter form, there is little market incentive for the development of a more tractable financial system, a classic "Catch-22."

Without financial development, there can be no market-led development, and without market-led or -constrained development there can be no sustainable growth. In many ways this is the first problem to be faced. It is more a matter of government attitude and will than of missing capital or infrastructure, though it is necessary to have modern telecommunications and air transport connections at a minimum for internationally competitive financial services. Generally, the issues involved and the solutions necessary are national, not regional. Still, development of financial expertise has been the subject of regional cooperation elsewhere (e.g., ASEAN).

Lack of Physical Infrastructure. At present, telecommunications linking the region internally and with the world are rudimentary. Similarly lacking is a developed transportation system for moving goods and people (see Chapter 7). Much of what exists, both railroads and highways, was originally designed to service Japan and European Russia, not the intraregional trade of Northeast Asia. The result is different railway gauges at many border crossings, with accompanying delays and storage costs, circuitous and incomplete linkages between production and consumption centers, and undeveloped feeder routes to main lines. Airports in the region often link with central cities but not across borders; missing are major conveniently located international airports. The transportation infrastructure that does exist is often in poor repair or out of date. This is especially so of highways. Except for the major Primorski ports, the region lacks adequate container and other cargo handling and storage facilities. Reliable electric power and water supplies are often a problem.

Thus, one of the major unfulfilled preconditions for successful trade in Northeast Asia is a satisfactory regional infrastructure. Without this infrastructure in place, investors from outside or within the region are going to be difficult to attract. If it is in place in one locale and not in others, the result will be the favoring of one part of the region over the others as a location of productive investments. Such choices are not likely to reflect regional long-run comparative advantages and will tend to undermine the mutual confidence and good will needed for successful intraregional trade expansion. Basically, the problems will be deciding how to internationalize existing infrastructure, what new infrastructure to try to finance, how to finance it, and how to avoid the competitive development of infrastructure. All these issues can be addressed best on a regional basis and in a regional forum.

Lack of Non-Financial Services. The services necessary as foreign trade grows, from housing, hotel, and medical services for international professionals to computer services, including supplies and repairs, are also mostly absent from developing Northeast Asia. So are customs institutions to facilitate the rapid movement of goods across borders. The many kinds of business services—accounting, warehousing, planning—that complement increased business activity need to be cultivated rather than stifled by the state bureaucracies. As with physical infrastructure, one goal of addressing these requirements in a regional forum would be to avoid as far as possible supply-led competition for the provision of non-financial services.

Lack of Information and Trade Support from Governments. Trade support activities or institutions are minimal—but especially lacking, except to some degree in Northeast China, are the data necessary for reasonably intelligent decision making. Prospective traders have very little information on what is out there to be exchanged, how reliable the supplies are, who is buying now, and so forth. Data needed for intelligent foreign investing are equally difficult to come by. Public sector institutions to collect and provide this information to nationals in the form of advice and economic intelligence are in the embryo stage in Northeast Asia. Essentially, there was little perceived need for, and so interest in, these activities in the command economies of the region. Now that reform brings the need, established habits and ways of viewing the world hold back their development.

For example, in the Russian Far East detailed information on mineral production and resources of the sort that would be necessary for foreign investors or purchasers to make a decision to invest or buy are available but remained confidential in 1992 when the UN tried to collect such information. This attitude applies to trade data as well. Such data—total or disaggregated by partners—are available on only a very incomplete and inconsistent basis, although only a few bureaucratic changes would solve the problem. Under current reforms the Primorski Statistical Office is beginning to receive import/export declarations from the five customs offices in the region, but product coding is not yet satisfactory.

In addition to the different definitions, different timing of release, and missing data resulting from the reporting of different categories of trade to different government agencies, the trade information problem is made more difficult by the fact that most trade is on barter terms and so is difficult to value consistently. Further confounding the provision of consistent trade data, especially in the RFE but also in Northeast China, are the many exchange rates in use, the continual depreciation of the currency, and very high and variable inflation rates.

Focus on the RFE. The Russian Far East shares all the problems mentioned above, and they all stand in the way of its trade development. For a long time the RFE was a client "state"—a beneficiary of the Cold War, especially the most populous Khabarovsk and Primorski provinces. The rest of Russia was taxed to make net transfers to the RFE to support the defense establishment. The rationale for these net transfers has disappeared, and the transfers themselves are rapidly disappearing or even reversing. National security is no longer the major export of the RFE.

A painful structural adjustment is now under way. To replace the lost net transfers, the region must somehow develop new exports from the resources tied up in the defense establishment (see Appendix 2 for one such effort). The RFE must look outward—there is no alternative—either within Russia or across the border to the rest of Northeast Asia and the world. Since a quick fix is needed, the best alternative seems to be the growing regional cross-border markets. But, so far, the RFE has not been given freedom to act by the central government, and it is not clear whether the attempt to gain that freedom unilaterally by declaring a Russian Far East republic will work. With the large Chinese presence nearby, what the RFE seems to want is economic autonomy under the protective umbrella of the Russian nation. But unless the RFE has a separate central bank and its own currency, it will have to labor under constraints posed by monetary and exchange rate policies concocted in western Russia to obtain western Russian goals. The important issues for RFE trade prospects and ability to attract capital—the "internationalization" of the ruble, its stability and convertibility, and the underlying rate of national inflation—will remain out of the region's control, even in a democratic political process.

Beyond this important autonomy issue, the RFE has numerous other problems to overcome in gaining sustainable economic growth. Key is the endemic financial backwardness and lack of business services (e.g., hotels), often because of inefficient state operation. Other important problem areas include the quota and export licensing systems, which penalize a major part of the RFE's potential exports, the shortage of capital to replace and convert existing military assets or to develop the region's copious natural resources, the lack of management with a bottom-line orientation, and the lack of reliable energy and water sources to service production and the civilian population. Further constraining the region's development are the absence of international-quality telecommunications and reliable access to international transportation networks, inadequate information for decision making, the lack of unskilled labor, and endemic uncertainty about the political structure and business regulations. Although some might be aided by regional agreements (say, for training), most of these problems are solvable only by domestic policy changes. Thus, the major role for regional cooperation is in creating an environment conducive to the political acceptance of the changes, in part by creating competitive pressures that raise the costs of maintaining the status quo. A resolution of the ongoing political conflict with Japan would also greatly help, since Japan is the major potential nearby market for RFE marine and mineral resources and a prime source of investment capital (see Chapters 5 and 8).

An important RFE comparative advantage is in minerals and mineral- or resource-based production. But these are not growth markets. If this fact is coupled with the relative inaccessibility of many of the mineral deposits, the bureaucratic inefficiencies still remaining—including the continuing confidentiality of information needed to make investment decisions—labor shortages, and the lack of needed infrastructure, it is clear they cannot provide a major short-run prop to trade and development. As the structure of demand continues to change away from traditional minerals and energy sources, the relative long-run value of this comparative advantage may be reduced if growth in total demand is insufficient to offset this substitution effect. This possibility heightens the importance of manufacturing based on conversion of the defense/military industries and of the promotion of Northeast Asian trade, a process that can be carried out independently but also can be greatly aided by regional cooperation.

Advantages of Regional Cooperation

In the preceding section I discussed the numerous problems the region and specifically the Russian Far East face in expanding interregional and world trade and in moving to a market-focused economic culture. It is now time to explore why many knowledgeable people expect regional cooperation in Northeast Asia to be a positive sum game and exactly how the RFE might be expected to benefit from this game.

Without regional cooperation, domestic development and international trade would clearly remain on their present pace, which for the four less developed countries and subregions of Northeast Asia is less than satisfactory. Although Northeast China leads the rest of developing Northeast Asia in both trade and development, it lags the rest of China and can expect to be more than averagely impacted if China's growth slows. Still, without regional cooperation but with internal reforms, including a competitive environment and integration into the world economy, a self-feeding growth process could be initiated in all parts of the region. No multicountry agreement would be needed—though bilateral relations and rules must be in place—for increased specialization to raise productivity or for joint ventures to occur and for foreign capital to come in. However, by reducing costs and gaining externalities not achievable through solo action, regional cooperation can both speed up the process and make it more likely in the first place.

For example, to lay the basis for expanded domestic production that increases value added and for the attraction of foreign capital to aid the process, the many existing infrastructural constraints must be removed. As discussed, these include insufficient or nonexistent port and transportation facilities, international air access, modern telecommunications, a financial system able to function internationally, business support services, and a reasonably settled contractual/property rights environment and ways of adjudicating the inevitable conflicts that arise in these domains. These constraints are regional in their impact, and intraregional trade cannot grow near its potential as long as they remain. The same can be said for extraregional trade. Self-feeding growth is not likely in developing Northeast Asia without improvements in infrastructure, and the prospects for the needed infrastructure are limited on a bilateral basis. The projects involved will all have major domestic components but will almost all cross international borders physically or in terms of necessary agreements. Thus, some form of regional cooperation is a necessary condition for effective system design and for attracting the funds and setting up the rules that will allow the efficient functioning of regional infrastructure networks.

Regional cooperation may also help in promoting necessary economic reforms. In a more perfect world, small positive steps would not be necessary; a giant one would do. However, especially for the command-oriented economies of Northeast Asia, the dislocations from simply and rapidly opening up to the world, in both trade and financial markets, may either have lasting negative effects on the growth possible (waste productive resources for many years) or lead to current hardships that bring about a reversion to the security blanket of "plan and command" and so end reform. In the provision of information on a complete and objective basis, in the opening of markets to obtain greater economies of scale, in the secure utilization of the potential production and trade complementarities in Northeast Asia, in achieving the externalities of agglomeration (e.g., in the Tumen project), regional cooperation can help ease the way. Regional cooperation may be both a precondition for successful reform and a way of encouraging and carrying it out.

Looking more directly at the ways regional cooperation might enhance economic growth, the broadest, most general impact will be from cooperation that increases trade, within the region and between the region and the rest of the world. International specialization is a major source of growth throughout the world and, with international specialization way below the regional potential, the possibilities for increasing productivity through increased trade are clearly important in developing Northeast Asia. The benefits will depend on the net additional trade generated, on the dynamic comparative advantage of the region, and on the resultant improved efficiency of production.

Greater international openness also generates externalities, or indirect benefits. Most important of these are the effects of meeting international competition. Also, the increased demand for improvements in the physical, policy, and legal infrastructure can make it easier to get support and funding for carrying out these improvements. And the experience of trade can help strengthen the thin fabric of economic relations and trust between the countries in Northeast Asia and provide sometimes needed rationalizations for difficult political changes.

Essentially, the gains come from production and trade following the lines of comparative advantage. In this context, with the essential information readily available, profit-motivated producers or trading companies can best identify the region's comparative advantage and help—with financial intermediation—support development along those lines. Supportive regional cooperation can help avoid the detrimental subsidization of misguided import substitution, such as that which would encourage capital-intensive production where labor-intensive output is the comparative advantage.

To the extent that regional cooperation opens regional markets, it can also increase growth by increasing the opportunities for economies of scale. This can attract both foreign and domestic capital by reducing uncertainty and giving "guaranteed" access to a market large enough—as in developing Northeast Asia—to make the risks involved to obtain the scale economies worthwhile. An "infant industry" argument based on the efficient attainment of scale economies could be used to justify Northeast Asian trade cooperation—as long as sufficient competition is encouraged and the region emulates Japan and does not get stuck in the import substitution phase. Regional cooperation that encourages growth will also help Northeast Asia attain the agglomeration economies that follow from having a critical mass of industrial and business operations in a particular geographic area.

Cooperation that opens regional markets can also help in the establishment of brand names able to compete in world markets. Recognizable brand names increase the market and decrease the price elasticity of demand for the products involved. The growth in their value added is enhanced, and they may achieve markets beyond the region in which they were originally introduced.

As noted, regional cooperation can increase the attractiveness of developing Northeast Asia to foreign investment, either because cooperation reduces production costs and so improves the region's competitiveness in world markets or because regional barriers to trade are reduced by cooperation. By raising returns to savings, it can increase domestic resources for both human and physical capital accumulation. In both ways, regional cooperation can increase the ratio of capital to labor in the region and so raise growth through increased capital deepening. And regional cooperation can help reduce costly supply-led competition for foreign investment and achieve economies in training skilled personnel for financial and business services.

Right now, the direction of capital flows from Japan, South Korea, and Taiwan implies that the perceived returns to capital are higher in the developed countries and in Southeast Asia than in Northeast Asia. A regional agreement, by demonstrating commitment to reforms and increased economic openness, could go a long way toward changing this situation.

Cooperation that attracts outside capital or makes the domestic acquisition of outside capital more profitable facilitates technological progress, one of the key sources of growth. In Northeast Asia this could result from trade-expanding regional cooperation and the economic efficiency it engenders. It could be fostered by a common approach to treatment of rights to technology and by the development of new technology through the pooling of regional resources. In the specific instance of developing Northeast Asia, increased access to the technical sophistication of the RFE would benefit the rest of the region. Closely related are the benefits from learning by doing, which have a direct cross-product with improved technology and increased economic activity.

Perhaps the major untapped source of economic growth in Mongolia, Northeast China, the RFE, and North Korea is simply better economic organization, both internal and external to the producing unit. All these countries and subregions are far off their production possibility curves.

Essentially, this means they can increase productivity and growth through better economic organization without increasing the resources available, including technology. No economic systems are perfect, but theirs has failed relative to the market economies. Many changes and much learning are necessary to tap this source of growth—as well, it seems, as the patience of Job—but regional cooperation that leads to freer trade and so increases cross-border competition can make a major contribution. For example, regional cooperation schemes that increase exposure of entrenched, government-supported monopoly power to greater competition will directly raise productivity. International competition will do this, helping make reforms necessary and demonstrating the advantages of improved economic organization and so pointing reforms, in evolutionary fashion, in the right direction. Of course, the costs associated with such reforms (and those that have prevented real reform to this date) will still be there. But being part of an international effort to make the reforms effective, with transparent gains in sight and a political constituency that will benefit, may make implementing them easier politically.

Key Problems for Regional Cooperation

Assuming that the political will to cooperate exists on all sides, what are the major problems any regional scheme in developing Northeast Asia must overcome? A beginning list follows. Other issues could be raised, and any particular form of regional cooperation would bring up problems specific to that form.

Differences in the Stage of Economic Reform. Incompatibility of economic systems is a major problem for Northeast Asian regional cooperation. North Korea is a classic command economy that eschews most rational economic calculations and would have a massive lack of experience at responding to the incentives of economic cooperation. The Russian Far East and Mongolia are in the process of change; things there are chaotic and there is little experience with rational economic calculations. China has undergone considerable economic reform and is aware of the requirements and opportunities of a market system and international competition. However, Northeast China lags the rest of the country in this respect. There is little reason to expect that much of the requisite experience or many of the requisite management skills have been developed in the Northeast.

Thus, even though all remain "socialist" countries, rules and regulations governing economic decisions and the relative prices and availability of different goods and services are very dissimilar. And the response to the opportunities presented—say, a regional free trade zone—may also be very dissimilar and possibly not at all what experience elsewhere might suggest. There has to be greater harmonization of relative prices and greater understanding of basic economics for regional agreements, other than the usual barter agreements, to work. Also capable of causing continuing differences in regional economies is the approach—very different in Russia and China—to the sequencing of reform or the relation between political reform and economic reform, and the importance of political stability vis-à-vis political freedom. On the positive side, because of the differences that do exist, there are many opportunities for improvements that will raise growth. Working through these issues with others facing similar problems or with those who have fought through them before provides a major reason for expecting regional cooperation to be more effective than going it alone.

Varying Legal, Social, and Economic Standards. As often noted, one of the major stumbling blocks to regional economic development is the existence of very different rules and regulations—so that what is an acceptable practice in one country is illegal or bad form in another. For Northeast Asian economic cooperation to work, there has to be agreement on an understandable, enforceable, and fairly level set of operating rules covering all aspects of economic activity. For example, codes covering production, labor relations, tax treatment and holidays, environmental concerns, loan subsidies and guarantees, and repatriation of earnings and currency operations will be necessary early on, as will a clear understanding of laws and courts and how they work in each part of the region. Also important everywhere but especially in Northeast Asia, there has to be some way of guaranteeing freedom from excessive bureaucratic regulation and delay.

For making investment decisions, the requirement of a common set of operating standards and conditions is especially clear. Investors make comparisons of different locations within the region covering proximity to market, land cost, the quality of workmanship, labor costs, and the availability of skilled workers for particular industries. Only the first of these is not subject to government control in Northeast Asia, making a regional agreement to avoid uneconomic competition important. Also important is the availability of managerial talent in different parts of the region, which raises concerns about regulations on the movement of management personnel from where they are to where they are needed, irrespective of nationality (see Chapter 4).

National Affiliations. An important question for any regional scheme is how Northeast China and the Russian Far East can be isolated from the rest of China and Russia for purposes of regional cooperation. Both Northeast China and the RFE depend on the rest of their respective countries much more than the rest depends on them. Thus, for example, the exchange rate that would keep the ruble in line with national policy goals may not work at all for the RFE as a participant in a Northeast Asian regional grouping. Or the monetary policy that works for China as a whole may be too restrictive or too expansionary for Northeast China in relation to its partners in a Northeast Asian regional grouping. Difficult problems can arise when fiscal policies and incentives differ markedly between members of a regional grouping, and most of all when relative prices bear little or no relation to relative opportunity costs. These issues do not preclude regional cooperation, but they definitely do limit its feasible forms.

Financial Instability. Regional cooperation works best when partners in the cooperating group have similar and relatively stable rates of inflation and stable exchange rates. Then, if generally set by market forces, changes in relative prices can more accurately reflect the real underlying determinants of comparative advantage, and the response to relative price differences will direct resources toward their long-run best use. In developing Northeast Asia, relative prices often have little relation to world opportunity costs, but they are improving in this respect with economic reform. However, both monetary policy and exchange rate policies are very unstable. Russia has had runaway inflation since the beginning of its political reforms. China has had high levels of inflation followed by stifling bouts of inflation control. Mongolia also suffers from endemic inflation, and North Korean price levels are not translatable to international benchmarks. China more or less continually depreciated its exchange rate in the 1980s to offset inflation and increase international competitiveness. The RFE exchange rate has until recently had very little relation to economic forces and is now depreciating at a horrendous rate as the country tries to move into the world economy. There is much uncertainty about the future of the ruble, compounded in Northeast Asia by the fact that non-Asian considerations are paramount in Russian monetary and exchange rate policy decisions. North Korea lives in a barter world and would have to come out of it and learn about exchange rates in any regional grouping. Where regional cooperation, as in the Tumen Project, has been initiated for other reasons than achieving relative financial stability, the problem of financial stability has to be faced. Making this problem explicit will increase the probability that in making policy decisions the cooperating countries will factor in the costs to or loss of benefits from regional cooperation of idiosyncratic financial policies.

Policy Differences and Arbitrage. Given the many price distortions still present in the command economies of Northeast Asia, there should be numerous opportunities for arbitrage as some parts or sectors liberalize and become market-guided. For example, with trade liberalization in a developing Northeast Asia free trade zone, goods might be imported into the RFE at a favorable zonal border price and then make their way through Northeast China to, say, Shanghai, where the remaining border tariffs raise prices sufficiently above the zone level to offset the greater transport costs and delivery times involved. Disguising such imports is easy (but not costless in economic terms) and the disguises are difficult to trace. Tracing the opportunities for financial arbitrage created by a regional zone would be even more difficult. Monitoring costs could be high. Offset against these nonproductive, even income-reducing activities are the gains that would come within the zone from the removal of controls and the rent-seeking activities they generate. The larger the region encompassed in the zone and the greater the reduction of administered controls within that region, the greater the benefits of regional cooperation will be relative to the costs.

The Infrastructure Horse, or Is It the Cart? Many observers hold that it will be difficult to proceed without a minimally satisfactory regional infrastructure, now missing or insufficient in most of Northeast Asia. The argument is that adequate infrastructure, at least physical infrastructure and financial services, must be in place for much to happen. Another viewpoint is expressed in UNDP (1992) for the Tumen Project as follows: "Only once existing resources are fully utilized, and once participant countries have shown that they can cooperate in the management and use of existing infrastructure, is there a need and justification for large new, cooperative investments." Or, on the issue of funding a first-stage international airport and large container port, "it is better to let the infrastructure development follow rather than lead demand."

A further reading of the potential for cross-border interchange without major infrastructure projects is necessary to resolve this issue of supply-led or demand-pull development. In fact, some infrastructure projects (e.g., the railroad from Hunchun, China, to Kraskino, Russia) are under way. My experience suggests that little positive in the way of trade development can happen without major improvements in the region's infrastructure, both within Northeast Asia's separate parts and across borders. Any regional cooperation, except to fund and generate physical infrastructure projects or to develop a modern financial system, including the complementary infrastructure, would be severely constrained by the current lack of such infrastructure. The question really is, how far can you go and how far do you have to go in generating demand for infrastructure before the requisite international funds can be raised for infrastructure projects?

Structural Adjustment Costs. If successful, regional cooperation that achieves economic reform and greater trade and economic growth must result in structural adjustments. Intraregional competition for some goods or services will increase if intraregional trade expands via regional cooperation. All factors in product lines competing with the now available imports stand to lose to some extent, and as a step in the adjustment process large-scale unemployment may result. Firms competing with new capital for the available supply of labor and other resources must face the resulting rise in resource costs, via prices or some state-run allocation mechanism. The point is that the benefits of regional cooperation are net: there will be losers as well as gainers in any effective regional cooperation process.

Types of Regional Cooperation for Northeast Asia

There are many forms regional cooperation can take. In this section I discuss a selection of approaches that address major problems in developing Northeast Asia, have been successful elsewhere, or have been suggested for developing Northeast Asia (see Chapter 8 for elaboration of these approaches in a maritime context).

Non-Government Associations

Although finding non-government representation is impossible in North Korea and difficult in the other parts of developing Northeast Asia, one can find non- or quasi-government host institutions. The key is to keep discussions informal and representation unofficial. To get the cooperative process going, there is a strong need for unconstrained discussions of the many issues involved in the most politically neutral arena possible. A frank and open interchange, reflecting different country concerns and not pulling too many punches, is required to clear the air and provide the basis for meaningful compromise and progress. This applies to discussion of possible approaches to regional cooperation and of the specific proposals so far presented. Trial balloons need to be run up and research needs to be organized, financed, and carried out. This is especially important where, as in developing Northeast Asia, government-to-government exchanges tend to involve even longer strings of ideological platitudes or carefully noncommittal statements than usual.

Several forms of institutionalized non-government organizations (NGOs), ranging from regional centers for information exchange to organizations covering academics and business representatives, with government officials as observers, have been suggested. A network of national Asia-Pacific institutes (in Japan, China, Russia, South Korea, and the United States) has initiated this process. The Northeast Asia Economic Forum was established by the second Changchun conference for this purpose. Its task is to encourage research on regional issues and facilitate the continuation of consultations and discussions between all interested parties and the dissemination of research results.

An Association of Northeast Asian Economies

The "rules of the game" have to be established for all forms of substantive regional economic cooperation, from joint ventures through international economic zones to European Union–type integration. At the beginning, since achieving an enforceable consensus on these concerns is both a necessary condition for economic cooperation and very difficult to accomplish, differences in the legal, social, and paralegal environments affecting economic decision making might best be discussed in a non-governmental setting. However, to take substantive steps toward at least clarifying the "rules" in existence and to organize the investigations and hold the meetings needed to reach agreement on what cross-border activities will be opened, a formal international commission—an Association of Northeast Asian Economies—would be best. The UNDP is organizing something like this for the Tumen Project.

Besides helping establish the "rules of the game" and setting regional product standards, such a regional organization could help in negotiating plans for cross-border infrastructure development as well as in moving to close the huge information gap now constraining regional decision making. This could be done by establishing the accepted definitions and reporting rules for data categories, by carrying out training proposals, and by providing research that would serve decision making. High on the agenda is research on ways to finance the immediate infrastructure requirements and, since substantive action requires a clear image of the costs and benefits, on feasibility studies of the projects or enabling agreements contemplated. These studies should emphasize economic returns, with and without economic reforms. The political process will supply the weights for the numerous other factors that will ultimately be involved. At some point an intergovernment regional association could provide an appeals court for businesses contesting the interpretation of the "rules" of regional cooperation or for settling the inevitable business conflicts between nationals of the different countries involved.

The cost of such a regional association would not be great, but it would be positive and sovereignty issues would surely be involved. But such issues are implicit in all regional cooperation schemes. If Japan and South Korea could be prevailed on to join as consultative but non-voting members, the cost problem could be solved. Location is more of an issue and most likely the most difficult to resolve.

Regional Financial Cooperation

Although the timing may be in question, funding infrastructure requirements and organizing financial modernization are both necessary conditions for realizing Northeast Asia's strong potential for successful economic development. The transportation, communications, and energy infrastructure projects needed for sustainable industrial development often involve externalities not captured by market returns and long payout periods that make raising private capital difficult unless the risk is shared. They require low-return, national or cross-border loans, which are difficult to arrange. There also is a clear need for start-up or seed money loans, both to determine the feasibility of specific lines of production and to foster learning by doing. Again, these loans can lead to externalities not captured by market returns. Finally, for rational investment decisions to be made and outside investors to be attracted, there is a need to carry out project-related research and evaluation and to monitor lending risks— necessary steps in the banking process.

Together, these circumstances or preconditions for self-feeding growth suggest the value of establishing a regional development bank to service developing Northeast Asia. Such a Northeast Asian Development Bank would facilitate the financing of infrastructure and start-up projects by raising and channeling funds, generating equity capital, serving as a lead broker or guarantor of loans, and helping upgrade general financial capabilities. It would have a broader mandate than existing multilateral banks, possibly providing trade finance and clearing services in addition to the activities just described.

The temporary provision of trade finance, especially for start-up businesses and in new markets, would help solve an expected start-up problem and would train regional bankers in the financing process. Operating a clearing union for intraregional trade in developing Northeast Asia to economize on the reserves held in the region or to clear transactions internationally would be difficult because parts of countries—Northeast China and the Russian Far East—are involved. Financial records of shipment origins and destinations should be enough. There are many precedents or prototypes for regional clearing unions. Intraregional trade is low now, and the substantive benefits of a clearing union would be low, but such unions are a win-win way of working together and gaining confidence in each other.

Finally, a Northeast Asian Development Bank could establish regional training centers and develop other ways to help regional nationals learn basic banking skills. A financial structure that can carry out the clearing of domestic and international accounts necessary to escape a barter world is a number-one priority for developing Northeast Asia, where the necessary level of banking sophistication is missing.

There are at least three reasons why there is a need for a regional bank even though except for North Korea, the countries of the region are already members of one or more of the Asian Development Bank, World Bank, or European Development Bank. First, infrastructure projects in

Northeast Asia will be better planned and carried out as multinational projects than on a country-specific basis, as required by the charters or self-imposed lending criteria of the existing banks. Second, given the very different economic systems involved and the transition problems being faced, it does not seem likely that any but a regionally specialized lending institution would be sensitive enough to the region's special economic requirements and political realities. Third, staff of a regional bank would concentrate on Northeast Asia and not be continually shifting back and forth between Northeast Asia and the many other regions covered by the World Bank, Asian Development Bank, or European Development Bank. As opposed to the private banking sector, development banks have been efficient in materializing project finance of the sort required in Northeast Asia, because they can more often overcome international political barriers and can better spread (or diversify) the risks of finance.

A regional bank, with initial "ownership" capital coming from the developed countries on the "edge" of developing Northeast Asia—Japan, South Korea, and possibly Taiwan and the United States—could raise funds in all the established financial markets and from multilateral lenders. The problem in setting up such a bank would largely be in getting the agreement of these funding sources. With that in mind and for other sound financial reasons, the Northeast Asian Development Bank might be located in Japan.

International Free Trade Zones

The broadest free trade zone would involve all the developing Northeast Asia region's borders being open for trade, with only a few exceptions—much as trade between states in the United States is open. NAFTA and the European Union are current examples of such an approach, but neither involves parts of countries, which could require customs checkpoints between the Russian Far East and the rest of Russia and between Northeast China and the rest of China. There would have to be a central committee of some sort to establish rules and fix border access as Brussels does for the Union. Because of the RFE/Russia and Northeast China/China problem, this approach is probably ruled out. If a large free trade zone of this sort could be established in developing Northeast Asia, it would yield the maximum benefits possible from regional cooperation. Given the initial starting point, there would probably be much more trade creation than trade diversion in such a zone, with major growth in productivity.

More likely, however, is an international free trade area limited to some narrow contiguous cross-border enclave of the countries participating, as is the case with the proposed Tumen Project. Within such a free trade zone a broad range of economic functions would be covered, perhaps involving manufacturing, transshipment, warehousing and storage, trade and marketing, regional headquarters, international finance, services, research, tourism, and shopping.

The Tumen River Project is the most widely discussed regional version of an international free trade zone. There is presently controversy over exactly how it will be organized and managed, though at the May 1993 Pyongyang meeting the National Teams agreed *ad referendum* to establish the Tumen River Development Corporation, with the riverine states agreeing to lease land to the corporation and to establish a coordinating committee (Whelan 1994). Before this, North Korea, had been arguing for separate national zones with separate national rules and with a commission representing the three riverine countries advising on relations across the zone borders. On the other side was China, supporting the idea of ceding sovereignty to some degree over a part of each riverine country's contiguous lands and placing the "international" zone thus created under the supervision of the Zonal Management Corporation, with control in the hands of riverine countries but with board positions open to others. Mongolia supported China and the RFE was closer to the North Korean position, apparently because of a belief that Moscow would not approve the loss of sovereignty involved in the Chinese position. South Korea, expected to be an important player in the zone, supported the Chinese position, which appears to have won out.

However, there has still been no formal approval of the Corporation concept from the capitals involved. In fact, it now appears that North Korea has become the major advocate, with Russia the least willing to agree and China backsliding from its earlier support. Obviously, it will make a considerable long-run difference whether there are three contiguous national free trade zones or one international zone covering the territory of three countries and whether or not there is a single authority able to grant investment rights, settle disputes, be responsible for infrastructure, and so on. The problems that come with moving goods, factors of production, even money between three national zones will greatly restrict what can be accomplished.

Whichever way the final treaty is structured, if indeed there is one, the zone will still retain some attractiveness, especially if North Korea participates and Northeast China is allowed by Beijing to push forward the infrastructure now planned for the zone. Just on the promise of international cooperation in the region, considerable investment funds have already moved into Hunchun from South China, Hong Kong, and South Korea.

Ideally, the zone or connected zones would combine factor inputs and partly processed goods accessed from all member countries and beyond, bypassing normal tariff constraints or quotas, in the production of goods for export outside the zone or zones. Labor would come mostly from Northeast China and North Korea. Technical skills and management would come from all members plus South Korea, or from outside the region (most likely Japan). Capital would mostly come from outside the riverine countries, with Japan joining Hong Kong, South China, Taiwan, and South Korea as the major providers. The goods produced would be sold in the participating countries or exported, either by rail to Europe or by ship worldwide through the container facilities planned for Rajin, Troizki, or Poisyet.

Benefits for Mongolia and the RFE would be possible transfers of technology and the utilization of the comparative advantage of natural resources that otherwise might remain in the ground. The RFE would also gain from the probable increased demand for its research capabilities and high-tech inputs. China and North Korea would have the productivity of their workers increased and get the workers' share of the resulting increase in value added. They would also get the training effects and a major share of the secondary ripple effects of the increased employment and wage bill. All members would benefit from any subsidization of infrastructure loans used to get the project under way. The land share of value added created and whatever taxes are relevant would presumably be distributed to all zone participants after collection by the Corporation, if a single zone is developed, or to the country in which the zone producing the traded product is located. The after-tax profits share of value added would go to whoever supplied the ownership capital for the processing operation, probably a South Korean or Japanese firm, but possibly one from South China, Taiwan, Hong Kong, or even the United States or European Union. The interest share would go to the banks or other lenders involved—almost certainly, in the absence of a regional development bank, from outside the region in the single-zone model, and from who knows where for all but the Chinese zone in the multizone model.

However organized, an important part of the Tumen Project would be the connection of the zone or zones with container port facilities in the RFE or North Korea, or both. These could involve significant reductions in transportation costs as well as increases in economic specialization for Northeast China. Similarly, Mongolia would gain access to an internationally controlled port. And, if the Tumen ports can be connected to existing transcontinental rail routes, there could be further advantages.

South Korea (and Japan) would further benefit from the additional market for their machinery and equipment, both in providing the necessary infrastructure component and in establishing producing/fabricating/assembly activities in the zone or zones. And, along with the rest of the world, they would benefit from any real economies made possible by zone activities.

In sum, the Tumen Project has initial government approval and serves as an example of the international free trade zone approach to cooperation. It clearly needs further careful evaluation, especially as to the advantages or disadvantages of a multicountry zone over national zones such as the ones suggested (the Greater Vladivostok Economic Zone) or in operation (Nakhodka) in Primorski (see Appendix 2). The main advantages may be that an international agreement can be used to push through otherwise politically difficult reforms, that the necessity of working together on a limited basis may suggest the gains possible from and open the door to more general trade liberalization, and that there may be efficiency gains outside the zone from the increased competition and from the diffusion of the technology transferred into the zone.

Russian/RFE Benefits from Regional Cooperation

The benefits to the Russian Far East from the minimal approaches—activities of NGOs, intergovernment conferences on specific sectors or regional plans—would not be great, but neither would the costs. These forms of regional cooperation are relatively easy to implement but run the risk of seeming not to build toward any substantive results. However, given the lack of any but essentially negative regional interchange for so many years, any working together that provides knowledge and builds trust will help open the economic activities, unilaterally or via some international agreement, which promise real growth and development for the region. Also, with regional RFE representatives involved in and taking responsibility for these early-stage activities, a beginning independence from Moscow can be established.

An Association of Northeast Asian Economies would be a step up in complexity and commitment and, if agreed to by Moscow, would convey a special status to the RFE. For Russia itself, it would provide a multilateral means of building economic relations in Asia and so help avoid the bilateral issues that will continue to cloud such activities with Japan. In fact, membership in such an organization could give Russia needed leverage in its negotiations with Japan. The RFE would also benefit from the information-sharing, rule-setting activities to the extent that such activities attract capital to it. An international commitment to provide information and to establish common institutions and rules to govern economic activities may seem more likely to hold in the long run than action by any one country, and so it may be more attractive to foreign investors.

Many of the reforms necessary for sustainable growth require either local autonomy or that Moscow want the same changes. Examples are liberalized property rights, removal of licenses and quotas and other government interventions in the economic process, legal and institutional arrangements supportive of legitimate business activities, and strong action, especially in the courts, against illegal activities. Being exposed to international competition and to the necessity of survival in international markets is one way of making these reforms palatable. However, the costs of the shock involved may be too great if the opening is to the whole world at once. A stepwise approach, with the initial competitive market limited to developing Northeast Asia, could ease the way and bring substantial benefits at the same time. In this way, regional cooperation may contribute to essential domestic reforms.

One of most necessary economic reforms, creating a financial system that can function at international levels, requires either action from Moscow or the creation of a regional central bank (as the regional Federal Reserve Banks in the United States) with a certain degree of autonomy. The RFE lacks the banking experience and skills needed for the most rudimentary financial activities. Letting foreign banks set up there and carry on a general banking business is one way to achieve this skill transfer; but there are predictable roadblocks to such openness being adopted in the near future. Accordingly, regional cooperation—perhaps under the auspices of a regional development bank—which helps train the RFE personnel needed to operate a regional banking system would provide substantial benefits, if complemented by the necessary domestic financial reforms.

Regionwide trade cooperation promises the largest gains, because it provides the largest possible area for increased specialization in production and the largest increase in competitive pressures. Any regional free trade area (e.g., the Tumen area) would provide these benefits to some extent, but the larger the area involved the greater the gains. Unilateral Russian openness would raise Russian and RFE incomes, but historically such drastic reform has been politically impossible. The most visible political alternative is to establish policies that are similar to those in other countries in the region, so that the results can easily be seen as "fair" and the benefits (e.g., transportation, economies of scale) easily understood through observation of other regional trade agreements.

For the RFE, an international free trade zone would increase the market for high-tech skills, in symbiotic relation to the basic resource endowments of the other participants. Energy, labor, and land and water from China could be joined with RFE mineral resources to fabricate resource-based products. Perhaps, with the technological skills available in the Far East, boutique (specialized and to order) metals products serving the rest of developing Northeast Asia and beyond would develop. Regional trade cooperation could provide a ready market for RFE marine products and the labor to process these products into worldwide exports in an international free trade zone. Once under way, the growth involved in these activities and the long-term opportunities presented could encourage migration to the Far East from the rest of Russia, adding a layer of semiskilled, resource-based manufacturing production to the economy.

In a trade grouping, the RFE would gain access to Chinese agricultural products and the economies of scale possible in the Northeast China market—this in addition to the benefits of greater specialization already noted. The development of RFE brand names for high-tech inputs, boutique metal products, and marine foods is possible. The nearby market for forest products would also be enhanced.

There would not be much loss to international trade diversion from regional trade cooperation since the RFE is not a major importer at present. Trade creation, for any size international free trade zone, should be far greater. However, there will be some shift from Russian sources to nearby developing regional sources—a necessary result of greater specialization. Why, then, would Russia agree to any Northeast Asian free trade zone, since such a zone involves at least some trade diversion from the rest of Russia and means loss of central control? First, growth in any part of Russia has positive feedback to the rest of Russia as long as national average productivity is raised, as it would be by an international free trade zone. And growth that promises to add to the hard currency earnings of the country is even more desirable. Finally, the competitive experience and learning by doing in a relatively easy market will provide externalities for all Russia, not just the Far East.

The RFE is short of capital of all kinds now that it can no longer count on net defense transfers to cover local capital needs. A regional development bank that succeeded in raising otherwise unavailable funds for infrastructure projects and industrial development would obviously be of benefit. So would the direct foreign investment attracted by trade cooperation and financial reforms.

For foreign interest to go beyond the exploratory stage, regional autonomy in approving projects is important. In general, timely action, absence of political risk and instability, and believable contract enforcement guarantees along with a low level of red tape are all the incentives required to bring in foreign capital once the regional agreements are in place. State-of-the-art communication facilities, easy movement of people and funds, and the ability to operate at world prices at the exchange risk associated with world currencies (i.e., with forward markets) are also important. And, as argued, all can be facilitated by some form of regional cooperation.

Many forms of regional cooperation would encourage international joint ventures designed to take advantage of the larger regional markets and input-combining opportunities. With the needed infrastructure in place, it should not be necessary to subsidize such ventures to meet competition from elsewhere except through initial tax breaks. Letting profit-driven businesses determine what is produced is important in avoiding the still present command–heavy industry–planning mentality that generally believes "picking winners" is easy in spite of its history, everywhere, of picking "white elephants."

A major difficulty for the RFE in any regional grouping, already discussed at length, is the problem of financial stability, which even with quasi-regional autonomy would still be Moscow's responsibility. Exchange rate and inflation uncertainties could undermine the expected benefits from a regional trade agreement by sharply reducing the willingness of both domestic and outside entrepreneurs to take on the risks of production for cross-border markets.

In sum, the RFE can gain from regional cooperation that fosters greater international specialization, creates opportunities that generate demand for improvements in the physical, policy, and legal infrastructure, and gives sometimes needed rationalizations for difficult political changes. The RFE can also gain from regional cooperation that allows inputs to be combined more cheaply by accessing them throughout the region, opens up economies of scale, and provides opportunities to develop products and technology prior to entering world markets. Entry, via any cooperative scheme, into even part of the world's third-largest market, China, promises present and future benefits. Greater capital inflows to the chronically capital-short RFE brought about directly by regional cooperation or indirectly through the optimism for growth created by the fact of regional cooperation or even discussion of cooperation and the technology that accompanies greater capital inflows will be an additional benefit.

There are obviously many possible gains for the RFE and, indirectly, for Russia through all the levels of regional cooperation discussed, though the gains would be more difficult to sell to Russia. This is understandable, since on the surface it would look like the rest of Russia gives up sovereignty and loses control over RFE policies while the latter gains the direct benefits. The arguments to show that the rest of Russia stands to receive large benefits as well are relatively sophisticated and thus difficult to see. So any cooperative process is likely to start slowly. In the RFE, it is important to have a positive attitude and to be able to see the forest, not just the trees.

It is also important not to oversell regional cooperation. If reforms and international openness could be carried out unilaterally in all parts of the region, most of the benefits of regional cooperation could follow. The key is ready access to capital and appropriate technology and few constraints on the introduction of either. The problem is getting past the vested interests opposed to reforms and the high short-run costs of the resulting structural adjustments. South China has so far successfully made such a unilateral move, benefiting from the relative absence of state enterprises, a large agricultural surplus of labor, ready capital next door in Hong Kong, and little red tape, once you know where to place the envelopes. However, the special circumstances involved there are not generally reproducible, and successful regional cooperation can be a useful step toward politically acceptable economic reform.

Advantages to Outside Investors

Why might capital be attracted from Japan and South Korea and regional cooperation supported in Northeast Asia? Japan might see support of developing Northeast Asian regional cooperation as helping defuse the North Korea problem. Developing a nearby supply of resources is a less significant but not zero-value rationale for Japan's interest. Having a nearby location for labor-intensive production, given Japan's rapidly changing demography, might also gather support. Certainly developing Northeast Asia is one region where Japan could take an international leadership role. The inertia of Japan's conservative bureaucracy in taking on new political initiatives or committing funds to regional problem solving would be an obstacle. The outstanding issues with Russia would be another major block, but these might be avoided in supporting a larger group that includes Russia. Other reasons for Japan's not supporting regional cooperation in Northeast Asia are the continued Japanese focus on the West along with regional stereotypes that may make working with Northeast Asia seem unattractive to the Japanese. If Japanese support is to be forthcoming, western Japan and the business organizations seeing the value of the region's markets and resources will have to be strong advocates.

South Korea could expect regional cooperation to help share the coming burden of modernizing North Korea. And South Korea's economic planners may be beginning to understand the importance of China to their own long-run economic performance, and of Northeast China as an entry point within China. Regional cooperation can open a large market for South Korea's move to higher technology, and one where South Korea has a special locational and cultural advantage for learning by doing. As with Japan, developing Northeast Asia can provide a home for South Korea's declining labor-intensive production. The major problems are somewhat similar to Japan's—a negative image of Northeast Asia's capabilities, a relative focus on developed country markets, and a conservative bureaucracy.

For geopolitical and economic (market) reasons, the United States might be interested in providing at least moral support to regional economic cooperation in Northeast Asia. The problem is that most U.S. business is unaware of what is happening or might happen there, and the U.S.

government is not filling the information gap. The European Union's interest in what regional cooperation might bring is economic, not geopolitical. The Union has a sufficient trade presence now in the region to monitor what goes on effectively.

The goals of the present leadership in developing Northeast Asia in pursing regional cooperation would definitely differ. Beijing wants very much to get something going outside South China, to balance off the growing inequalities in regional economic performance. Beijing would also like to see change that could offer opportunities for rationalizing the inefficient state enterprises in Northeast China and that could reduce the present net resource transfers to North Korea. Within Northeast China, Jilin and Heilongjiang leaders have the most to gain and have provided the major support to regional cooperation. Liaoning faces the Yellow Sea and is less involved with and less interested in developing Northeast Asia; in fact, it would find some of the suggested cooperation (e.g., the Tumen Project) competitive with its own interests.

The possible economic reasons for Moscow's interest or lack of interest in Northeast Asian regional cooperation have been discussed. In geopolitical terms, the added importance of Primorski's ports now that both Baltic and Black Sea ports are no longer under the Russian flag may encourage a go-slow attitude in Moscow toward greater autonomy for the RFE or toward "sharing" the region's ports with China in a regional cooperation agreement. Perceived short-term strategic and longer-term economic interests may well conflict here.

In North Korea, regional cooperation may be seen as needed to achieve a beginning breakthrough out of its stagnating if not imploding economic performance, helping smooth the intergenerational transfer of leadership—seemingly the main motivation of the country's leaders. An opening that involves cooperating with its old comrades may seem the least threatening path to take in doing this. However, until demonstrated otherwise, the commitment of North Korea to real change and cooperation must remain suspect. In Mongolia's equally dire circumstances, anything that promises ways to jump-start growth and so give the newly elected president a long-run grip on power is going to seem desirable. There are not many options to regional cooperation for this purpose or for gaining some independence from China or Russia.

Although a combination of a Northeast Asian Development Bank and a Developing Northeast Asia Free Trade Zone supported by an Association of Northeast Asian Economies would provide most of the possible benefits from regional cooperation described in this chapter, the concerns and motivations driving regional leaders suggest that such wide-ranging cooperation is not in sight. It can be the goal, but initially the steps are going to be tentative and small. The largest and so most promising is the Tumen Project, if it does not self-destruct on sovereignty issues.

References

Asian Development Bank. 1992. *Key Indicators of Developing Asian and Pacific Countries*. Manila: ADB.

China Resources Advertising Company. 1988. *Almanac of China's Foreign Economic Relations and Trade, 1988*. Beijing.

Chinese State Statistical Bureau. Various years. *Chinese Statistical Yearbook*. Beijing.

Eberstadt, Nicholas, and Judith Banister. 1992. "North Korea: Population Trends and Prospects." Unpublished manuscript.

Jensen, Robert G., Theodore Shabad, and Arthur W. Wright, eds. 1983. *Soviet Natural Resources in the World Economy*. Chicago: University of Chicago Press.

Kim, Won Bae, and B.O. Campbell. 1992. *Proceedings of the Conference on Economic Development in the Coastal Area of Northeast Asia, August 1991, Changchun, China*. Honolulu: East-West Center.

Republic of China, Directorate-General of Budget, Accounting and Statistics. 1992. *Statistical Yearbook of China*. Taipei: Executive Yuan Republic of China.

UNDP. 1992. "Preliminary Reports of the Tumen River Area Development Programme." New York: UNDP (circulated but not published).

U.S. State Department, Bureau of Public Affairs. 1989. "Background Notes: [North] Korea." Washington, D.C.: GPO (July).

Whelan, John J. 1994. "Status of the Tumen River Area Development Programme: Progress, Accomplishments, Remaining Tasks." In *Regional Economic Cooperation in Northeast Asia: Proceedings of the Yongpyeong Conference, Yeonpeyeong, South Korea*. Honolulu: Northeast Asia Economic Forum.

World Bank. Various years. *World Development Report*. Oxford: Oxford University Press.

World Resources Institute. 1988. *World Resources 1988*. New York: Basic Books.

3

Economic Reform in Russia

Pavel A. Minakir

During 1991, traditional Russian problems of interregional economic ties were transformed into serious problems of relations between the center and the provinces (see, e.g., Murphy et al. 1992).[1] During the first quarter of 1991, industrial output decreased because of union-republic political conflicts, national conflicts within republics, refusal to produce nonprofitable products, and erosion of government control of prices.

The central government provoked these changes by supporting an unlimited free market and privatization of government enterprises. It tried to improve the situation by increasing prices. But this strategy, rather than achieving price structure optimization, destabilized the ratio of production to consumption. The first cycle of inflation had begun, and prices increased in 1991 by 2.18 times.

Producer reaction was logical for such a situation: production decreased because of increased risk, the costs of materials and semifinished products, and increased prices of consumer goods. This strategy had severe consequences for capital accumulation and investment. The consumption share of the national income increased from 73.6 percent in 1985 to 79.3 percent in the early 1990s, and investments dropped.

Since 1988, in the former USSR, the general strategy had been "neither plan nor market." Enterprises obtained freedom in the sense that they no longer had a hard central plan. But they also had no real possibility of market operations. In such circumstances, they had no choice but to increase the nominal income of workers, for example, in the form of barter exchange.

The economic crisis deepened in 1991. Officially, industrial production in the USSR was 93–95 percent of that in 1990. But the real production decrease was larger. The oil and coal extraction rate was down 11 percent, production of light and food industries down 12 percent, meat production down 18 percent, and milk production down 14 percent.

The decrease in production and the increase in prices produced stagflation. The confidence of consumers and producers in the ruble began to fall, as did the value of the ruble. The populace began to search for protection from the devaluation of their money, and the volume of commodities in regional markets decreased. Barter exchange replaced monetary exchange. Regions introduced special consumer coupons and severe limits on consumption.

The private sector was not ready to support general economic development without first developing the nongovernmental sector of the economy. It was in these circumstances that the August 1991 coup, basically an attempt to reintroduce government control of the economy, was attempted. But the foundation of the government economy had already been destroyed, so the coup was doomed to failure. The command economy could be reconstructed, but only as a "command private" economy; too many people had embraced the concepts of business and property and were absolutely opposed to a return to the old economy. Now they were waiting for the transformation of government property to private property. Thus, very few supported the putchists. The disintegration of the USSR as a result of the failed coup accelerated the process of radical economic reform in Russia.

The Macroeconomic Situation: Reform 1992–1993

The main task of the radical economic reform in Russia begun in January 1992 was the construction and introduction into the Russian economy of market regulations (Lipton and Sachs 1992; McKinnon 1993). The reform government declared that the key problem for the revival of the economy was financial stabilization. To accomplish this it was necessary to increase the cost of money by cutting the state budget, restricting credit, and reducing demand through price liberalization. But implementation of this strategy was faulty, and the consequences were the opposite of what was expected.

In Russia there had not been overactive investment before the beginning of reform. In fact, for many years the Soviet economy "decapitalized" itself. Now new regulations were formulated to accelerate reconstruction. But it was impossible to change the fundamental economic structure without investment funds (Sachs and Woo 1993). Government enterprises had only one possibility for reducing expenses—reducing jobs. But enterprise directors thought they were cleverer than the government. They reduced jobs, but not on the same scale as their increase in financial troubles. Consequently, production in January 1992 dropped 14 percent, but general demand dropped more than 300 percent.

In February and March, government enterprises could not pay for supplies, and the severe financial crisis had begun. Theoretically, with an increase in bank interest, such enterprises should have reduced their costs. Instead, they stopped paying each other. Debts became a new form of exchange, "shadow money." The total sum of such debts in mid-1992 reached 3 trillion rubles. Faced with this situation, the government adopted a "stop and go" policy. The central bank increased credit. Although this increase was not enough to cover all debts and the modernization of production, it was enough to increase the inflation rate in industry and an increase in budget income. The latter meant increases in both budget expenses and budget deficits. In the first half of 1992 the deficit of the Russian federal budget was more than 100 billion rubles, or 7.5 percent of GNP.

Differences between the theoretical model of economic behavior and the real economy were the most serious problems in 1992–93 (Table 3.1). According to theory, the universal regulator would be severe financial conditions: supply becomes greater than demand, prices decrease, profits drop, production modernization begins, production costs decrease, demand increases, production increases, and the financial situation stabilizes. In reality, some regulations influenced the economy in unpredictable ways.

The most serious impediment to regulation was the real behavior of producers and consumers. After Yegor Gaidar retired in December 1992, the new government suggested no new alternative economic policy. In January 1993 it declared the following measures as key points of its stabilization policy: restrictive and centralized financial regulation; reduction of credit expansion; centralization of the regulation of foreign economic activity; and reduction of federal budget expenses.

But this seems no more than Gaidar's policy. Of course, the lack of change is understandable: substantial corrections of economic policy are more political than economic. Modern economic policy can change only along with society's development, so it is no simple matter to achieve economic results similar to those in developed countries. First it is necessary to change the society's standards of economic and political behavior.

The Macroeconomic Situation in the Russian Far East

From early 1992, general economic activity in the Russian Far East decreased (see Table 3.2). In comparison with 1991 production levels, oil decreased 8 percent, coal 10 percent, timber 22 percent, construction materials 26 percent, paper 27.5 percent, meat 27 percent, and milk 28 percent.

The reduction of industrial output was considerable in the northern and island regions, where it has always been strongly dependant on external

TABLE 3.1 Economic Policy: Sequence of Events

Theory	Reality
Money market regulation	
Decreased money quantity	Decreased money quantity
Reduced consumer and production	Reduced demand
demand	Reduced production
Reduced production costs	Increased debt level
Increased supply	Increased money quantity
Increased production	
Credit market regulation	
Increased interest rate	Increased money demand
Decreased credit demand	Increased interest rate
Reduced commodity demand	Increased prices
Reduced prices	Increased debts
Reduced interest rate	Increased interest demand
Increased production	Increased interest rate
Investment regulation	
Increased prices	Increased prices
Reduced demand	Increased wages
Limited consumer funds	Reduced investments
Increased investments	Reduced production
Reduced production costs	
New production output	
Increased demand	
Price and production stabilization	
Structural regulation	
Increased prices	Increased prices
Reduced demand and profit	Reduced demand
Bankruptcies	Increased debts
Privatization	Increased money demand
Modernization of enterprises	Increased interest rate
Increased effectiveness	Increased prices
Price and production stabilization	

TABLE 3.2 RFE Economic Situation in 1992 (million rubles)

	1991	1992	1992 as % of 1991
Industrial production	580,838.7	491,384.5	84.8
Production of consumer goods	264,236.4	229,130.9	86.7
Investments	266,058.7	172,188.1	65.0

Source: Data from the Ministry of Economy of the Russian Federation, Far East Representative, Khabarovsk, 1993.

TABLE 3.3 Economic Activity of the RFE Territories, 1992 (% compared to 1991)

	Industrial Output	Consumer Goods Output	Investment	Housing Const.	Retail Sales
Sakha Republic	79.0	89.6	58.0	81.4	57.7
Primorski Krai	90.2	90.8	48.0	69.4	57.8
Khabarovsk Krai	88.3	83.3	67.0	66.0	67.1
Amur Oblast	84.3	74.3	93.0	86.0	67.6
Kamchatka Oblast	73.9	88.0	93.0	50.0	67.6
Magadan Oblast	92.7	114.5	53.0	45.0	46.5
Sakhalin Oblast	72.2	78.4	76.0	61.0	39.0

Source: Data from files of the Economic Research Institute, Far Eastern Branch of the Russian Academy of Sciences, Khabarovsk.

inputs. The social sphere has been suffering there much more than in the south. Housing construction and retail sales decreased in Magadan and Kamchatka oblasts to half that in 1991 (Table 3.3). Demographic statistics might be more precise indicators of the crisis. After 1992 the RFE population began to decrease. Immigration virtually ceased. Only Primorski and Khabarovsk krais received some influx. Amur, Kamchatka, and Sakhalin oblasts lost people. In the northern regions—Magadan oblast and the Sakha Republic (Yakutia)—the population was down in 1992, but the actual beginning of the decrease from Magadan Oblast began in 1988, and that from Yakutia in 1991.

The cash income of the RFE population during the economic reform period increased more rapidly than in the rest of Russia. In 1992 cash income increased 10.9–24.7 times (depending on territory), while the average growth in Russia was 12.3 times. Cash income may distort the real situation in terms of the quality of life because inflation rates differ in particular territories. But according to official statistics, the rate of inflation in RFE territories was lower than the average in Russia. This means that the economic situation was not the only reason for population reduction. Rather, changes in the economic position of the RFE within Russia, and pessimistic perspectives on its development potential, were major factors.

In mid-1993 the RFE economy underwent deflation. All enterprises had begun to increase prices for their products in early 1992. In addition to increased production costs, enterprises tried to include insurance against future price inflation. This tactic had two important consequences: an increase of profitability for some enterprises, and an increase in the proportion of unprofitable enterprises. There were 13.4 percent unprofitable enterprises in the RFE in 1991 and 27.9 percent in 1992. In the same years, the profit rate for profitable enterprises increased from 19.6 to 53.2 percent. But because of higher transportation costs and wages, the average profit in the RFE is less than in other regions. The increase in profit for Russia as a whole in 1992 was 1,360 percent, but only 760 percent for RFE enterprises.

By mid-1992 the main reason for the decrease in industrial production was a massive failure to pay by the government sector of the economy. Nevertheless, the general balance of payment was positive due to the high profit rate for the majority of enterprises. But enterprises preferred to increase debts rather than cut jobs. Because of the anti-inflation policy of the central government and central bank, a new cycle of regulation efforts appeared. To increase demand for money, the government and central bank created a deficit to support a minimum production level, and enterprises began to increase debts. To resolve the debt problem, new credits and subsidiaries were created. The inflation rate increased, as did the debt.

It is usual to describe the great potential for the Russian economy and its brilliant future in terms of its skilled population and huge natural resources. In fact, there is little hope for substantial growth in the population of the RFE (the region has only 8 million people and this number has decreased during the past three years), though the natural resource potential is real. The region has 280.6 million ha of forests with 21.3 billion m^3 of wood and vast reserves of fresh water with a hydroenergy potential equal to 1.0 trillion kwh. Marine resources include 6 million tons of fish and 2 million tons of other marine animal products per year. Known fossil energy and mineral reserves are 18.1 billion tons of coal, 308.2 million tons of oil, 1.5 trillion tons of gas, 4.4 billion tons of iron ore, 99 percent of Russian diamonds, the majority of Russia's gold and silver, 88–95 percent of its tin, antimony, and boron, 41–63 percent of its fluorspar and mercury, and 24 percent of its tungsten. The resources are forecast to be at least as great as the known reserves (for more on resources, see Chapters 5, 6, and 8).

It is also important that in many areas natural resources are located together and complement each other, allowing the creation of territorial production complexes that could meet interregional demands in raw materials and export substantially to other regions. The role of the RFE as the supplier of natural resources can increase. In such a situation, it will be not only a competitor but also a partner that can contribute to an integrated economy in Northeast Asia.

The resource base of the RFE economy is not, however, as significant as it was some years ago, when its raw materials were used mainly for the domestic market and the central government invested money in extraction industries mainly to support domestic consumption. For one thing, the best deposits have been exploited, and now large investments are needed to increase the natural base of many industries (timber, fish, nonferrous minerals, coal, oil, gas). But government investment is no longer a possibility, Russian private investors are too weak, and foreign investors are moving only slowly into the poor investment climate of Russia. Furthermore, the domestic market in Russia and CIS countries for RFE raw materials was and remains huge and unique for many products. But for Pacific Basin countries, these resources are not unique and must compete for markets, which again requires modernization and thus huge investments.

Investment has thus become critical for the survival of the RFE economy. Some years ago investments were necessary to increase production and strengthen the position of local leaders in the party and state bureaucracy. Usually there was fierce competition between such leaders for additional investment funds, but a minimum level of investment in each region was supported by the central government—thus guaranteeing some level of regional production and infrastructural and social facilities although ignoring the problem of development.

In 1988 the situation began to change with government attempts to reduce budget expenses. In early 1992 the investment situation became worse. The general strategy of minimizing federal budget expenditures meant the loss of investment, especially in the production and infrastructure spheres. Generally, then, the investment situation in the RFE is not optimistic. The decrease of investment activity in the production sphere was about 35 percent in 1992. The financial crisis and the collapse of the banking system excluded the possibility of increased investments from domestic sources, and so the attraction of foreign investments became one of the main goals for local administrations.

Foreign Trade and Direct Investment

Foreign Direct Investment

Recently, foreign direct investment has become an important factor in the economic development of the Russian Far East. At present, about 1,000 foreign-affiliated firms are registered in the region. The majority are concentrated in the service sector, but foreign trade is the main sphere of joint venture activities.

Fisheries are of particular interest for foreign investors (see Chapter 8). Joint ventures in that sector are oriented toward fishing, processing, and export. Fish products account for about 80 percent of the total export volume of foreign-affiliated enterprises. Joint ventures are the major contributor to the expansion of fish exports from the RFE, accounting for over 25 percent of total export income in this sector. The number of joint ventures

TABLE 3.4 Foreign Trade Activities of Foreign-affiliated Firms in the RFE

	1989 (million rubles)	1990 (million rubles)	1991 (million rubles)	1992 (US$ million)
Foreign trade turnover	5.2	40.7	405.8	602.7
Exports	13.0	31.3	221.8	386.9
Imports	2.2	9.4	184.0	215.8

Source: Data from files of the Economic Research Institute, Far Eastern Branch of the Russian Academy of Sciences, Khabarovsk.

in the timber industry is considerably smaller. Nevertheless, that industry as well as construction are also of interest to foreign investors.

Exports serve as a main source of hard currency recoupment for foreign capital enterprises in the RFE. The volume of exports exceeds that of imports and domestic market sales. It should be noted, however, that at present the imports of joint ventures are growing faster than their exports (Table 3.4).

Actually, joint ventures are becoming an important channel for the reorientation of Russia's foreign economic ties in favor of Asia-Pacific countries (see Appendices 1 and 3). Foreign-affiliated enterprises now account for 22 percent of RFE foreign trade. Although sometimes joint ventures contribute to diversification of the commodity structure of Far Eastern exports, in most cases they compete with domestic enterprises in traditional commodity markets, particularly fish and sea products. As a result, the share of fish products in regional exports is increasing.

As a rule, the major technologies transferred via foreign capital firms are those connected with the primary processing of raw materials. This situation is entirely different from that in Asian countries, where Japanese direct investment has made a noticeable contribution to the expansion of manufacturing exports. Nevertheless, the activities of foreign investors in traditional industries of the RFE are sometimes useful in penetrating new markets. For instance, the United States has substantially expanded its economic ties with the RFE through the activities of U.S.-affiliated firms. In 1992, American capital enterprises accounted for 66 percent of trade volume between that region of Russia and the United States. The corresponding figures for such countries as Vietnam and South Korea were 74 and 81 percent, respectively. Japanese firms dominate foreign investment in some RFE territories. In contrast, Chinese-affiliated firms rely heavily on simple barter transactions.

Among the positive influences on the process of joint venture establishment and expansion of foreign trade are the plans for establishing free economic zones and eliminating some legal limitations to foreign inves-

TABLE 3.5 Major Foreign Trade Channels of the RFE (%)

	1988	1989	1992
Centralized	94.4	74.2	19.3
Independent	5.6	25.8	80.7
Border and coastal trade	2.6	2.0	3.7
Direct ties	3.0	22.2	52.7
Exports of joint ventures	—	1.6	24.3

Source: Data from files of the Economic Research Institute, Far Eastern Branch of the Russian Academy of Sciences, Khabarovsk.

tors' access to natural resources and the inner market of the RFE. So it is quite understandable that the commodity structure of foreign capital firms' imports consists not only of capital goods but also of such goods as personal computers, cars, and office equipment, the demand for which is particularly high. The process of economic liberalization in Russia brought new opportunities for domestic enterprises for expanding foreign trade operations and increasing sales of imported goods on the domestic market, thus providing new stimuli for competition between national and foreign capital enterprises.

However, the preferential treatment of foreign capital firms in Russian economic legislation enables them to be more competitive than local enterprises. For example, foreign capital firms with a foreign equity share of more than 30 percent have the right to export their own products freely; in 1989–91 the exports of foreign capital firms grew almost 10 times, while regional exports through other channels grew by only 100 percent.

Foreign Trade

Up to the end of the 1980s, the development of RFE foreign trade proceeded mainly in a centralized system in which the state ordered enterprises to produce goods for export. This state order was imposed by central ministries and related bodies. Imports were also highly centralized. In later years the reforms aimed at decentralization of external trade and resource management led to a dramatic decrease in the share of centralized exports and imports. Thus, new opportunities for independent economic exchange appeared. The share of independent economic exchange in total exports in 1988–92 increased from 5.6 to 80.7 percent (Table 3.5).

New opportunities for expanding independent economic exchanges have been used by RFE enterprises for promoting direct ties with foreign partners, particularly on a barter basis. The main reason for such economic behavior has been the possibility of obtaining extra profits stemming from the existing gaps between domestic and international prices

TABLE 3.6 Commodity Composition of Imports to the RFE (%)

	1989	1990	1992
Machinery and transportation equipment	34.4	39.5	24.0
Fuels, minerals, metals	0.1	0.2	1.6
Foods, beverages, tobacco	36.7	23.9	27.1
Other consumer goods	8.2	19.1	41.7
Construction materials	4.1	1.5	0.6
Other	16.5	15.0	5.0

Note: Excludes imports of joint ventures.
Source: Data from files of the Economic Research Institute, Far Eastern
Branch of the Russian Academy of Sciences, Khabarovsk.

for export and import commodities. At the same time, such transactions enable stabilization of the regional consumer market. Barter transactions also overcome some limitations imposed by existing foreign exchange and trade legislation. The development of direct ties was also positively influenced by the central government's provision of export quotas to RFE territories. On the other hand, the formation of a domestic foreign exchange market provided access to hard currency for individual enterprises and fostered the expansion of decentralized imports for satisfying the Far East's own demand for capital and consumer goods as well as for reimport operations (Table 3.6).

As a result, in recent years the growth rates of regional imports have been higher than those of exports. The fact that until recently import tariffs had been relatively low also stimulated import growth. In general, tariff regulation was more liberal than in other countries of Northeast Asia. Market-oriented reform and the growing importance of market signals have decreased the competitiveness of locally produced goods in the domestic market of Russia and the CIS. But an optimization of RFE economic ties is emerging. The role of foreign trade in economic development is increasing. The current reorientation of economic relations from the domestic market toward the international market is a more important factor for the prospects of economic integration with the Asia-Pacific than export expansion through increased centralized investment in primary industries, which had been the previous mainstay of RFE foreign economic policy.

Over the past decade, economic relations of the RFE with the inner regions of the country have been characterized by a negative balance of trade. External trade is, however, entirely different. For example, in 1992 the volume of foreign trade amounted to US$2.5 billion, with a trade surplus of more than $300 million. The current surplus in foreign trade is connected with sluggish investment activities, which lead to a decrease in de-

TABLE 3.7 Commodity Composition of Exports from the RFE (%)

	1988	1991	1992
Machinery and transportation equipment	2.1	1.9	17.8
Fuels, minerals, metals	20.7	17.2	26.7
Chemical products	1.0	7.3	9.1
Construction materials	0.6	0.1	0.2
Raw materials and semifinished goods	34.5	24.2	13.4
Foods and beverages	34.2	44.9	29.4
Other commodities	6.9	4.4	3.4

Note: Excludes exports of joint ventures.
Source: Data from files of the Economic Research Institute, Far Eastern Branch of the Russian Academy of Sciences, Khabarovsk.

mand for capital goods. At the same time, demand for consumer goods is increasing. Imports of capital goods began to decrease at the end of the 1980s. In the following years, the share of consumer goods in imports began to rise rapidly. The leading position of nonfood consumer goods in imports can be partially explained by their use for further sale in Russia's internal market. As for foods and beverages, they are mainly designated for local consumption. These commodity groups are already of importance in the RFE local market.

The major export commodities are timber, mineral fuels, and fish products. But the commodity structure of exports is far from stable, with several remarkable changes occurring at the end of the 1980s and the beginning of the 1990s (Table 3.7): (1) The share of industrial raw materials, for example timber and timber products, has decreased substantially. In 1992 these commodities accounted for only 13.4 percent of total exports (the figure for 1988 was twice as high). However, the structure of timber-related exports itself is rather stable: timber products with low value added occupy the leading position. (2) The share of coal, crude oil, and petrochemicals in total exports increased from 5.6 percent in 1980 to 20.5 percent in 1992. The growth rate of exports for the entire commodity group of fuels, minerals, and metals was even higher due in part to expansion of exports of ferrous and nonferrous metals. Their share in total exports rose from 0.8 percent to 6.2 percent during the same period. These figures do not include centralized exports of gold and silver. (3) In recent years there has been an increased share of reexports in total exports of the RFE. This is particularly important for machinery and equipment and for mineral fertilizer. Mainly due to reexport operations, the share of machinery and equipment in exports grew from 2.1 percent in 1988 to 17.8 percent in 1992. The growth of the share of chemical exports from 1.0 percent to 9.1 percent during the same period is also connected with reexports of min-

Pavel A. Minakir

TABLE 3.8 RFE Exports by Destination (%)

	1980	1985	1990	1992
Asia-Pacific region	68.0	78.0	85.0	89.8
Japan	61.0	62.0	65.0	47.2
China	—	10.0	17.0	29.5
Other countries	7.0	6.0	3.0	13.1
Other destinations	32.0	22.0	15.0	10.2

Source: Data from files of the Economic Research Institute, Far Eastern Branch of the Russian Academy of Sciences, Khabarovsk.

eral fertilizer. At the same time, the commodity structure of exports became more diversified, as exports of other chemicals grew, particularly boron components produced in Primorski. The available statistical data do not cover exports of machinery from military enterprises in the RFE. (4) A more noticeable trend in RFE exports is the emergence of the fisheries industry as the leading exporter. In 1991 it accounted for more than half of total exports. Exports of other commodities have been characterized by a lack of stability or growth. In most cases volume has decreased, particularly for furs and construction materials.

Overall, the current trends in foreign economic relations of the RFE imply some changes in the commodity structure of its exports and imports while the general pattern of foreign trade remains unchanged, that is, a horizontal division of labor. This situation can be explained in terms of the existing industry structure in the local economy and the crisis in military-industrial enterprises, which possess considerable potential for expanding economic ties with Pacific economies through industrial cooperation.

Current changes in the geographical structure of RFE foreign trade are more fundamental than those in commodity structure (Table 3.8; see also Chapter 2). The most important change is that Japan has been surpassed by China as the leading trade partner. Though Japan remains the largest single market for such export commodities as fish, timber products, and mineral fuels, its share in total exports decreased from 62 percent in 1985 to 47 percent in 1992. However, the RFE still accounts for about 25 percent of total Russian exports to Japan.

RFE trade relations with China are dynamic. In 1992 the trade turnover between Russia and China grew by 27 percent and was a little less than US$4 billion, representing about 5 percent of the total volume of Russian foreign trade. The RFE accounted for some 25 percent of this figure. From 1985 to 1992, the share of China in RFE exports grew from 10 to 30 percent, mainly due to the rapid expansion of reexport operations and barter trade. For example, the share of China in total barter transactions of the

RFE was 58 percent, about two times greater than that of Japan. It should also be noted that by the beginning of the 1990s China had become the RFE's leading import market, which can be explained by taking into consideration stable demand for foodstuffs and nonfood consumer commodities in the region and the relatively low prices of Chinese goods.

The importance of the Republic of Korea is also rapidly increasing. At present, that country accounts for about 9 percent of total trade turnover in the RFE. The large Korean corporations became the leading economic partners in the RFE from the very beginning of bilateral economic cooperation. In many cases they display interest in the same export items as small and medium-sized Japanese firms. Under the conditions of sluggish investment activity in the RFE, the major export items of Korean firms are consumer products. As a result, the share of South Korea in regional imports has notably increased, and competition between Chinese, Japanese, and Korean products is growing.

An orientation toward Japan as a single large trade partner was a peculiar feature of foreign trade in the RFE for almost two decades and proved to be an impediment to the development of the external economic relations of the territory. Taking into consideration the narrow range of export goods and their relatively low quality, it is quite understandable that RFE exports are extremely vulnerable to demand fluctuations in the Japanese market.

In this view, partial reorientation of exports and imports toward other markets can be considered an important factor for further expansion of Russian Far Eastern external trade. This is particularly true for economic ties with the countries of Northeast Asia, which account for about 80 percent of the total foreign trade volume of the RFE.

Prospects for Economic Cooperation with Northeast Asia

Decentralization of foreign economic activities in Russia facilitated the expansion of trade between the RFE and neighboring economies but also exposed some serious problems, mainly connected with the decline of foreign trade efficiency at the macroeconomic level. This situation is typical for Russia as a whole in that dumping of exports of natural resources in exchange for imports of profitable goods that are not of vital importance to the national economy further aggravates the economic problems of this country.

To raise the efficiency of foreign economic relations and strengthen control over foreign exchange circulation, the central government toughened foreign trade regulations and introduced higher export and import tariffs and a system of licensing for strategically important exports. Those measures can limit further development of independent economic exchanges of the RFE and hinder the process of reorientation of the region's economic ties with Northeast Asian countries where competitiveness of RFE products is higher than in Russia's internal market.

On the other hand, the growth of internal investment activities in the RFE may lead to a deficit in the balance of payments. However, the worsening balance of payments seems to be inevitable if the region chooses to reorient its economic ties and attract large-scale foreign investment. Under such conditions, the need for well-coordinated export and investment promotion policies will become absolutely clear. The same holds true for the promotion of foreign investment in export and import substitution industries and for the rationalization of foreign exchange spending. Therefore, the main problem is to find an optimal scenario for economic integration of the RFE with Northeast Asia. This kind of scenario must envisage partial liberalization of export and import tariffs as well as maintenance of non-tariff regulations. This approach is aimed at providing new stimuli for foreign economic activities on the micro level in order to promote independent economic exchanges with neighboring economies and at raising the efficiency of external ties on the macro level.

Economic Tendencies

There are both negative and positive results and tendencies in Russian Far Eastern development under the new economic reforms. Among the negative are these:

1. True regional self-financing is required in the RFE as well as many other regions in Russia. Traditionally the RFE received guaranteed subsidies of food and other products according to accepted development plans. Now regions and enterprises have to fill financial and supply needs by themselves. Obtaining local budget sources to do so, and to balance payments with other regions, has become the primary problem. Thus the RFE has to support intense, competitive production.

2. Noncompetitiveness is the strategic problem for the region. The RFE has few ways to improve its competitiveness because, with the general change in the structure of the price system, commodities such as oil, gas, coal, electricity, grain, metal, transportation services, and raw materials for industry are determining prices. Thus the increase of production costs for the RFE is larger than in other regions. Furthermore, enterprises have to pay additional wages to workers from their budgets; previously the central budget provided these directly or indirectly.

3. Investment in the economy has diminished. Up to 1992, central budget investments were relatively significant in the region. For the RFE the period 1988–91 was one of relative growth in investments, through the Long-Term Program of Economic and Social Development of the Far East

to the year 2000. But since 1992 the situation has changed. The federal budget was practically eliminated as an investment source. Four possible sources of investments remain: corporate profit and amortization of funds; bank loans; local budget investments; and foreign investments.

Corporate profit and amortization funds are very limited sources because of inflation and the financial troubles of almost all enterprises. In fact, they are mirages; there is a profit in the balance but not in the bank. Banks are now mainly giving short-term loans because of high inflation and the negative interest rate on an annual basis. Local budgets in the RFE are traditionally negative: scales of deficit in 1993 in the territories are 10 percent and more. Foreign investments need an attractive climate, which can be established only by governmental decision.

4. The economic life of the RFE is disintegrating. This process began in the second half of 1992 after President Yeltsin nominated territorial heads of administration and dispersed the administrative power of the country. New governors wanted to prove that they were more professional and stronger in ruling their territories, and the central government gave incentives to some territories without basis save for the personal persistence of governors and their relations with central leaders.

The following are positive tendencies:

1. The reorientation of economic ties in the region began in 1992. The RFE had received the majority of foodstuffs and other commodities and goods for production and consumption from European Russia and from other republics until 1990. In 1991 and especially 1992, government obligations and promises had been forgotten. As a result, RFE territories had to find new ways to obtain the necessary resources, especially food. One way was to increase imports. In 1992 the general increase of imports was 320 percent, though the volume of exports increased only 30 percent. The problem of stabilizing the balance of payments by developing exports cannot be resolved without a flexible federal policy in this field.

2. A new sector of specialization in the RFE appeared—international transport and transit services. With the dissolution of the USSR, Russia lost more than half its seaports in the western part of the country. Thus Russian foreign trade began to reorient toward the Pacific, and so Russian and also many CIS producers are trying to use Far Eastern ports to export commodities. Accordingly, RFE investments are beginning to reorient away from heavy industry toward transport infrastructure, including seaports and ferry facilities on the Chinese border.

3. The public mentality is changing. Because of propaganda by companies in favor of private property, the majority of the population looks forward to privatization. But privatization will not by itself bring wealth to the people and the country. In fact, the future of the former Soviet countries may be poverty if the present general strategy remains the same. In-

deed, government capitalism may not be much better than government socialism. In principal, however, the reorientation of public opinion offers a chance to change the current strategy without returning to totalitarianism.

The near future of the RFE depends on furthering these positive tendencies and eliminating the negative. It is necessary that the model of development and management be changed to create an open, mixed economy with flexible regulations sufficient to attract foreign capital.

Notes

1. All source citations in this chapter have been added by the editor. The general analysis, including statistical and tabular information, is supported by the 1993 *Russian Far East Economic Yearbook*, Part 2 (1992), produced at the Economic Research Institute, Academy of the Russian Federation, Far Eastern Branch, Khabarovsk. Another useful source is State Committee of the RSFSR for Statistics, *Economic Situation in the Russian Federation, 1992*, Moscow.

References

Lipton, D., and Jeffrey Sachs. 1992. "Prospects for Russia's Economic Reforms." *Brookings Papers on Economic Activities* 2:213–83.

McKinnon, Ronald I. 1993. "Gradual versus Rapid Liberalization in Socialist Economies: The Problem of Macroeconomic Control." *Proceedings of the World Bank Annual Conference on Development Economics*. Washington, D.C.: World Bank.

Murphy, Kevin, Andrei Shleifer, and Robert Vishny. 1992. "The Transition to a Market Economy: Pitfalls of Partial Reform." *Quarterly Journal of Economics* 57(3):889–906.

Sachs, Jeffrey, and Wing Thye Woo. 1993. "Structural Factors in the Economic Reforms of China, Eastern Europe and the Former Soviet Union." Economic Policy Panel Meeting in Brussels, Belgium, 22–23 October.

4

Migration

Won Bae Kim

The level of cooperation and interaction across national boundaries in the North Pacific has been extremely low until recently because of political barriers and incompatible ideologies. But many of the factors that prevented interaction in the past have been disappearing, especially ideological differences, and a more pragmatic approach has been developing, setting the stage for dynamic growth of the region's economies. As China, Russia, Mongolia, and to a lesser extent North Korea move away from command economies to a mixed economy, there will be more reforms and deep industrial restructuring. One consequence will be considerable flows of population within these countries and eventually into neighboring countries.

A Changing Economic Environment

International labor movements in Northeast Asia are likely because of differences in resource endowments and levels of development (Table 4.1). The countries/areas of the North Pacific can be grouped into three basic economic levels: high-income, labor-deficit economies; low-income, labor-deficit economies; and low-income, labor-surplus economies. If land resource is added, it is possible to divide these groups further. Russia (especially the Russian Far East), the United States, Canada, Mongolia, and a portion of China represent large land masses, rich in mineral and forest resources; Japan, North Korea, and South Korea are relatively small countries in terms of area, and a large portion of their land is too mountainous for settlement. The tremendous rise in land prices and associated problems in Japan, Taiwan, and South Korea in the 1980s illustrate the severity of population pressure on land. The recent rush of Japanese, Hong Kong, and Taiwan investors to the west coast of North America reflects the underlying forces of capital and population movement in the North Pacific. In this regard, the Russian Far East has a great potential to host temporary

TABLE 4.1 Population and Economy of the North Pacific, 1990

Subareas	Area (1,000 km²)	Population (million)	Density (persons/km²)	Per Capita GNP ($)
China	9,561	1,143.3	120.0	326
NE China[a]	1,970	121.6	60.5	392
Japan	378	123.5	326.7	25,430
North Korea	125	21.4	170.6	1,095
South Korea	99	42.8	439.5	5,569
Mongolia	1,565	2.1	1.3	na
USSR (1989)	22,402	288.0	13.0	na
RFE (1989)	6,216	7.9	1.3	na
Canada	9,976	26.5	2.7	20,470
United States	9,373	250.0	26.7	21,790

[a]Lioaning, Jilin, Heilongjiang, and Inner Mongolia.
na = not available.
Sources: Sallnow (1989) for Soviet Union and Russian Far East; State Statistical Bureau (1991) for China; Hankuk Ilbo, 8 November 1991, for North and South Korea; World Bank (1992) for other information.

migrants (for both capital-associated and residential purposes), provided that its infrastructure and social facilities are upgraded and expanded. It is natural to expect, from economic logic, that the United States and Canada will be the most likely destinations for long-term migration. Japan, because of its superior economic power, could be an alternative destination for potential migrants from Asia and beyond.

If political barriers are removed and free movement of labor is allowed in the North Pacific, there will be a substantial redistribution of the region's population. Clearly this free movement of labor is not going to be allowed in the immediate future, and therefore real wages are not going to be equalized by labor movements. Still, the pressure to migrate will soon build up in labor-surplus areas if political barriers are lifted. China seems most susceptible to potential emigration, since it has suppressed people's mobility for over three decades. Furthermore, China as a whole is not a land-rich country, because of its huge population. As seen in Table 4.2, China ranks well below Canada and the United States and is closer to land-poor economies in terms of agricultural land available per capita. As mentioned by Chinese planners, there are more than 100 million "surplus" laborers in China's rural areas, indicating an enormous number of would-be migrants from rural to urban areas within China as well as would-be emigrants to other countries. Albeit to a lesser extent, North Korea shares these attributes.

Demographic factors determine the long-term pattern of migration between countries. Industrialized countries in the North Pacific have al-

TABLE 4.2 Rural Population and Crop Land per Capita, 1990

	Share of Rural Population (%)	Crop Land per Capita (ha)
China	66.6	0.08
Japan	33.0	0.04
North Korea	40.2	0.09
South Korea	28.0	0.05
Mongolia	47.7	0.63
Soviet Union	34.2	0.80
Russian Far East (1989)	23.0	na
Canada	22.9	1.73
United States	25.0	0.76

na = not available.

Sources: World Resources Institute (1992); and Sallnow (1989) for the Russian Far East.

ready gone through demographic transition, and their population growth is expected to be slow. Japan began to experience labor shortages in the 1980s, and these will worsen because of very slow labor force growth. South Korea and Taiwan have begun to see labor shortages in some sectors, and shortages of blue collar workers should become more pervasive in the 1990s; labor force growth is projected to be slow (Bauer 1990), and these two countries appear to be socioculturally closed and biased against immigrants.

Along with the trend of regionalization in the global economy, one would anticipate a regionalization of migration pressures, determined not only by geographical proximity but also by political and economic linkages. Within the North Pacific, such pressures will intensify toward North America, which has been the major destination for international migration. More narrowly, recent trends indicate increasing pressures for migration toward Japan and more dynamic countries within Asia (Stahl 1991; Martin 1991). This is particularly so because of growing economic interdependence in Asia through capital and commodity flows. The penetration of Japanese capital throughout Asia has been considerable in the 1980s, and the presence of Japanese capital and businesses in these countries has in turn stimulated emigration toward Japan.

Political Concerns

Migratory pressures based on economic forces do not automatically result in migration, because border control usually intervenes as a determining factor. International population movements are often impelled, encouraged, or prevented by governments or political forces. Moreover, governments control entry and exit of their citizens. States do play an important role in both creating and responding to international migration. Governments may force emigration as a means of achieving cultural homogeneity, dealing with political dissidents, extending control over foreign territory, or destabilizing neighboring states (Weiner 1992/93). In such ways, migration is used as an instrument of the state and often constitutes a threat to the security and stability of other states.

In an ideal situation, migration across borders will strengthen ties of interdependence, promote social openness, and improve mutual understanding. It can contribute to the economic and social stability of the countries involved and thereby enable them to enjoy a higher level of security. In reality, however, international population movements often create conflicts within and between states, posing serious threats to national stability and international security. Globally, a reappraisal of the whole issue of international migration and labor movements and their implications for security and stability is under way in the industrialized states (Weiner 1992/93; Widgren 1990). In the North Pacific, Japan has expressed serious concerns about the rapid increase of illegal foreign labor in recent years. Illegal entry of aliens is an important issue for economically depressed Americans. Recent arrivals of Chinese by boat to the U.S. mainland have heightened America's social awareness about migration. Immigration policies in the United States might become more restrictive in the future, because ethnic conflicts and racism there have been rising and economic protectionism has been gaining momentum.

Conceptually, there are five categories of situation in which migrants may be perceived as a threat: (1) refugees and migrants opposed to the regime of their home country (e.g., permission for Chinese students to remain in the United States after the 1989 Tiananmen incident because of possible persecution in China was regarded by China as interference in its internal affairs); (2) refugees and migrants perceived as a political threat to the regime of the host country; (3) immigrants seen as a cultural threat; (4) immigrants seen as social and economic problems for the host society; and (5) immigrants used by the host society as an instrument of threat against the country of origin (Weiner 1992/93). Although some nations, such as North Korea and China, restrict exit, generally policies of potential receivers determine whether movement can take place and of what kind. Often these immigration policies are intertwined with international politics. Mitchell (1989) summarizes a few of these relationships: international relations help to shape international migration; migration may influence and serve the goals of national foreign policies; and domestic immigration laws and policies may have unavoidable international political repercussions. The prohibition of exit that prevailed among socialist states (and still prevails in China and North Korea) during the past decades has acted as a negative determinant of population movements across national borders in the North Pacific. Such restrictive emigration policies have begun to change in Russia and China, and it is likely that there will be further liberalization in the near future. A new Russian immigration law took effect in 1993. China adopted a new emigration and immigration law in 1986 and for the first time relaxed exit restrictions (Wakabayashi 1990); specifically, the law allows exit for the purpose of "residence," "visits," "wealth inheritance," "privately funded study," "employment," and "tour." Because of the change in the law, the propensity to emigrate has increased since 1986, especially in large urban areas.

Past and Present Migration in the North Pacific

Pre–World War II Migration

Historically, migration in the North Pacific, particularly in Northeast Asia, was dominated by planned migration for purposes of colonization. Russia's colonization policy included transplantations of Russians in Central Asia, Siberia, and the Russian Far East and relocation of indigenous ethnic minorities from their homelands to other areas. Relocation of Korean residents from the RFE to Central Asia is one example.

The immigration of Koreans to China in large numbers started in the 1880s, when tens of thousands of poor farmers crossed the border. It accelerated after 1910 when Korea was annexed by Japan. The Japanese colonial economic policy in Korea left many Korean farmers landless, and a large number of poverty-stricken farmers in the northern provinces moved to the Yanbian area in China and to the RFE to avoid economic hardships at home. Other Korean immigrants were recruited as laborers by the Japanese colonial government once the latter had control over Manchuria after its occupation (1931–32) and the establishment of Manchukuo in 1932.

During Japan's external aggression in the early twentieth century, Japanese migration to its overseas territories was actively promoted by the government. The prewar military regime regarded Manchuria as Japan's lifeline and the major source of supply of natural resources. Transplantation of Japanese people to Manchuria, Korea, Taiwan, and Sakhalin was national policy. The number of nonmilitary Japanese in Manchuria was about 1.2 million, with 713,000 in Korea, 322,000 in Taiwan, and 277,000 in Sakhalin just before World War II. A total of 3.2 million nonmilitary Japanese repatriated from Japan's overseas territories after the war, in addition to 3.1 million military and paramilitary personnel (Watanabe 1993).

In contrast, the immigration of foreigners into Japan during the prewar period was mainly from Korea and Taiwan, which were under Japanese rule. The fact that large numbers of Koreans were not voluntary migrants reflects Japan's two-edged migration policy: sending out Japanese to colonize overseas territories, and bringing in Koreans and Taiwanese to supplement the manpower gap caused by the outflow of Japanese. In 1940, Koreans who resided in Japan numbered 1,304,286 and Chinese 60,549 (Watanabe 1993).

During the first half of the twentieth century, migration was an important element in Russia's expansion toward Siberia and the Far East. The population of the RFE increased rapidly through active promotion of migration from Europe: 1.26, 2.56, and 4.35 million in 1926, 1939, 1959, respectively (Kirby 1971). Russians and Ukranians who came as peasant pioneers formed the major settler groups. Certain remote Far Eastern territories were colonized by convicts through forced labor. There was also "military colonization": discharged soldiers settled down with their families in the fertile border regions on the Ussuri River (Kolarz 1954). With the beginning of large-scale development under the five-year plans, efforts to increase the population of the RFE appeared at many levels, including calls to the Young Communist League for loyalty and moral appeals to many workers (Mandel 1944).

Indigenous peoples and oriental immigrants living in the area were few, less than a million in total. About 30,000 Chinese and 180,000 ethnic Koreans lived in the RFE around 1930. After the occupation of southern Sakhalin at the end of the war, some 400,000 Russians moved into that territory, replacing the Japanese. Around 180,000 Korean residents were relocated from the RFE to Central Asia by Stalin in 1937. Soviet authorities considered Koreans a potential threat in the east after Japan's move into Manchuria.[1]

Policies regarding ethnic minorities differed between countries. For example, Min (1992) attributes the differential levels of ethnic identity between the Korean groups in China and Japan to the differences in minority policy between the two countries (China's pluralistic minority policy emphasizing ethnic autonomy versus Japan's assimilationist policy[2]) in addition to differences in the context of migration and levels of influence from the home country.[3]

Recent Long-term Migration

The major direction of permanent migration within the North Pacific since World War II has been toward North America. In terms of annual average, the United States accepted 0.5–1.5 million, Canada 100,000–190,000, and Australia 150,000–250,000 between 1980 and 1990 (Table 4.3). These figures amount to 0.5 and 0.2 percent of the total population of the United States and Canada. Recent statistics show that Koreans and Chinese are

TABLE 4.3 Long-term Immigrants (thousands)

	Canada	United States	Japan	Australia
1980	143	531	40	170
1981	129	597	41	205
1982	121	594	52	211
1983	89	560	56	173
1984	88	544	62	145
1985	84	570	64	163
1986	99	602	63	186
1987	152	602	69	204
1988	162	643	82	242
1989	192	1,091	na	250
1990	na	1,536	na	232

na = not available.

Sources: Australia figures adapted from Madden and Young (1993); Canada figures from Ministry of Industry, Science and Technology (1991); U.S. figures from U.S. Department of Justice (1991); Japan figures from United Nations (1991).

among major immigrant groups from Northeast Asia to the United States (U.S. Department of Justice 1991). The importance of Asians as a source of business immigrants to Canada, the category Canadian immigration policy emphasizes, has been rising (Kunin 1991). Hong Kong is by far the single most important source area because of its reversion to China in 1997 (Ministry of Industry, Science and Technology 1985, 1988, 1992), and China and Taiwan are potentially important sources as well. Similarly, Hong Kong, Chinese, and South Korean immigrants figure heavily in recent migration into Australia (Stahl et al. 1993). Although absolute numbers are small, there have been increasing flows of immigrants into the United States and Canada from the former Soviet Union since 1989, a trend that is likely to continue in the coming years because of the homeland's unstable economic situation.

Within Northeast Asia, China's open-door policy and its establishment of diplomatic relations with Japan appear to have promoted migration toward Japan. Between 1980 and 1988, there was an annual average inflow of almost 10,000 Chinese into Japan, totaling 129,000 in 1988 (Ministry of Justice 1990). Considering the increasing numbers of Chinese visitors to Japan (over 100,000 per year in 1988 and 1989), growing numbers of Chinese immigrants in Japan are likely. The Korean community in Japan was established mainly by prewar non-voluntary migrants, and their numbers reached 677,000 in 1988.

Migratory pressures have been increasing in China, where a large proportion of its 1.2 billion population is underemployed. Reforms undertaken in the 1980s such as decollectivization of farms, relaxation of migration to towns, new regulations on temporary residence in cities and towns, and changes in labor assignments and the employment system also contribute to migratory pressures within the country. Since the Chinese government cannot afford to accept these potential migrants as registered residents of its cities, some spillover to neighboring economies is inevitable. Large numbers of long-term migrants—legal and illegal—have been flowing into Hong Kong, Japan, the United States, and Australia.

Prospective Migration Based on Labor Demand and Supply

Key variables that will determine the quantity of labor demand in the North Pacific region are economic growth rate, industrial structure, and major infrastructure projects supported by international agencies. The economies of China and South Korea are projected to grow around 10 and 6–7 percent, respectively, during the 1990s, whereas projection figures for the Japanese economy are around 3 percent, which is still higher than the U.S. and Canadian industrial economies (Asian Development Bank 1993). The slow growth expected for the United States and other advanced economies will form unfavorable attitudes and policies against immigrants, particularly illegal entrants, in these countries. The high growth trajectory in China and South Korea will certainly require a large number of workers in various categories. Considering changing industrial structures in advanced parts of Northeast Asia, there will be much greater demand for technicians and skilled workers in the 1990s. North Korea, Mongolia, and the Russian Far East have highly uncertain prospects for economic growth, and, as argued throughout this book, growth in these countries will depend greatly on the extent to which these economies are integrated with market economies of the North Pacific and other regions.

Labor demand in the current labor-deficit countries such as the United States, Canada, Japan, and South Korea will not increase as rapidly as it once did since the industrial structure of these economies will move toward high value-added production and high technology. However, demand for menial labor, especially for the low-pay, unskilled service sector jobs, will increase and continue to attract migrant workers from poor countries, because these jobs are shunned by residents of these countries. Similarly, because of slow labor force growth projected for the 1990s and beyond, the domestic supply of labor in Japan and South Korea will not be enough in sectors such as social and domestic services, especially 3-D (dirty, dangerous, and difficult) jobs. Labor force growth projections suggest that Japan and South Korea will have to resort to raising the labor force participation of women and the elderly, importing foreign labor, or a combination of both (Kim 1993). It will take time to raise the labor force participation rate of women substantially because of rigidities involved in social structures in the Confucian societies of Japan and South Korea. For a rapidly aging society like Japan's, maintaining employment opportunities for older workers will be costly (Ono 1990). Even with increased labor force participation of women and the elderly, there will be labor shortages in the 3-D jobs, which will still require importation of foreign labor. For South Korea, another source of labor supply will be military personnel. If there is any genuine arms reduction or peace agreement on the Korean peninsula, tens of thousands of young men can reenter the labor market. This increase in labor supply will lessen the labor demand in most sectors, except for 3-D jobs.

China and North Korea, unlike Japan, South Korea, and the RFE, have large rural populations. In absolute numbers, China has a huge reserve of labor for nonagricultural employment. Northeast China alone can supply millions of laborers to other areas. Furthermore, there are about one million unemployed young persons in China's urban areas. During the 1990s there will be an annual average of 150,000 newly entering the labor force. Because per-capita cultivated land has been shrinking and agricultural mechanization has been advancing in China, there will be less demand for agricultural labor there. This situation also holds for Northeast China. For example, Jilin Province will require only 5 million laborers in agriculture in 1995, but the estimated rural labor force will be up to 7 million (Wang 1991). Therefore, there will be more than a million surplus workers in Jilin. The situation in Liaoning and Heilongjiang is not much different. During the 1980s, the total labor force increased by 4.6 million in Liaoning, 4.5 million in Jilin, and 3.5 million in Heilongjiang. Among these increases, the urban sector absorbed about 2.9, 1.7, and 2.6 million in Liaoning, Jilin, and Heilongjiang, respectively. The substantial portion of labor absorption in the urban areas was through the rapid growth of the collective sector (56, 46, and 42 percent, respectively, in the three provinces). But such a rapid growth of employment in that sector may not be possible in the 1990s, considering the recent performance of the collective sector in the three provinces (during 1986–90, collective sector employment grew annually by 0.9 percent in Liaoning, 1.3 percent in Jilin, and -0.2 percent in Heilongjiang).

Anticipated reform in the state enterprises and the consolidation of rural industries imply a moderate growth of nonagricultural employment in Northeast China in the 1990s. Industrial transition, in particular the growth of the service sector, which was underdeveloped in China's prereform period, may help absorb some idle labor, but the magnitude will not be sufficient to absorb all the currently unemployed, underemployed, and new entrants. Other measures to absorb labor need to be sought actively.

The labor demand and supply situation in North Korea cannot be assessed with any accuracy because of a lack of relevant data. Population growth projections by age group in North Korea suggest that the labor force will grow quite fast (2.8 percent in the 1990s) and that the dependency ratio will increase until the year 2000 (Eberstadt and Banister 1990). The large rural population and underdeveloped nonstate sectors indicate a potential labor surplus. As in China, there is certain to be disguised unemployment in rural areas and redundant workers in the urban sector. Reduced tensions on the Korean peninsula will add tens of thousands of demobilized servicemen to the potential labor surplus pool, since North Korea has about 1.2 million military personnel, approximately 6 percent of the total population (Eberstadt and Banister 1990). North Korea may, then, be a source of labor for the construction of factories, hotels, airports, and seaports in the special economic zones considered for Vladivostok and Nakhodka (see Appendix 2). North Korean labor also figures heavily in the recent development proposals for the Tumen River Basin, where the Russian, Chinese, and North Korean borders meet.

In sum, the labor-deficit economies of Japan and South Korea can respond by capital export, labor import, or both. Although transferring low value-added jobs abroad is one way of dealing with domestic labor shortages, the extent to which it can be a general solution to the problem is circumscribed by the immobility of capital in many of the industries affected by labor shortages. In other words, even with extensive offshore investments such as Japan made in the 1980s, imported foreign labor is still needed to meet increasing demands in social and domestic services, construction, and some labor-intensive manufacturing operations. The capacity of Japan and South Korea to absorb foreign labor is limited by social and political factors, but there exists a sufficient pool of skilled and unskilled workers in China and, to a lesser extent, in North Korea. The key issue is how to achieve a regionwide balance of labor demand and supply in the midst of imbalanced labor demand and supply at the state level. The rationale for regional cooperation or integration lies in the advantages of joint use of resources, including labor.

The need for a regionwide perspective on labor supply and demand does not, however, square with government positions prevailing in the region, especially in the market economy states. For example, Japan has been reluctant to open its door to foreign labor because of alleged social and cultural problems. Conservatives argue for banning foreign workers; they think that inflow of people of different cultures and traditions will undermine the unique organizing principles of Japanese society—a homogeneous, monoethnic society. The liberal argument acknowledges the inevitability and the benefits and costs associated with inflow of foreign workers and stresses Japan's international responsibility to deal with the poverty in the surrounding region. The mainstream argument advocates inflow limited by strict regulations, citing both associated social and economic benefits and costs (Lie 1992). Meanwhile, Japan's domestic labor shortage and other international economic factors have already made the presence of foreign laborers a reality in Japanese society. There is little doubt that the number of foreign workers will increase in the future because of sheer economic necessity. The lack of a national consensus on the subject of labor migration undermines the government's ability to formulate and implement a clear policy. Avoiding or delaying action will merely result in a choice by default (Spencer 1992).

The Korean position is not much different from Japan's. Employment of foreign workers is largely limited in South Korea, except in a few categories. Immigration law does not allow unskilled foreign labor to enter the country. Nevertheless, it is estimated that more than 100,000 foreign workers are illegally engaged in employment there. The major rationale for not allowing foreign workers to enter South Korea lies in the perceived long-term social and economic burden arising from legalizing foreign workers. However, South Korean labor-intensive industries are reported to require foreign workers to sustain their operation. Because Korean workers shun 3-D jobs, it is increasingly difficult to find workers for manual production jobs. In addition, hiring foreign workers provides wage cost savings for enterprises, since foreign workers are paid about half the average wage of domestic workers. Considering the demand from businesses and industries for foreign workers, the Korean government appears to have adopted a status quo policy, implicitly endorsing the use of foreign workers to smooth Korea's economic adjustment process but not actively promoting an explicit policy of foreign labor importation. A recent discussion by policymakers to accept foreign workers as trainees indicates the dilemma facing the Korean government on this issue (Park 1993).

Obviously, China is very much interested in labor export. Since 1985, China has used a new strategy for the export of labor and for contracting overseas construction projects. Authorities have relaxed restrictions on the recruitment of laborers by overseas cooperations and now allow foreign firms to recruit directly in China. The strategy includes the employment of foreign engineers and managers to improve the efficiency of the corporations and increase their ability to contract for more technology-intensive projects. It also includes diversifying markets for overseas contracts (Fang 1991). China can earn badly needed foreign exchange by exporting labor. This is also a way of enabling workers to get on-the-job training, which is costly within China. Furthermore, labor export helps to relieve unemployment and underemployment problems in China; there is now an estimated 100 million or more surplus laborers, and there will be an additional 22 million new entrants each year in the 1990s (Fang 1991). Even in Northeast China there will be more than a million underemployed agricultural workers by 1995, and there will be an annual stream of 150,000 and more new entrants to the existing labor force (Wang 1991). This all indicates increasing migration pressure in China. The RFE is and will be an alternative outlet for increasingly mobile Chinese labor.

Migration Dynamics in Russia and the Russian Far East

The approximately 32 million expatriates of the fifteen former Soviet Union republics are now regarded as potential ethnic migrants, although it is uncertain how strong the various pressures will be for each to move and how strong the physical or financial deterrents. Russians will be the main group moving on ethnic grounds, followed by Ukranians and Belorussians. The selection of a destination within the home republic could be expected to be economic and distance-related (Cole and Filatotchev 1992).

In addition to ethnic migration, there will also be increasing economic migration. Several factors may influence economic migration within the former USSR and beyond its borders: the varying development of the reform process in different sovereign republics, the inflow of foreign capital, and the ways the former union's uniform economic space disintegrates. It is clear that the reform process in general and the liberalization of economic relations in particular are increasing the mobility of people in the post-Soviet republics. In contrast to the former system of centrally planned flows of labor between different regions, decision making with respect to migration is more decentralized and is increasingly dependent on microeconomic factors rather than on the decisions of central planning authorities.

Professionals and technicians with high levels of education are known to be sensitive to economic incentives. Since the simplification of emigration and immigration procedures, many such potential economic migrants are looking for opportunities outside the CIS countries. For these highly mobile professionals, then, international migration is another option in addition to migration within the former USSR. Indeed, there is an increasing number of professionals and technicians working abroad, including those with temporary employment. Russian pilots and engineers are frequently seen in major airlines in Asia.

International labor movement is not, however, limited to professionals and technicians. Thousands of young Russian women are reported to be engaged in entertainment and service activities, including prostitution, in Europe and Asia. A few hundred Russian girls are known to be working at bars and restaurants in major Chinese cities. They usually come to China for fun as well as work. The dismal situation in Russia clearly pushes people abroad.

In terms of internal migration, people from less affluent regions are likely to move to areas of growth and relative prosperity with the transition toward a free labor market and an increase in the mobility of the labor force. The intensity of these migration flows will depend on the income-earning opportunities and the availability of social amenities at both origin and destination. Since nearly all domestic resources of the economy are being channeled simply toward the survival of existing enterprises, the availability of foreign capital will be an important factor affecting the new pattern of internal migration in the CIS.

Foreign investment in Russia may be attracted by three considerations: resource exploitation, technology and skilled labor, and market access. Foreign investment in Siberia and the Russian Far East are likely to be motivated by the first consideration. The intensity of migration flows, however, will depend on labor requirements of the new ventures (which are not expected to be very high because resource exploitation in general is capital-intensive) and on the development of economic and social infrastructures in the potential growth region (which will require more long-term investments and generate high demand for labor). Foreign investment targeted for technology/skilled labor and domestic markets in the CIS is likely to flow into centers of population and manufacturing industries. Siberia and the RFE are at a disadvantage in this regard. The establishment of free economic zones in Nakhodka and Vladivostok may attract the inflow of foreign capital and consequently attract workers from other regions.

Even though population growth in the RFE has been higher than the average population growth rate of the former Soviet Union, the small base of population will not guarantee a smooth supply of labor in the area. During the period 1979–88, the population growth of the RFE was largely dependent on natural increase (more than 70 percent). Migration played a small role in population growth, except in Kamchatka and Yakutia (Table 4.4). Sakhalin experienced net outmigration during the period. Migration into and out of the RFE has been largely by Russians, and recent Russian arrivals and departures reveal a few interesting characteristics (Table 4.5). Very large gross migration figures indicate that the RFE is the most active region of migration in the former USSR (perhaps because of wage incentives), but at the same time the region is unstable in terms of labor supply because of high turnover. In 1989 outmigration exceeded immigration for the RFE. In 1991, for the first time in its history, a negative population growth was registered in all territories of the RFE (Admidin 1993). If the trend of net outmigration by Russians holds for the future, this implies

TABLE 4.4 Population Change in the Russian Far East, 1979–1989

| | Population Increase (000's) | | % Contribution by | | | |
| | | | 1979–88 | | 1989 | |
	1979–88	1989	NG	M	NG	M
Russian Fed.	985.0	662.9	81.53	18.47	87.49	12.51
RFE	112.2	69.8	70.18	29.81	100.29	-0.29
Primorski	28.1	23.2	65.66	34.70	67.24	32.76
Khabarovsk	25.8	15.7	66.28	33.72	90.45	9.55
Amurskaya	12.1	8.8	92.56	7.44	104.55	-4.55
Kamchatka	8.8	3.8	53.41	46.59	97.37	2.63
Magadan	7.7	-3.4	81.82	18.18	161.76	-258.82
Sakhalin	5.5	3.7	110.91	-10.91	148.65	-48.65
Yakutia	24.2	18.0	61.57	38.43	91.11	8.89

Note: NG = natural growth; M = migration.
Source: Economic Research Institute (1993:174).

TABLE 4.5 1989 Total Net Migration and Net Migration of Russians

	Total Net Migration	Russian Arrivals	Russian Departures	Net Russian Arrivals
Primorski Krai	18,477	67,712	58,602	9,110
Khabarovsk Krai	12,113	51,587	45,657	5,930
Amur Oblast	6,622	36,083	32,668	3,415
Kamchatka Oblast	1,575	11,705	11,846	-141
Magadan Oblast	-3,675	18,943	22,391	-3,448
Sakhalin Oblast	1,992	21,896	20,515	381
Yakut AR	3,878	28,868	28,126	742
Total Far East	40,982	236,794	219,805	15,989

Note: Urban settlements only.
Source: Data from Panel on Siberia (1991).

dim prospects for a stable supply of educated labor (assuming migrants are better educated than nonmigrants). The high turnover reported is closely related to the lack of social infrastructure such as housing, education, and other social facilities. Unless social infrastructure is significantly improved in the area, a stable labor supply in the RFE will be difficult to achieve (Sallnow 1989). In contrast, ethnic Koreans are recently moving back to the RFE from Central Asia. Most of them are young and engaged in businesses or in commercial agriculture.

There have been foreign guest workers in the RFE since at least the mid-1960s. For example, the former Soviet Union has had joint timber activities with North Korea since 1967 in Khabarovsk Krai and since 1975 in Amur

Oblast.[4] North Korea supplies labor for many of these operations, while Russia supplies the machinery and transport. Chinese and North Koreans are farming at three places in Primorski Krai. These guest workers are employed mainly in forestry, construction, agriculture, and light industry; they total approximately 30,000. Workers are contracted under institutional agreements made between Russian organizations and sending-country organizations, usually in the form of barter compensation: sending-country organizations are paid by commodities for the labor rendered; wages are not directly paid to workers by host institutions. The use of foreign labor has also been required for the improvement of housing and social facilities in the RFE (Admidin 1993; Helgeson 1990).

Recent political events in the former Soviet Union suggest the possibility of domestic supply arising from potential unemployment and thus a lesser need for foreign workers. A rapidly deteriorating Russian economy, especially after the failed Moscow coup in August 1991, is expected to bring about considerable unemployment (Minakir 1991). Another possible source of supply is the servicemen to be released as part of Russia's troop reduction program. Still, there are problems of both labor shortage and surplus in the RFE (Minakir 1991; see also Chapter 2). Highly paid skilled jobs are in short supply, whereas low-wage manual jobs have a high vacancy rate. Considering the relatively harsh climate and lack of housing and social amenities in the RFE, it is unlikely to see large numbers of skilled and unskilled workers migrating from European Russia.

The collapse of the Soviet Union and ensuing disintegration between republics and within the Russian Federation damaged the linkages between the Far East and other regions. Cuts in military spending resulted in a decline in production by military-related industries. In the RFE, the economy is still dominated by state enterprises; nonstate enterprises make up only 12 percent of the total (Schevchenko 1992). All these factors have weakened the potential attraction of the RFE in internal migration.

Riding the waves of independence and ethnic identity, the idea of an independent or autonomous Siberia and Far East has recently reappeared.[5] For Moscow, which has lost control of important natural resources such as oil and gas in Central Asia, an autonomous Siberia and Far East region may not be acceptable. Regardless of the likelihood of an independent RFE, the very idea can discourage Russians from migrating to that area.

In contrast to the situation vis-à-vis European Russia, burgeoning border trade between China and Russia—naturally accompanied by increasing flows of petty traders, businessmen, entertainers, and so on across the border—suggests labor migration in one form or another. Four Chinese cities—Manzhouli, Heihe, Hunchun, and Suifenhe—were designated as "open border cities" in 1992. In 1991 about 8,000 Russians visited Manzhouli, and the number reached 15,000 in the first half of 1992. Similarly, the number of Russian visitors to Heihe and Suifenhe exceeded 100,000 in 1992 (Schevchenko 1992). A railroad linking Hunchun in Jilin Province and Kraskino in Russia that will be completed in the near future, together with the expansion of the port of Zarubino, is expected to stimulate trade and business and thus population movements across the border.

There is, however, a fear in Russia with regard to increasing movements of Chinese into the RFE. Labor import from China may not be entirely welcome, since it may eventually mean the domination of the RFE by the Chinese population (Sakamoto 1994). Also, the idea of the resettlement of ethnic Koreans in the Far East has not been received well by Russians, although it is uncertain that Koreans would want to return. Whether Koreans will leave Central Asia depends on internal conditions such as discrimination against ethnic Koreans within the republics as well as opportunities in the Russian Federation. If a law currently being drafted by the Russian Parliament is enacted, Koreans may well be able to return to the Far East. In its current draft form, the law offers Russian citizenship to Koreans living in all former Soviet republics and permits them to settle anywhere in Russia.[6] The prospect of jobs in the RFE, specifically in Nakhodka, where a Seoul-Moscow agreement will create an industrial park for some hundred South Korean companies, is likely to attract Koreans. The possibility of a Pacific reunion of ethnic Koreans is, however, perceived to be a potential threat to ethnic Russians in the RFE, who already feel threatened by an influx of traders, laborers, and businessmen from across the Chinese border (Lilley 1992).

This perception of migrants as a threat stems from Russian concerns with the integrity and sovereignty of the RFE. Given the dire economic performance accompanied by radical reforms, both central and local governments of Russia face a dilemma of balancing their security against economic opportunities. The choice is not simple because of the many actors and multilevel decision-making process involved. A closed-door policy favored by a nationalist faction in Moscow and a local independence group in the RFE implies a loss of opportunity to cooperate economically and integrate with neighboring Asia-Pacific economies, although this may prevent the wholesale of resources to other countries at a long-term loss to the RFE. An open-border model with a substantial degree of economic interdependence presents an opportunity to push forward economic development of the RFE. Russian hesitance to adopt the open-border model derives from lack of confidence in its role in the coming international division of labor. Despite Moscow's friendly gesture toward China, the prospect of economic integration of the RFE with neighboring economies, in particular China's northeast region, is not well regarded in the RFE. The structure of economic interdependence and the pace of economic integration in the region around the RFE will depend on the interplay between regionalism, centralism, and internationalism in Russia.

Conclusion

With a continued opening of socialist economies and their improved relations with market economies in the North Pacific, there will be greater interactions across national borders, in particular trade, capital flows, and movement of people. Further liberalization and democratization in China and other socialist countries in Asia will stimulate long-term emigration likely destined for North America. In addition, political liberalization of socialist economies and a reduction of international tensions make exit from socialist countries more likely and therefore may produce political asylum seekers from those countries. In brief, political and economic circumstances in the North Pacific suggest increasing migration pressure from labor-surplus, low-income economies.

On the receiving end, internal political pressure may build up against migrants and thus help make immigration a serious problem. In recent years, ethnic conflicts have frequently flared up in the United States, particularly including Asian Americans in conflict with other minority groups (Gardner 1992). There are signs of rising racism in Europe and the United States, which could be transformed into hatred and violence between ethnic groups, especially during economic hard times.[7]

Unlike the United States and Canada, which have relatively open immigration policies, the prosperous states of Northeast Asia are rather closed when it comes to foreign migrants. The shortage of land in Japan and South Korea is known to be another factor inhibiting large numbers of foreign immigrants. Therefore temporary migration, including special student and training programs, which now constitute de facto labor import policy, is more likely in Japan and South Korea.

Still, the potential migration pressure from China is serious. Japan's population specialists point out increasing migration pressure in China after economic reform started in 1978 (Wakabayashi 1990; Sugimoto 1991). They conjecture that, if China had not adopted the one-child policy and tightly controlled exit of its population, migration pressure would have been much higher. Blind pursuit of emigration from China to prosperous countries such as the United States and Japan has indeed been increasing and arousing anti-immigration attitudes in the host countries.

As seen in the cases of Eastern Europe, political upheaval and internal conflicts might trigger massive population movements regardless of the social and political barriers confronting potential migrants.[8] For example, some 1.3 million people moved from ex-COMECON countries to the West in 1990. A few million people a year are expected to emigrate from the former Soviet Union itself. Likewise, internal conflicts in China and a collapse of the authoritarian regime in North Korea would instigate outflows of population and therefore could destabilize the North Pacific region. This possibility demonstrates the need for potential host countries to assist peaceful transitions in China and North Korea.

There are possible avenues for containing population movements in the North Pacific by concerted efforts of the nations involved. Regional economic cooperation will certainly help develop the underdeveloped areas in the North Pacific—especially the Russian Far East, China's northeast, Mongolia, and North Korea—and consequently will help manage potential migration flows. If the political situation of Russia stabilizes and the development of the RFE gets under way with the assistance of capital-rich countries, frontier development and settlement could be an important outlet for migratory pressure in the North Pacific in the twenty-first century. However, as the history of the early twentieth century reminds us, such a situation can be abused as disguised foreign economic policy to extend a country's control over others' territory. Multilateral arrangements regarding the joint management of labor migration may be necessary to materialize the benefits of migration.

Specific to the RFE, permanent migration appears not to be an acceptable proposition to the Russians, or in general to the other countries in Northeast Asia. Instead, temporary migration with some guarantee of return seems more feasible. Project-tied migration as commonly adopted in the Middle East would be suitable for the RFE since it involves employment for a specific assignment with a limited duration. Uncontrolled migration could be a destabilizing factor for the RFE because of historical legacies and cultural sensitivity in the region. This calls for joint efforts to manage flows of people across borders between the countries involved. To achieve this goal, monitoring the flows and stock of migrants will be a first essential step. Second, multilateral or bilateral agreements with regard to appropriate channels and levels of migration will be necessary. Third, setting up labor training and information centers in major origins and destinations will help enhance efficient and organized utilization of labor resources. These centers can be established and operated by cooperative efforts of both government and private sectors, especially those enterprises interested in joint ventures or in using foreign workers in home countries.

Notes

I thank Changzoo Song for his careful checking of the historical facts of migration in and around the Russian Far East.

1. There is a controversy around this issue. For the analysis given here, see Huttenbach (1993). For other explanations of the forced relocation of Soviet Koreans, see Kho (1990).

2. Weiner (1989) argues that prejudice and discrimination against Koreans in Japan originated in the years after the Meiji Restoration of 1868. A new concept of a nation based largely on racial mythology was necessitated by Japan's confrontation with the wealth and power of the West. Subsequently, the sense of racial superiority engendered by the mythology was reinforced by the introduction of an educational system that promoted nationalism. Throughout the pre-1945 period, the Japanese people were socialized into accepting a view of the world in which their country was portrayed as the only Asian nation capable of creating a viable alternative to Western civilization. Such beliefs are still shared by many Japanese.

3. According to Min (1992), the Koreans in Japan were a colonized minority, whereas the Korean Chinese were voluntary migrants. The concentration of Korean Chinese in the Yanbian area as a territorial and psychological base for Korean culture facilitated their ethnic identity and ethnic attachment, whereas Korean Japanese do not have a comparable ethnic enclave. The Korean Chinese community has been influenced by North Korea and recently by South Korea, while neither South Korea nor North Korea has had much influence on the Korean Japanese community. Others, however, argue that some Koreans went to Japan voluntarily for a better income and opportunity and that the Japanese government actually tried to divert their flow to other areas such as Manchuria (see Kim 1990).

4. North Korean workers had been sent to the Soviet Union since late 1940s. Many of them remained there rather than returning to North Korea.

5. During the period 1920–22, the Far Eastern Republic was an independent state recognized by many countries, including the United States.

6. Soviet Koreans have different desires and opinions according to their occupation and family situation. Educated professionals want to move to big cities such as Moscow and Leningrad, while farmers prefer places that are good for farming. Many others seem to prefer to stay where they are as long as there are no serious political disruptions.

7. *The Economist*, November 16, 1991.

8. The political uncertainty of Hong Kong after 1997 has already triggered an annual outflow of 60,000 residents a year to other countries, notably Canada, the United States, and Australia.

References

Admidin, Andrei. 1993. "Utilization of Foreign Labor Force in the Russian Far East: Problems and Prospects." Unpublished manuscript.

Asian Development Bank. 1993. *Asian Development Outlook*. Manila: ADB.

Bauer, John. 1990. "Demographic Change and Asian Labor Markets in the 1990s." *Population and Development Review* 16:615–45.

Cole, John P., and Igor V. Filatotchev. 1992. "Some Observations on Migration within and from the Former USSR in the 1990s." *Post-Soviet Geography* 33:432–53.

Eberstadt, Nicholas, and Judith Banister. 1990. "North Korea: Population Trends and Prospects." Unpublished manuscript.

Economic Research Institute. 1993. *Russian Far East Economic Yearbook*, Part 2 (1992). Khabarovsk: Academy of the Russian Federation.

Fang Shan. 1991. "Mainland China's Overseas Construction Contracts and Export of Labor." *Issues and Studies* 27:65–75.

Gardner, Robert. 1992. "Asian Immigration: The View from the United States." *Asian and Pacific Migration Journal* 1:65–99.

Helgeson, Ann C. 1990. "Population and Labor Force." In Allan Rodgers, ed., *The Soviet Far East*. New York: Routledge.

Huttenbach, Henry R. 1993. "The Soviet Koreans: Products of Russo-Japanese Imperial Rivalry." *Central Asian Survey* 12:59–69.

Kho, Songmoo. 1990. "Koreans in the Soviet Union." *Korea and World Affairs* 4:137–74.

Kim, Ki-Hoon. 1990. "Japanese Policy for Korean Rural Immigration to Manchukuo, 1932–1945." Ph.D. dissertation, Department of Political Science, University of Hawaii.

Kim, Won Bae. 1993. "Population and Labor in Northeast Asia." In Won Bae Kim et al. (eds.), *Regional Economic Cooperation in Northeast Asia*. Northeast Asian Economic Forum.

Kirby, E. Stuart. 1971. *The Soviet Far East*. London: Macmillan.

Kolarz, Walter. 1954. *The Peoples of the Soviet Far East*. New York: Archon Books.

Kunin, Roslyn. 1991. "The Economic Impact of Business Immigration into Canada." Paper presented at the conference on International Manpower Flows and Foreign Investment in the Asian Region, September 9–12, 1991, Tokyo, Japan.

Lie, John. 1992. "Foreign Workers in Japan." *Monthly Review* 44:35–42.

Lilley, Jeffrey. 1992. "Pacific Reunion." *Far Eastern Economic Review* 11 (March):26–27.

Madden, Ros, and Susan Young. 1993. *Women and Men Immigrating to Australia: Their Characteristics and Immigration Decisions*. Canberra: Bureau of Immigration Research.

Mandel, William. 1944. *The Soviet Far East and Central Asia*. New York: Dial Press.

Martin, Philip L. 1991. "Labor Migration in Asia." *International Migration Review* 25:176–93.

Min, Pyong Gap. 1992. "A Comparison of the Korean Minorities in China and Japan." *International Migration Review* 26:4–21.

Minakir, Pavel A. 1991. "Economic Cooperation in the New World: The Soviet Far East." Paper presented at the International Conference on Economic and Technological Development in Northeast Asia, August 29–31, 1991, Changchun, China.

Ministry of Industry, Science and Technology, Canada. Various years. *Canada Yearbook*. Communications Division of Statistics.

Ministry of Justice, Government of Japan. 1990. *Statistics on Immigration Control*. Tokyo.

Mitchell, Christopher. 1989. "International Migration, International Relations and Foreign Policy." *International Migration Review* 23:681–708.

National Statistical Office, ROK. 1990. *Korea Statistical Yearbook 1989.* Seoul.

Ono, Akira. 1990. "Labor Cost in an Aging Economy." *Japanese Economies Studies* 18:30–57.

Panel on Siberia. 1991. "Economic and Territorial Issues." *Soviet Geography* 32:380.

Park, Young-bum. 1993. "Turning Point in International Migration and Economic Development in Korea." Paper presented at the conference on Turning Points in International Labor Migration, April 6–7, 1993, Seoul, Korea.

Sakamoto, Masahiro. 1994. "Kyokuto roshia, chugoku izon takameru." *Nihon Keizai Shinbun,* February 5, p. 24.

Sallnow, John. 1989. "The Soviet Far East: A Report on Urban and Rural Settlement and Population Change, 1966-89." *Soviet Geography* 30:670–83.

Schevchenko, Nicklai V. 1992. "Russia in East Asia." Unpublished manuscript.

Shimada, Haruo. 1991. "The Employment of Foreign Labor in Japan." *Annals of the American Academy of Political and Social Science* 513:117–38.

Spencer, Steven A. 1992. "Illegal Migrant Laborers in Japan." *International Migration Review* 26:754–86.

Stahl, Charles. 1991. "International Migration in the Asian Region." Paper presented at the conference on International Manpower Flows and Foreign Investment in the Asian Region, September 9–12, 1991, Tokyo, Japan.

Stahl, Charles, Rochelle Ball, Christine Inglis, and Pamela Gutman. 1993. *Global Population Movements and Their Implications for Australia.* Canberra: Australian Government Publishing Service.

State Statistical Bureau. 1991. *China Statistical Yearbook 1990.* Beijing.

Sugimoto, Takashi. 1991. "China's Population Growth and Its Consequences for Regional Stability." Paper presented at the NPCSD workshop on Nonconventional Security in the North Pacific, December 11–12, 1991, East-West Center, Honolulu.

United Nations. 1991. *Demographic Yearbook 1989.* New York.

U.S. Department of Justice, Immigration and Naturalization Service. 1991. *1990 Statistical Yearbook of the Immigration and Naturalization Service.* U.S. GPO.

Wakabayashi, Keiko. 1990. "Blind Movement of Chinese Population: Background for the Recent Influx of Chinese Working Students and Disguised Refugees into Japan." *Journal of Population Problems* 46:35–50 (in Japanese).

Wang Shengjin. 1991. "On Resources of Labor Force in International Economic and Technical Cooperation in Northeast Asia." Paper presented at the international conference on Economic and Technological Development in Northeast Asia, August 29–31, 1991, Changchun, China.

Watanabe, Susumu. 1993. "The Lewisian Turning Point and International Migration: The Case of Japan." Paper presented at the conference on Turning Points in International Labor Migration, April 6–7, 1993, Seoul, Korea.

Weiner, Michael A. 1989. *The Origins of the Korean Community in Japan, 1910-1923.* Manchester: Manchester University Press.

Weiner, Myron. 1992/93. "Security, Stability, and International Migration." *International Security* 17:91–126.

Widgren, Jonas. 1990. "International Migration and Regional Stability." *International Affairs* 66:749–66.

World Bank. 1991. *World Development Report 1991*. Oxford: Oxford University Press.

World Bank. 1992. *World Development Report 1992*. Oxford: Oxford University Press.

World Resources Institute. 1992. *World Resources 1991–92*. New York: Basic Books.

5

Energy and Mineral Resources

James P. Dorian, David Fridley, and Kristin Tressler

One of the world's last frontiers for the development of energy and mineral resources, Northeast Asia has promising potential for multilateral resource cooperation. Vast resources ranging from offshore oil and gas to alluvial gold are being made available for investment to foreign companies for the first time in decades. Commercial opportunities are now being assessed by many of the world's largest energy and mineral firms. In this chapter we define the present resource industries in Northeast Asia, review the region's history of resource cooperation and identify current viable opportunities, and examine some of the potential obstacles to joint development. Aside from the Russian Far East, Mongolia, Northeast China (Heilongjiang, Liaoning, and Jilin provinces), North Korea, South Korea, and Japan, we refer to the U.S. state of Alaska, since its resource industry may have an impact on commercial development projects within the Russian Far East.

Economic and Resource Base

Resources

Northeast Asia includes many mineral- and energy-rich regions, particularly the Russian Far East, Mongolia, Northeast China, and North Korea (Figures 5.1 and 5.2). The area produces significant quantities of coal (North Korea, Northeast China), crude oil (Alaska, Northeast China), cement (Japan), and gold (RFE, Northeast China). Table 5.1 reviews recent Northeast Asian production figures of coal, crude oil, natural gas, iron ore, cement, pig iron, and gold. Much of the region is still relatively lightly explored, so ample mineral and energy reserves may yet be discovered through newer, more advanced geological prospecting techniques.

compiled by willy icay ('94 prem, ewc)

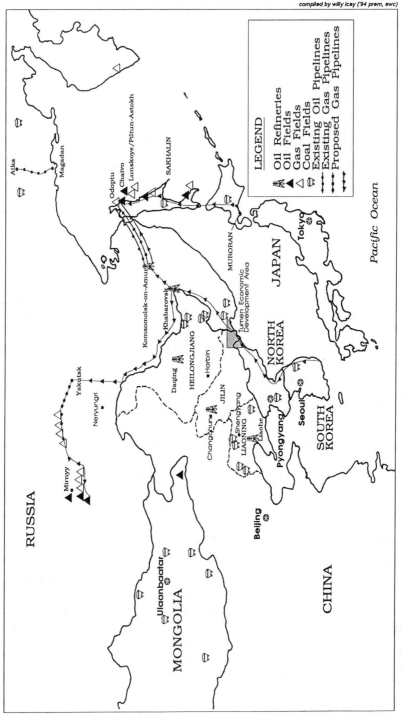

FIGURE 5.1.   Major energy-producing mines and deposits of Northeast Asia.

compiled by willy Icay (prem, ewc '94)

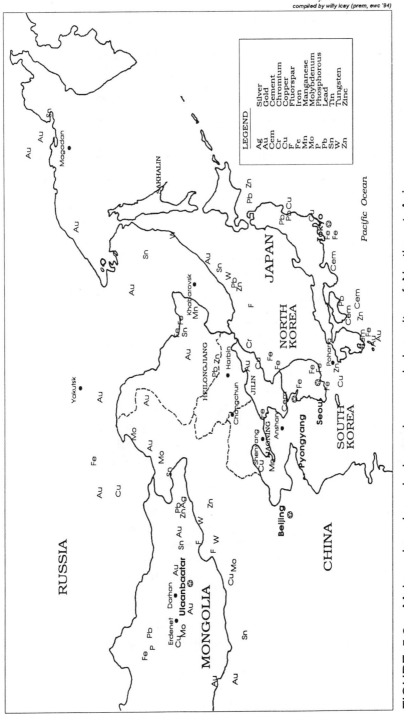

FIGURE 5.2. Major mineral-producing mines and deposits of Northeast Asia.

TABLE 5.1 Mineral and Energy Production in Northeast Asia

	Coal (10³t)	Crude Oil (10³t)	Natural Gas (10⁶m³)	Iron Ore (10³t)	Cement (10³t)	Pig Iron (10³)	Gold (t)
Japan	8,300[a]	700[b]	1,900[c]	25[d]	112,435[c]	73,000[c]	8.3[a]
North Korea	43,300[a]	na	na	3,600[e]	16,000[d]	6,500[d]	5.0[b]
South Korea	19,800[c]	na	na	379[d]	44,092[c]	19,000[c]	21[a]
Russian Far East	49,800[b]	2,300[d]	3,200[b]	na	4,873[b]	na	na
Alaska	1,531[c]	85,312[c]	na	na	na	na	7.44[c]
Mongolia[f]	9,000[a]	0	0	0	513	0	1.0[c]
Northeast China	162,938[a]	72,788[a]	4,454[a]	50,270[a]	23,387[a]	13,609[a]	na
Liaoning	52,350[a]	13,742[a]	2,055[a]	47,660[a]	13,120[a]	12,280[a]	na
Heilongjiang	85,000[a]	55,623[a]	2,273[a]	397[b]	5,536[a]	592[a]	na
Jilin	25,588[a]	3,423[a]	126[a]	2,213[a]	4,732[a]	737[a]	na

[a]1991
[b]1990
[c]1992
[d]1989
[e]1988
[f]Mongolia produces a variety of metals and nonmetals not listed in this table, including copper, molybdenum, tungsten, tin, fluorite, and coal.

Note: Figures may be rounded. na = not available.
Sources: U.S. Bureau of Mines (1993); British Petroleum (1992); World Bureau of Metal Statistics (1992); Economic Research Institute (1991); Liaoning Statistical Bureau (1992); Heilongjiang Statistical Bureau (1992); Jilin Statistical Bureau (1992).

The RFE and Mongolia are two of the last frontiers for resource exploitation. The RFE enjoys a considerable comparative advantage over other resource-rich areas: over 120 different types of metallic, nonmetallic, and energy resources are known, and the region is well endowed with large reserves of antimony, boron, brown coal, diamonds, fluorite, gold, platinum, silver, tin, and tungsten. The area contains the largest reserves of gold and diamonds in the former Soviet Union, giving it an obvious lure for enticing foreign investment. Overall mineral development in the RFE appears to have promising long-term potential. But in the intermediate term the outlook is modest, and the short-term potential is limited, primarily because of inadequate infrastructure, capital scarcity, and outdated mining technology (see below, and Chapter 2).

In Mongolia, a huge landlocked nation with a population of more than 2.3 million people, the mining sector continues to grow in importance and now accounts for 20 percent of GNP. Currently there are about 200 mines or deposits being worked. The largest mines are for copper/molybdenum, fluorspar, lignite, coal, tin, and tungsten ore. Mongolia is a major exporter of copper, molybdenum, and fluorspar. There are about 150 gold deposits in the country (nearly twenty under development), including one of the biggest placer deposits in Asia, with reserves of 100 metric tons. Total gold resources are estimated at 3,000 tons.

Mongolia also possesses valuable coal resources, with the coking coal reserves at the Tavan-Tolgoy deposit estimated at more than 5 billion tons. The quality is on par with deposits in Australia and Canada, major players in the world coal industry. Oil deposits are estimated to be 400 million tons, which is sufficient to meet domestic demand. Today there is significant interest in exploring for and developing oil deposits in the southeast and western regions of Mongolia.

North Korea and Northeast China also have abundant resources, mostly underdeveloped. Although the government of North Korea issues no official information on mineral production and trade, enough data are released to characterize the mining industry. Raw material resources in North Korea include anthracite, bituminous coal, iron, magnesite, manganese ore, zinc, nickel, lead, copper, gold, silver, and molybdenum (Korea Resources Institute 1992). Anthracite coal is by far the largest domestic mine output in terms of quantity. Large amounts of anthracite are produced for domestic use in addition to export, but the country must import some bituminous coal. North Korea possesses no domestic resources of oil or natural gas.

Much of North Korea's mining industry is based on the extraction and processing of its own raw materials. The mining industry is sluggish owing to inefficient capital and outdated technology. North Korea's principal exports include coal, iron and steel, and nonferrous metals. It is a large producer of magnesite and exports large quantities to Japan, Poland, and the former Soviet Union (U.S. Bureau of Mines 1988). North Korea also exports graphite and zinc in both concentrate and metal form, to acquire much needed foreign exchange. Because zinc, lead, and copper have significant international markets, the government intends to increase their production capacity.

Heilongjiang, Jilin, and Liaoning provinces are well endowed in energy and mineral resources. Combined, they account for slightly more than half of China's total oil output, which reached 144 million tons in 1993. Daqing, China's biggest oil field, located in Heilongjiang, produces about 1.1 million barrels of oil per day. This huge field alone contributes 40 percent of national petroleum output. Liaoning province yields about 275,000 barrels of oil per day, and Jilin produces about 70,000. One resource assessment study of China concluded that based on geological conditions Heilongjiang and Jilin are likely to contain substantial metallic and nonmetallic mineral resources, including copper, gold, manganese, molybdenum, nickel, platinum, uranium, and asbestos (Clark 1987).

Economy

The countries or regions of Northeast Asia have a combined population of nearly 306 million people and a combined land area of 10 million km². By 2010, the region is expected to have a total population of 344 million people (under a medium growth scenario), representing an increase of just under 13 percent over today's figures. Approximately 42 percent of the population lives in Japan, while China holds 33 percent of the remaining population, North Korea 8 percent, South Korea 14 percent, and Mongolia 0.5 percent (United Nations 1991).

The whole Asia-Pacific region experienced the fastest economic growth in the world in the 1980s. Today, while all other economies are growing at an average rate of 2 percent per year, the region from the South Asian subcontinent to Japan and from Southeast Asia to Northeast China is growing at 6 percent annually. Not every country or region in Northeast Asia has participated in Asia's recent economic expansion, but all expect strong economic growth by the early twenty-first century. The abundance of natural resources and labor in such areas as the Russian Far East suggests the capacity for economic expansion long after present political problems subside.

As Northeast Asia prospers in the years ahead, consumption of energy and minerals will rise to meet growing industrial demand. Oil consumption in the Asia-Pacific region is now projected to grow at an average annual rate of 3.6 percent over the remainder of the century (Fesharaki and Wu 1993). Similarly, demand for nonferrous and ferrous metals is expected to rise sharply in Asia, particularly in South Korea and China. Economic expansion will also increase import demand for energy and mineral products as well as capital resources available for investment. Such a growing demand for energy and minerals seems likely to enhance prospects for multilateral resource cooperation.

Regional Resource Cooperation: A Brief History

In the following paragraphs we discuss some of the past relationships among trading partners in Northeast Asia and provide examples of historic regional cooperation in the energy and minerals industries of the respective countries. Table 5.2 presents a brief chronology of Northeast Asian economic cooperation since 1957.

Russia–China

Since the 1700s trade activities have been conducted along the borders between Heilongjiang Province and eastern Russia. Relations were officially suspended in 1968 (although still carried out to a limited extent) with the

TABLE 5.2 Chronology of Northeast Asian Economic Cooperation and Trade

1957: Russia and Japan establish the first Trade Payments Agreement.

1965: South Korea and Japan normalize relations.

1968: Sino-Russian relations suspended because of border conflicts.

1972: China and Japan normalize relations.

1972: Russia and Japan agree to develop a coking coal mine and coal-washing plant at Neryungri.

1974: South Korea and Japan agree to explore undersea oil on the continental shelf between the two countries.

1975: Russia and Japan agree to develop oil and gas fields off Sakhalin Island.

1978: China and Japan agree to build the Baoshan Iron and Steel Complex in Shanghai.

1979: Trade between Russia and Japan declines after Russia's invasion of Afghanistan and ensuing economic sanctions.

1981: A Mongolian-Russian joint venture, Erdenet Mining and Processing Complex, is put into full production.

1982: Sino-Russian relations improve as part of Gorbachev policies.

1983: Usibelli Coal Mine of Alaska and KEPCO of South Korea establish coal agreement.

1984: North Korea proclaims an opening of international trade and a law on joint ventures.

1985: Baoshan Iron and Steel Complex begins operations.

1985: China and South Korea establish trade links.

1988: The International Chemical Joint Venture Corp. is established by North Korea and Japan to extract and refine rare-earth metals.

1989: The Red Dog and Greens Creek mines in Alaska begin limited production for export.

1990: SVZAL, a joint mining venture between Russia and Alaska, is formed.

1991: Russia and South Korea normalize relations.

1991: China, North and South Korea, Mongolia, and Russia begin formulation of a plan for long-term development of the Tumen River Basin.

1992: The Russian government selects Japan- and U.S.-based companies to undertake a feasibility study of Sakhalin oil/gas development.

1994: After six years and $US80 million, the Russian government and MMMSM consortium agree on contract terms for the Sakhalin oil/gas project.

onset of border conflicts, and they resumed in 1982 with the ascendancy of Mikhail Gorbachev in the Soviet Union and "open door" economic reforms in China. Sino-Russian trade continued to expand throughout the 1980s with the easing of political tensions, primarily along lines established across the pre-1968 border and barter trade. Total trade, excluding barter, rose from US$363 million in 1982 to $1.92 billion in 1985 and further to $4.38 billion in 1990 before dropping to $3.90 billion in 1991 (EIA 1992). It is likely that official trade figures would be much higher with the inclusion of barter trade, particularly in China. Exports from China include crude oil, coal, iron and steel products, tungsten ores, and copper products, while imports include rolled steel, chemical fertilizers, nonferrous metals, and cement.

Heilongjiang Province has been important in Sino-Russian trade throughout the past three decades because of its close proximity to the Russian Far East. In 1992 Heilongjiang's total export value reached US$1.9 billion, compared to $324 million in 1984 (Editorial Board 1987–88). Exports to the USSR from Heilongjiang also rose rapidly, from $150.2 million in 1984 to $359.0 million in 1990. Border trade has continued to be significant, with outlets in Heihe, Tongjiang, and Suifenhe along the eastern border and with additional trade outlets opening up in Mishan, Hulin, Raohe, Lushui, and Jiaijin for interaction with the Russian trade outlets of Kamen Rybolov, Lesozavosk, Bikin, Amurzet, and Pashkovo.

China and Russia also collaborated on energy and mineral projects in China before relations were disrupted in 1968. The Karamay Oilfield in Xinjiang Uyghur Autonomous Region and the Daqing Oilfield in Heilongjiang Province, two of the largest operations in China, were developed with Russian assistance, as was the Bautou iron and steel/rare earth mine in Inner Mongolia. Since 1982 no new projects have been developed, although talks pertaining to joint ventures and technology transfers are currently being conducted, including the possible joint construction of a nuclear power plant in Liaoning.

Russia–Japan

Trade and cooperation between Japan and Russia began along the coasts of the two countries in the late nineteenth century and continued on a small scale until World War II. Although no formal peace treaty was signed between the two nations to end the war, trade relations resumed in 1957 with the first Trade Payments Agreement. Throughout the 1960s and 1970s bilateral trade increased steadily; Russia showed a trade surplus in the 1960s, Japan a surplus in the 1970s. The two countries seemed economically compatible. Russia planned to develop Siberia and the Russian Far East and needed Japanese capital investment and advanced technology.

Japan's economy was growing rapidly, and the country thus needed large quantities of industrial raw materials such as those available in the RFE. But trade decreased in the early 1980s with the Soviet invasion of Afghanistan and the resulting economic sanctions imposed by the United States and Japan. Several large-scale projects being negotiated between the two countries were canceled, and the Japan Export-Import Bank banned the issuance of new credits and the export of high-tech products to the Soviet Union. Still, trade in the later 1980s continued its upward trend, from US$4.3 billion in 1985 to $5.5 billion in 1989, and with the political and economic reforms of the former Soviet Union it is likely that cooperation and trade beneficial to both sides will continue to grow.

Japan and Russia have collaborated on the development of several projects within the energy and minerals sectors of both countries. A few were initially discussed, but because of numerous problems involving estimation of reserves, financial support, and appropriate import-export laws, they were eventually postponed or canceled; examples include the Udokan copper deposit, the Yakutia natural gas project (see Chapter 6), and the Molodezhnoe asbestos mine development project. Other projects have been undertaken but with limited success.

In 1972, Japan and Russia signed an accord for the development of a coking coal mine and coal-washing plant at Neryungri in southern Yakutia (Troner 1988). The project was designed to supply 5 million tons per year of coking coal to Japan and to provide the remaining low-grade coal to a local thermal power plant. The first coal was not exported until 1984, at which time Japan implemented an energy-saving plan that reduced its demand for coking coal. In addition, the local power plants were not equipped to use the low-grade Neryungri coal. It is also clear that little attention was paid to this project's long-term effects on the environment and local communities. Japan is currently importing approximately 4 million tons of coal annually from Neryungri and will continue to do so until 2003, when the resources are expected to be exhausted.

Another project, which began in 1975 and is still being discussed, is the Sakhalin oil/gas project. An accord was signed for the exploration and development of offshore deposits by the Sakhalin Oil Development Cooperation Company (SODECO) and promising discoveries were made in 1977 and then again in 1982–83. However, project delays have pushed target start dates further into the future (current developments in Sakhalin are discussed later in this chapter).

Russia–Mongolia

Mongolia was a communist nation with a centrally planned economy until the July 1990 multiparty elections and the move toward a market-based economy. From the early 1960s until the mid-1980s, the Mongolian government concentrated on developing a modern industrial economy with the help of Soviet technical and financial assistance, estimated at $600 million annually. During the Seventh Five-Year Plan (1981–85), Soviet aid to Mongolia rose 40 percent over the previous plan period, and it amounted to nearly US$3 billion during the Eighth Five-Year Plan (Dorian 1991). The Soviet Union was also Mongolia's chief trading partner, and so Russian officials exercised extreme influence in all sectors of the Mongolian economy, particularly mining.

Cooperation between the Soviet Union and Mongolia in the energy and minerals industries began in the late 1940s. Mongolneft was established in 1949 to develop the Dzuunbayan oilfields, and Sovmongolmetall was to mine and process tungsten deposits. By 1957 these two joint enterprises were controlled solely by the Mongolian government. In the 1970s, Mongolian-Russian joint ventures once again emerged, with the help of the Soviet foreign trade association Tstvetmetpromexport. These large ventures helped to increase industrial output and establish infrastructure, and in some cases whole communities grew around large mining areas.

The largest Russian-Mongolian joint venture is the Erdenet mining and processing complex, which accounts for approximately 12 percent of Mongolia's gross industrial output. The Erdenet complex is based on a large copper/molybdenum deposit at Erdenetiyn-Ovoo located 340 km northwest of Ulaanbaatar. It was put into full production in 1981 and mines approximately 17 tons of ore and produces 350,000 tons of copper concentrate and 3,000 tons of molybdenum concentrate annually (Damdinsuren 1991). A second major Russian-Mongolian mining venture is the Mongolsovtsvetmet corporation, which includes the Bor-Ondor fluorspar mining and ore dressing operation, three smaller fluorspar enterprises—Berh, Harayrag, and Ulaanhajuu—and the Tolgoyt alluvial gold mine. Total annual output of the corporation amounts to 470,000 tons of fluorspar ore, 115,000 tons of 92 percent CaF_2, and 2 million m^3 of gold-bearing sands (Clark and Dorian 1992). Together, Erdenet and Mongolsovtsvetmet account for approximately 40 percent of Mongolia's exports. The majority of these joint Mongolian-Russian mines use Russian-made equipment, but they hire and train Mongolians to work along with the Russians. Some 8,500 Russian and Mongolian specialists are employed by these two mining complexes.

The external trade of Mongolia has been concentrated mainly toward the former Soviet Union and other COMECON nations, which accounted for about 97 percent of trade turnover during the period 1970–83. But the recent changes in these countries' economic and political structure will bring a substantial decrease of foreign aid and loans from them, and so too will Mongolia's dependence on them decrease. As Mongolia seeks to attract new foreign investors and trading partners in the near future, new opportunities will open up for the other countries of Northeast Asia, particularly in the energy and minerals industries.

Russia and China–South Korea

After the 1960s, trade and cooperation between South Korea and the Asian communist countries was indirect, with Hong Kong and several Western European nations used as intermediaries. Direct trade was also hampered by political tensions between North and South Korea and the friendly relationships of China and Russia with the former. But in 1985, after the Chinese sent a delegation to the IBRD/IMF meeting in Seoul and the Koreans participated in a Chinese trade fair, South Korea and China finally established direct trade links (Kim 1991). Sino-South Korean trade in 1985 was US$1.16 billion and reached $5.06 billion by 1992. In 1992, China granted most-favored-nation status to South Korea and lowered or removed tariffs on traded goods, so increased exports and imports between the two countries can be expected.

Total informal trade between South Korea and Russia amounted to just $257 million in 1988 (Lho 1989). But trade barriers are relaxing, and direct trade between the two countries has begun. South Korea's largest import item is coal, and some of its needs are already being met by Russian supplies, including Neryungri coal from the Far East. Russia is also interested in South Korean technology and investment to help it develop the energy and minerals industries of Siberia and the RFE.

China–Japan

Before China and Japan normalized relations in 1972, Sino-Japanese trade was generally conducted on a small scale and between small and medium-sized trading companies. In 1950, for example, trade volume measured US$40 million, compared to nearly $1 billion in 1972. After the reestablishment of diplomatic relations in the latter year, trade expanded quickly to $10 billion in 1981 and $25.4 billion in 1992 (Editorial Board 1987–88). Thanks to the energy complementarity of the two countries, trade flourished in the 1970s. Japan was importing nearly all its oil from outside sources, and China was producing more oil than it could use domestically. But the oil price decline, along with an increasing domestic energy demand in the early 1980s, disrupted oil trade and contributed to a $6 billion deficit for China in 1985. Since that time, China has attempted to diversify trade and is now emphasizing the export of processed goods rather than primary products in order to reduce the trade deficit and to meet domestic demand. Exports to Japan in 1992 amounted to $11.7 billion, and imports measured $13.7 billion, for a deficit of nearly $2 billion (IMF 1992).

The Baoshan Iron and Steel Complex in Shanghai is probably the largest and most costly project involving foreign participation ever undertaken in China. It is also a historic Sino-Japanese joint venture that will likely influence future cooperation between the two nations. Seven and a half years after the initial memorandum was signed in April 1978, the plant began operation on 15 September 1985, with the help of more than 500 Japanese experts and $2.5 billion worth of imported technology and equipment (U.S. Bureau of Mines 1990). In its first year, Baoshan surpassed its target production levels; the second phase of construction began and was completed in June 1991. In addition to increasing China's iron and steel output, Baoshan is a model for future joint ventures. China recently negotiated with Japan to build a $5 billion iron and steel plant at Shijuisuo, Shangdong Province, near Rizhao with a capacity of 3 million tons per year of steel for domestic use. Partners in what will be the new largest Sino-Japanese joint venture in China are China Hang Hua Development, MMI, the Shangdong provincial government, Nippon Steel, Industrial Bank of Japan, and Asahi Trading Company. China will still continue to be a major importer of iron and steel products up to the year 2000, but opportunities for joint venture development with Japan could be prominent in the growth of the energy and minerals industries of both countries.

North Korea–Northeast Asia

North Korea, one of the world's last centrally planned economies, still follows the *juche* ideology (self-reliance) and maintains an inward-looking development strategy. In the past, it has traded with the COMECON countries and with China, primarily by barter, but its ex-socialist partners now demand cash payment. North Korea's economy is based on heavy industry, with machine-tool building given the highest priority. But the country has to import advanced equipment and technology to keep the industry operational, and it exports no finished products, so the resulting trade deficit is huge. In 1990, North Korea's foreign trade was just US$4.65 billion, with a deficit of $600 million (Pacific Basin Economic Council 1992).

Although foreign trade is minimal in North Korea, it is an area in which the government is slightly flexible and outward-looking. On 26 January 1984, an official proclamation on trade policy stated that, for North Korea to increase economic development and earn foreign exchange, it must increase trade with foreign countries regardless of the diplomatic relations between them. In addition to this liberalization of trade policy, on 8 September 1984 the Law on Joint Ventures—similar in structure to the Chinese joint venture law—was proclaimed. Since this law was made effective, one hundred joint ventures have been created in North Korea, with preference for participation given to Koreans living in foreign countries (Park et al. 1987). North Korea's three biggest trading partners are the former Soviet Union (60 percent of total foreign trade), China (14 percent), and Japan (12 percent).

In the energy and minerals industries, North Korea exports coal, iron and steel, and nonferrous metals. In 1988, Japan's International Trading Corporation and the state-owned Korea Ryongaksan General Trading Company set up a joint venture company, the International Chemical Joint Venture Corporation, to extract and refine rare-earth metals in North Korea. The company built a US$12 million plant capable of processing 1,500 tons per year of monazite and extracting 400 tons of rare-earth metals and oxides.[1] This is one of the few mineral joint ventures currently in operation in North Korea, but assuming the North Korean government continues to permit such activities and given the high potential of certain commodities, continued cooperation is likely.

South Korea–Japan

Since South Korea and Japan normalized diplomatic relations in 1965, the two countries have become major economic powers. Trade between the two has grown considerably, from US$210 million in 1965 to $12 billion in 1984 and to $33.5 billion in 1991. Japan is South Korea's main supplier of intermediate and capital goods, and South Korea supplies manufactured goods to Japan. However, throughout the 1970s and through much of the 1980s, South Korea has built up a huge trade deficit with Japan. Many analysts attribute this to the differing stages of economic development in the two countries. Japan is said to be a more diversified economy, while South Korea, in the process of industrializing, has put enormous emphasis on heavy industry which requires large investments in plant and equipment largely supplied by Japan. Since the late 1980s and South Korea's aggressive export-oriented economic plan, this deficit has decreased.

Both countries have relatively few natural resources, but opportunities for joint venture development continue to be promising. For example, Mitsubishi is supplying equipment for the fourth expansion of the Pohang Iron and Steel complex. An agreement ratified in 1977 has paved the way for the joint exploration and production of undersea oil on the continental shelf between the two countries (Clough 1987).

Northeast Asia–Alaska

The countries of Northeast Asia have been involved in trade and cooperation with Alaska since the early 1980s: Alaska's Office of International

Trade, with offices in Tokyo, Seoul, and Taipei, was established in 1983; the Alaska Center for International Business began operation in 1984. These two organizations evaluate trade opportunities and other forms of cooperation between Alaska and Asia and promote Alaska's exports to Asian markets. Since 1975, Alaska's economy has depended considerably on oil, and thus it is vulnerable to fluctuations in world oil markets. Recently the state has looked for help from the nations of Northeast Asia to diversify its economy by developing its vast supplies of nonfuel minerals (Dorian et al. 1989).

In 1989 two extremely promising mines began production and could provide export and joint venture opportunities with the Northeast Asian region. The Red Dog zinc/lead/silver deposit in northeast Alaska is the second-largest known zinc reserve in the world after the Mt. Isa deposit in Australia. Production began at Red Dog in October 1989 and is expected to reach 680,000 tons per year of zinc, lead, and polymetallic sulfide concentrates. The Greens Creek polymetallic deposit in southeast Alaska began production in April 1989. Despite difficult economic conditions at both mines, the Greens Creek and Red Dog operations produced about half the U.S. domestic mine production of zinc, 12 percent of the lead, and 17 percent of the silver for the 1992 calendar year. Greens Creek will eventually become the largest silver producer in the United States as well as a major producer of gold, zinc, and lead.

Of Alaska's total exports in 1992, Japan received 69 percent (US$2.34 billion). The majority of the remaining exports went to Korea ($292 million) and China ($122 million). These exports included petroleum products, coal, and minerals. Within the minerals industry, export commodities included waste and scrap aluminum, nickel, stainless steel, and zinc. Alaskan coal exports to South Korea amounted to around 500,000 tons in 1992, or a value of $20 million. Metal scrap exports to Asia reached $2.63 million during the same year.

Many countries in the Northeast Asian region have expressed interest in establishing joint ventures with Alaskan firms. For example, in early 1990 a joint venture between Russia and Alaska was formed. The organization, SVZAL, is made up of Severovostokzoloto, the largest gold mining association in the Russian Far East, the Bering Straits Trading Company, headquartered in Nome, and Ronald Sheardown, a mining consultant based in Anchorage. The goal of SVZAL is to develop deposits and advanced technology on both sides of the Bering Strait. The joint venture is valued at $2.3 million and has already begun to develop Little Eldorado Creek, a placer deposit near Fairbanks, and several granite and limestone quarries in Magadan. The Russians have a much more advanced permafrost technology and the Alaskans offer more highly efficient automation technologies.

South Korean and Chinese entrepreneurs have also begun to establish joint venture ties with Alaska. Since the early 1980s, Alaska has geared coal mine development toward markets in Asia with the knowledge that U.S. intrastate demand for coal was insufficient. In January 1983 a long-term contract was signed for the development of the Usibelli Coal Mine, with partners including the State of Alaska and South Korea's Sun Eel Shipping and Korean Electric Power (KEPCO). In 1992 production at Usibelli reached nearly 1.39 million tons; more than half was used to fuel six interior power plants, and the remainder was exported to South Korea. SVZAL and Usibelli-KEPCO have both been successful and will likely serve as models for future cooperative efforts between Alaska and Northeast Asia.

Major Opportunities for Joint Development

Despite historical achievements, the mining industry in much of Northeast Asia operates below capacity and is plagued with a feeble infrastructure, outdated technology and equipment, rising production costs, and capital and labor shortages in addition to general economic deterioration. Behind these problems are shortages of essential materials, transport difficulties, labor disputes, and years of inefficient centralized planning. In the Russian Far East, the largest gold producer in the former Soviet Union, inadequate mining and processing techniques strand thousands of tons of otherwise usable gold ore in dumps or stockpiles. Commodities developed to the year 2000 and immediately beyond in the Far East will generally be restricted to those in short supply and of high quality. Poor transport facilities will continue to constrain minerals development (see Chapter 7).

Thus, Northeast Asian countries and regions are now encouraging foreign participation through joint ventures and technology transfers, and opportunities for regional cooperation in mining development are rapidly emerging. Leaders in the RFE, Mongolia, and Northeast China hope to expand their mineral industries and improve the efficiency of raw materials utilization by introducing capital, technology, machinery, and science from abroad (see Appendix 3 for a review of regional cooperative projects).

It has become typical for Northeast Asians to use imported technology and equipment to renovate existing enterprises and thereby tap their potential and promote production, economic growth, and technical development. During the 1990s, technology transfers could be pivotal in promoting domestic economic growth and structural change as well as cooperation with foreign nations. Though economic restructuring is under way in many of the Northeast Asia countries, technological advancement of industry is needed to achieve success in facilitating economic growth in the long term. It was estimated that, by the time of the collapse of the Soviet Union, as much as three-quarters of all equipment used in Soviet industry was in need of renovation or replacement to improve efficiencies in operations (Akopian 1992). Such an accomplishment would require massive capital investments as well as technology transfers for years to come.

Two projects that demonstrate the great potential of regional cooperative prospects in minerals and energy are the Sakhalin Oil and Gas Project and the Tumen River Development Project. Billions of dollars are being proposed for investment in these two projects by several Northeast Asian nations, and UN officials have indicated that with development the Tumen River Basin can become a center of world trade such as Rotterdam or Hong Kong. In the rest of this section we briefly describe these two proposed megaprojects (see also Appendix 1).

Sakhalin Island

Oil and gas field developments off Sakhalin Island requiring more than $10 billion over a period of years could represent the most significant opportunity for regional resource cooperation in Northeast Asia. Oil analysts have estimated that the fields off Sakhalin Island could produce up to 3 billion barrels of oil and at least a trillion cubic feet of gas. By comparison, Alaska's North Slope will have produced approximately 18 billion barrels of oil by 2010.

Hydrocarbon resources have been under exploration in Sakhalin for two decades. The four fields proposed for development are positioned off the east coast of the island and have been thoroughly evaluated with more than one dozen wells per field. Oil reserves lie within 15 miles of Sakhalin's coast in waters less than 100 m (328 ft.) deep.

Given the deterioration of the Soviet oil industry in the 1980s, government officials began asking international oil companies to submit bids to develop the offshore Sakhalin fields with the advent of perestroika. The Russian Far East has been plagued with energy shortages for more than a decade, and timely development of offshore Sakhalin could have, at least in part, prevented such difficulties. Sakhalin's onshore oil and gas resources are near depletion, leading to widespread concern in the Far East about long-term economic growth prospects of the region.

Development of offshore Sakhalin would represent a tremendous multilateral project involving a multitude of companies, countries, and financial lending agencies. The Sakhalin plan is above all a gas project. The proposal is for gas to be delivered by pipeline both to Russia (Khabarovsk Krai) and to Japan (Hokkaido) and South Korea (Pusan), with liquefied natural gas being sold to countries of the Asia-Pacific region including Japan, South Korea, and Taiwan. Slightly more than half the gas produced would be consumed domestically in the RFE, leaving about 1.2 billion cubic feet per day for export, mainly to Japan and South Korea.[2] Local RFE officials have also requested that any development of offshore Sakhalin be accompanied with infrastructure construction, perhaps including a railway, airports, power stations, and hospitals.

Although the Sakhalin project is critical to the energy future of the RFE and a potential financial windfall to the local economies, negotiations between oil company consortiums and Russia have been long, difficult, and trouble-filled. In 1991, when Moscow opened the bidding for rights to complete a feasibility study on the development of Sakhalin oil and gas reserves, major oil companies visited the island with tremendous enthusiasm and aspirations. Six international oil consortia or companies made bids in late 1991 for development of Sakahalin's offshore resources, including (1) the government-affiliated SODECO of Japan, Exxon of the United States, and C. Itoh of Japan, (2) Japan's Mitsui and McDermott International and Marathon Oil, both of the United States, (3) Showa Shell Sekiyu KK, Royal Dutch Shell, Showa Shell Sekiyu Development, Nissho Iwai, and Mitsubishi, (4) Amoco of the United States, BHP Petroleum of Australia, and South Korea's Hyundai Group, (5) Mobil Oil of the United States, and (6) Idemitsu Kosan.

On 27 January 1992, an established Russian government committee ruled that the MMMSM Group—Marathon Oil, McDermott International, Mitsui, Royal Dutch/Shell Group, and Mitsubishi—would be selected as a foreign partner to undertake a feasibility study to develop the Piltun-Astokhskoye and Lunskoye fields and further exploration in the tender zone. The Piltun-Astokhskoye and Lunskoye fields contain 50 million tons of oil, 30 milion tons of gas condensate, and 300 billion m^3 of gas. The selection was complicated when Russia's Supreme Council backed opposition to the Sakhalin Island award from local political interests in Sakhalin and created a new committee to reconsider bids for the work. The Russian Council also suggested that two unsuccessful bidders, Mobil Oil and SODECO, be reconsidered for inclusion in the project. Mobil bid for the feasibility study without a partner, and SODECO, which has Japan National Oil as a major partner, sought the contract jointly with Exxon.

By April 1993, the MMMSM plan for developing the oil and gas fields on the Sakhalin shelf received final approval by Russian authorities. One year later, in May 1994, a contract between the Russian government and the consortium was finally set to be signed. Pending ratification by the Russian and Sakhalin parliaments, the project holds the promise of huge profits for the foreign firms and could eventually establish Russia as a major player in Asian energy markets. About two-thirds of the yearly production, slated to commence by 2000, will be targeted for neighboring Asian markets, notably Japan, China, Taiwan, and South Korea.

Tumen River Basin Project

Under the auspices of the UNDP, a project that will transform the swamplands of the Tumen River delta dividing North Korea, China, and Russia into a hub of economic growth and international commerce is being formulated. At an estimated cost of US$30 billion over 15–20 years, the Tumen River Basin Development Project aims at improving economic cooperation between North Korea, China, Mongolia, South Korea, and Russia via a huge duty-free shipping and processing zone. The project would allow capital-rich Japan and South Korea to tap the region's tremendous national resources; it would also open a land route from the Sea of Japan to Europe and thereby improve Asia-Europe trade.

An international corporation will be created to manage the industrial zone in the Tumen River delta, which straddles the borders of China, Russia, and North Korea. In 1992, these three countries agreed to give land leases to foreigners to attract investment for the proposed economic development zone. The participating countries will respect the sovereignty of the three bordering countries over their respective land used in the program.

Each country participating in the planning for Tumen River development has defined its broad interests in the project. China's primary interest continues to be acquiring access to the Sea of Japan for exporting goods from its northeastern provinces, as well as creating employment in the area. North Korea desires to expand the existing Rajin port near the North Korea–Russia border and to construct a major airport, river port, and railway to serve the area. Desperate for hard currency, the North has offered to establish a special economic zone with preferential tax and investment laws in a 621-km^2 region that includes two existing ports. Mongolia, landlocked and remote, hopes to improve its railway links to the Pacific Ocean, taking advantage of the recently completed Ulaanbaatar-Harbin-Dumen-Hunchun railway project. Russia, and particularly the RFE, hopes to improve rail connections to China and upgrade the port facilities at Vladivostok and Nakhodka. The country also plans to create its own special economic zone in nearby Posyet in conjunction with the Tumen project.

The development of an operational free trade zone in the Tumen River is obviously a very long-term proposition—but one strongly motivated by the availability of energy and mineral resources on the Northeast Asian mainland. A comprehensive resource assessment of the participating countries must be completed to determine an economically and environmentally sound strategy for managing and utilizing the resources. The long-term exploitation of natural resources in North Korea, China, Russia, and Mongolia will have to be facilitated by removal of trade barriers, improved infrastructure, new industries, renewed economic growth, and financial and tax incentives. Mining-related activities in the Tumen River neighboring countries can eventually increase the volume of freight in the region, but not until substantial infrastructural improvements are made. Owing to an abundance of high-valued mineral and energy commodities, the RFE (gold, diamonds, tin, oil, and gas) and Mongolia (copper, gold, coal) enjoy more immediate prospects for increased resource development.

Tumen River Basin development depends largely on the willingness of Japan and South Korea to supply capital. But the 38,600 square mile project will also require Western capital and technical expertise, for the first time on such a scale in largely socialist territory. Political differences—for example, between North and South Korea, China and Japan, and Russia and Japan—may need to be overcome for the project to materialize. Economic conditions in the RFE and North Korea must also remain stable or improve to facilitate an attractive investment climate and allow project talks to continue. A favorable aspect of the megaproject is that the economic interests of all participating countries would benefit by improved international ties, increased foreign investment, and greater trade.

Major Obstacles to Joint Development

Despite efforts by Japan, the United States, and Germany to facilitate improved conditions, in recent years much of the world has experienced slow economic growth, or recession. As the world's leading economies continue to struggle to improve their own domestic conditions, capital for overseas investment has become increasingly scarce. Yet considerable funds are needed to reconstruct the former Soviet Union and Eastern Europe, and also to restore the global environment and curb the rise of pollution. Even in its first years, the decade of the 1990s has already shown great potential for capital scarcity and competitiveness. Most capital importers, for example, Latin America, Africa, South and Southeast Asia, and China, will face tighter capital supplies in the years ahead, higher interest rates, and higher degrees of capital repatriation associated with their direct foreign investment, and the burden of financing internal investment will tend to fall increasingly on their own domestic savings.

Tens of billions of dollars of investment will be required to accommodate growth in nonfuel minerals development alone during the 1990s. Based on planned expansion of global minerals capacity to 2005, at least US$66 billion may be required to build or expand nonferrous mines and

processing facilities (Dorian and Plummer 1992).[3] Moreover, maintenance, replacement, and environmental capital may be somewhere in the
range of two to four times the size of the investment required to increase
capacity. The issue of capital scarcity and its potential impact on Northeast
Asia regional cooperation projects raises several important questions:
What will the sources of capital be? What will total capital requirements
be for the energy and mineral sectors (including maintenance, replacement, and environmental control)? What forms of investment will pre-
dominate in the 1990s? Will mining companies be expected to increase
capital expenditures on environmental protection substantially? Will the
so-called transitional economies of Northeast Asia receive the massive
funds they seek to develop their mineral industries further? Through
1992, US$4.5 million was raised for the Tumen River project, with one mil-
lion dollars contributed by Finland.[4]

Much of the hope for developing Sakhalin oil and gas and the Tumen
River Basin, as well as the other cooperative ventures in energy and minerals, is predicated on substantial inflows of Japanese and South Korean
investment. Japan is the most crucial link to creating a foundation for regional trade and business.

To provide an indication of whether Japan is likely to invest the capital
needed for joint resource development in Northeast Asia, Table 5.3 lists
Japanese foreign direct investment in Asia, disaggregated by category. As
shown, less than one-quarter (22.8 percent) of Japanese direct investment
into Asia in the past three decades has been in resource development projects, amounting to US$7.34 billion. Moreover, most of this investment was
directed at the Indonesian energy and metal sectors, notably oil and gas
and bauxite and aluminum. Although Japanese investment in resource
development overseas has increased in nominal terms since the 1950s and
1960s, the pace of growth slowed considerably after the second oil shock
of 1979–80. Structural adjustment of the Japanese economy has led to less
energy consumption, thereby reducing the need to secure stable and diversified sources of supply. Clearly, based on changing directions of investment, the relatively small amount going into resources development,
and a slowdown in its growth, Japanese foreign investment is moving
away from resource-related projects.

South Korea, while placing importance on investment in mining and related activities,[5] actually provides little capital to resource development
projects. Between 1968 and 1985, Korea's direct foreign investment in mining totaled just US$235.3 million, spread over thirteen projects (Kwon
1987). In 1988, South Korea's investment in mining approached $13.7 mil-
lion, compared to Japan's investment of more than $12 billion. Relatively
few investments have been made by South Korean firms into metal mining, since Korea's nonferrous metal refining industry is not competitive,

TABLE 5.3 Japanese Foreign Direct Investment in Asia, 1951–1988 (US$ million)

	Manuf.	Resource Dev.	Commerce/ Services	Other	Total
NIEs					
Hong Kong	492	33	5,515	127	6,167
S. Korea	1,589	21	1,506	132	3,248
Taiwan	1,473	4	246	68	1,791
ASEAN					
Singapore	1,990	5	1,744	73	3,812
Indonesia	2,955	6,441	400	8	9,804
Thailand	1,456	38	416	82	1,992
Malaysia	1,350	179	294	11	1,834
Philippines	510	455	144	11	1,120
Other					
China	349	48	1,575	64	2,036
Other Asia	207	119	85	12	423
Total	12,371	7,343	11,925	588	32,227

Source: Export-Import Bank of Japan.

but significant investments have been directed to energy prospecting and development because of Korea's heavy reliance on imported energy. The country produces no oil and gas, and it seeks to obtain as much energy as possible from joint ventures in foreign countries in addition to other imports. Because of a shortage of capital among individual firms and a lack of mining technology and experience, all Korea's overseas mining development projects are in the form of production-sharing joint ventures, with the exception of the Usibelli and Tanoma projects in the United States. The number of projects and the amount of overseas investment in mining have increased substantially since the mid-1980s, but Korean investment is still only beginning and will therefore likely grow further in the future.

Conclusion

Although many factors favor regional cooperation in Northeast Asia (abundant natural resources and labor, growing demand for energy and minerals), potential barriers to joint activities are also numerous. These include imbalance of military and economic power, differing political systems, differing pricing systems, competing demands for capital, infrastructural constraints, political conflicts, incomplete legal regimes, and incompatible ideologies. Economic or political disintegration of Russia into its component parts would severely hinder the Russian Far East's ability to actively participate in any regional cooperation projects.

Because of these and other problems, relatively smaller projects involv-ing energy and mineral exploitation may be more suitable to regional co-operation activities than the multibillion dollar megaprojects. Smaller projects may offer less uncertainty, fewer risks, and a quicker pay off, while providing the experience in international cooperation necessary to establish large projects in the future. Such ventures, including some of those listed in Appendix 3, have a more reasonable chance of coming to fruition; in these cases, individual companies are selecting projects for which they have extensive experience, a strong desire to participate, or a comparative advantage in developing a product. Regardless of the size of the project, capital will be crucial for joint ventures involving resources.

Notes

An early version of this chapter was published in the *Journal of Northeast Asian Studies* (Dorian et al. 1993).

1. *Mining Annual Review 1991*, pp. 83–103.

2. "Field Development Eyed Off Soviets' Sakhalin Island," *Oil and Gas Journal* 89, no. 11 (1991):33–36.

3. This figure is likely an underestimate, however, since only selected commodi-ties are considered (copper, tin, nickel, aluminum, bauxite, lead, and zinc), and the value is based soley on known projects for which expenditures have been an-nounced.

4. FBIS, EAS-92-200, 15 October 1992.

5. The South Korean government has issued a set of policy directions for over-seas resource development. For designated minerals (bituminous coal, uranium, copper ore, and iron ore), the diversification of projects by country and region has been stressed. Consistent with this diversification policy, the government has rec-ommended politically stable countries such as Canada, the United States, and Australia as target areas. In its effort to minimize risk, it has recommended that Korean firms seek production-sharing joint ventures with minority equity shares of less than 30 percent.

References

Akopian, A. 1992. *Industrial Potential of Russia*. New York: Nova Science Pub-lishers.

British Petroleum. 1992. *BP Statistical Review of World Energy*. London.

Clark, Allen L., and James P. Dorian. 1992. "Mineral Investment Conditions in Mongolia." In *Mineral Investment Conditions in Selected Countries of the Asia-Pa-cific Region*. New York: United Nations.

Clark, Allen L., James P. Dorian, and Pow-foong Fan. 1987. "An Estimate of the Mineral Resources of China." *Resources Policy* 13 (1):68–84.

Clough, Ralph N. 1987. *Embattled Korea: The Rivalry for International Support*. Boul-der, Colo.: Westview Press.

Damdinsuren, M. 1991. "Mongolia." In *Mining Annual Review 1991*. London: Mining Journal Publications.

Dorian, James P. 1991. "USSR-Mongolia: A Minerals Association About to End." *Resources Policy* 17 (March):42–53.

Dorian, James P., David Fridley, and Kristen Tressler. 1993. "Multilateral Resource Cooperation among Northeast Asian Countries: Energy and Mineral Joint Venture Prospects." *Journal of Northeast Asian Studies* 12 (Spring):3–34.

Dorian, James P., and Michael G. Plummer. 1992. "Global Investment and Future Minerals Production." *GeoJournal* 27 (2):207–16.

Dorian, James P., Jay Slivkoff, Helen C. Caldwell, and D. Lyn Henagan. 1989. "The Potential Impact of Chinese Minerals Development on Alaska's Export Competitiveness and Economic Future." Unpublished report, prepared for the Alaska Center for International Business, Anchorage.

Economic Information and Agency. 1992. *China's Customs Statistics*. Hong Kong: EIA.

Economic Research Institute. 1991. *Russian Far East Economic Yearbook* (in Russian). Khabarovsk: Academy of the Russian Foundation.

Editorial Board. 1987 and 1988. *Almanac of China's Foreign Economic Relations and Trade*. Hong Kong: EIA.

Fesharaki, Fereidun, and Wu Kang. 1993. "Energy Demand and Supply Outlook in the Asia-Pacific Region: An Update," Energy Advisory no. 109, 15 January 1993. East-West Center, Honolulu.

Heilongjiang Statistical Bureau. 1992. *Statistical Yearbook 1992* (in Chinese). Harbin, China.

International Monetary Fund. 1992. *Direction of Trade Statistics Yearbook*. Washington, D.C.: IMF.

Jilin Statistical Bureau. 1992. *Statistical Yearbook 1992* (in Chinese). Changchun, China.

Kim, Won Bae. 1991. "Report on Regional Development in the Yellow Sea Rim." Submitted to the Korea Research Institute for Human Settlements and Asia-Pacific Institute of China, Population Institute, East-West Center, Hawaii, September.

Korea Resources Institute. 1992. *A Study on the Metallic Minerals Industry of North Korea* (in Korean). KR-92(B)-17, Republic of Korea, December.

Kwon, O. Yul. 1987. *The Korean Mineral Market: Opportunities and Marketing Strategies for Canada*. Ontario: Centre for Resource Studies, Queens University.

Lho, Kyongsoo. 1989. "Seoul-Moscow Relations: Looking to the 1990's." *Asian Survey* 29 (December).

Liaoning Statistical Bureau. 1992. *Statistical Yearbook 1992* (in Chinese). Shenyang, China.

Pacific Basin Economic Council. 1992. "Will North Korea Open Its Economy?" *International Bulletin*, January 10.

Park, Jae Kyu, Byung Chul Koh, and Tai-Hwan Kwak. 1987. *The Foreign Relations of North Korea: New Perspectives*. Seoul: Kyungnam University Press.

Troner, Alan J. 1988. "Soviet-Japanese Joint Cooperation Ventures: A Study in Far East Mineral Development Projects." Master's thesis, Department of Geography, University of Hawaii.

United Nations. 1991. *World Populations Prospects.* Population Studies no. 120. New
     York.
U.S. Bureau of Mines. 1988. *Mineral Industries of the Far East and South Asia.* Wash-
     ington, D.C.: GPO.
U.S. Bureau of Mines. 1990. *The Iron and Steel Industry of China.* Washington, D.C.:
     GPO.
U.S. Bureau of Mines. 1993. *Mineral Commodity Summary.* Washington, D.C.: GPO.
World Bureau of Metal Statistics. 1992. *World Metal Statistics Yearbook 1992.* Lon-
     don.

6

Yakutiya Gas

Allen S. Whiting

This chapter examines the possibility of providing natural gas by pipeline to the Russian Federated Republic, the People's Republic of China, North Korea, South Korea, and Japan. The gas would come from the Republic of Sakha (Yakutiya). The estimated cost would be $15 billion with delivery beginning ten years after the start of feasibility studies. Despite daunting obstacles, the potential gain in the reduction of CO_2 by substituting natural gas for coal warrants serious consideration of the project.

Background

Yakutiya gas was first discovered in 1936 but permafrost 1.5 km (0.9 miles) thick impeded exploration.[1] Subsequently the Vilyui River area was tested at various points, with promising deposits being found in its upper region. In the early 1970s negotiations with Japanese and American firms advanced interest in joint development. Tentative agreement was reached to schedule deliveries of 10 billion m^3 of liquified natural gas (LNG) to each of the participating countries, including the USSR.

Before negotiations could be finalized, a minimum resource of 1 trillion m^3 had to be proved. American skepticism of Moscow's claim of 825 billion m^3 prompted an invitation to a joint Japanese-American team for an independent survey. The Japanese accepted the Soviet figure; the Americans questioned it but privately expressed confidence that the necessary reserves would eventually be established (Conolly 1976:82). By 1979, 850 billion m^3 of gas had been identified, and the remainder was expected to be found in the near future.[2] As of the early 1980s, 273.5 billion m^3 had been proven and an additional 190 billion m^3 were probable or potential (C1 reserve category) with another 161 billion m^3 as speculative reserves (C2) (ZumBrunnen 1990:93). The total inferred reserves have been estimated at 13 trillion m^3 (Shabad and Mote 1977:44).

The proposed project involved a 3,200-km (1,984-mile) pipeline and a liquefaction plant to provide 10 billion m^3 of gas (7.5 million metric tons of LNG) annually to both Japan and the United States for twenty-five years. But in the absence of urgent demand and with protracted haggling over details, interest in Yakutiya gas waned. Finally, the Soviet invasion of Afghanistan in 1979 prompted the American and Japanese termination of negotiations.

Justification for Renewed Study

Major changes in the international system and in Northeast Asia together with new global energy and environmental concerns justify renewal of attention to Yakutiya gas supplying the region. Significant improvement in the political interaction among the five relevant countries makes multilateral cooperation feasible on a scale impossible to contemplate previously. The Tumen River Basin Development Project provides an encouraging precedent in this regard (see Chapter 5).

First and foremost, Russo-Chinese economic relations have progressed steadily since the mid-1980s, collapse of the USSR notwithstanding. Joint development of the Heilongjiang or Amur River basin, first proposed and surveyed in the latter 1950s, was abandoned for thirty years because of the Sino-Soviet dispute. This multipurpose project aimed at improved shipping facilities, flood control, irrigation, and electric power. Renewed joint interest, announced in the late 1980s, prevailed over continued disagreement on the border channel opposite Khabarovsk.[3]

Conclusion of a Russo-Japanese peace treaty remains blocked because of the so-called Northern Territories issue, Moscow's occupation of the southern Kurile Islands being disputed by Tokyo. Recently, however, Tokyo has relaxed its linkage of economics and politics. In 1992–93, Russia's Gas Industry Concern signed on for $700 million in seamless pipe and gas industry machinery, made possible by Export-Import Bank loans to Japanese trading firms with the Ministry of International Trade and Industry (MITI) insuring Japanese suppliers against possible risk and losses.[4] The fall of the Liberal Democratic Party after nearly forty years of uninterrupted rule complicates forecasting Japanese foreign policy, especially where nationalistic sensitivities invite domestic political exploitation. But the trend of Russo-Japanese economic relations over the past two years gives room for cautious optimism in this regard.

Moscow's relations with Seoul took a dramatic turn under President Gorbachev, moving from economic to diplomatic ties in short order. Seoul responded with $3 billion in credits and loans while private investors anticipated major opportunities, especially in Siberia. This enthusiasm waned as the Russian failure to pay bills due combined with growing uncertainty over the fiscal and legal investment environment. Nevertheless Kim Woo Choong, chairman of the powerful Daewoo business complex, reportedly is attempting to move Russian, North Korean, and South Korean players toward a Yakutiya natural gas pipeline to serve the Korean peninsula.[5] Meanwhile, Russian relations with North Korea, although seriously strained by Moscow's recognition of Seoul, have fallen short of complete rupture. At the same time, Seoul and Pyongyang have sustained a high level dialogue that offers promise of lowered tension on the peninsula despite a continued concentrated military confrontation.

This trend of rapprochement and detente is of multiple benefit to the exploitation of Yakutiya gas. It increases the number of potential contributors for funding the initial project. It also increases the number of potential consumers for the final product. Rapprochement and detente tend to reduce the burden of military expenditures for each country, thereby freeing funds for economic development. More particularly, these international political changes make possible the transportation of natural gas by pipeline on land from Yakutiya through Northeast China and Korea to the Tsushima Strait and Japan. This eliminates the more complicated shipping of LNG by tanker and also avoids winter weather hazards to shipping as well as possible off-loading risks. The feasibility of the Tsushima Strait pipeline has already been attested to by Tokyo Gas.[6]

Concomitant with the change in international relations has come a change in national priorities. Since the end of the Cold War, the major concern in foreign policy for Northeast Asian countries has shifted from military to economic security, with an attendant concern on how to meet growing energy needs with lessened pollution. One study by Tokyo Gas projects demand for natural gas in Northeast Asia to reach the limit of present and anticipated supply from sources in the region by the year 2000.[7] This projection is based on three new LNG trains—Indonesia in 1994, Malaysia in 1995, and Abu Dhabi in 1994—plus 4 million tons from the Total North Field in Qatar in 1997 and 5 million tons from Australia's Northwest Shelf around the year 2000.[8] However, greater dependence on Middle East sources raises questions in view of the Iran-Iraq war, the Gulf War, and continuing evidence of a regional arms race there, possibly nuclear as well as conventional.

MITI is seeking to reorganize the LNG chain of exploration, development, transportation, and import so as to center it on end users. With that in mind, it is prompting utilities to look beyond the safe end of this decade to more problematic prospects as commercial energy demand from South Korea, Taiwan, and other East Asian consumers is calculated to grow more than 5 percent annually. Japan's LNG requirement of 34 million tons in 1990 will hit 50 million tons by 2000 and 70–80 million tons in 2010.[9] The natural gas share of energy consumption is expected to increase from 10.6

percent in 1989 to 12.2 percent in 2010, while energy consumption is anticipated to increase by 1.2 percent annually.[10] This latter calculation depends on doubling the weight of nuclear energy from 8.9 percent in 1989 to 16.9 percent in 2010. But in recent years nuclear accidents in Japan have raised public concern, complicating site choices and slowing construction of power plants. Any further trend in this direction will place greater demand on natural gas. As a final consideration, Japan has pledged to play a leading role in trying to solve worldwide environmental problems and has specifically targeted stabilizing the CO_2 emission level from the year 2000 on at the 1990 level.[11]

China has abundant supplies of coal, which now provides 70 percent of the nation's energy with more than 900 million tons in annual consumption.[12] However, the National Institute of Environmental Health and Engineering reports death from lung cancer in Liaoning Province to be four to five times that of developed countries, with 2,000 dying annually in the provincial capital of respiratory diseases.[13] Per unit of fuel burned, coal releases 60 percent more CO_2 than natural gas, and natural gas conversion technologies can be made more energy-efficient than coal conversion technologies, significantly reducing the greenhouse effect (Williams 1991). The heavy industrial centers of Northeast China can be serviced from a Yakutiya pipeline. These centers produce the most pollutants in winds born eastward to Japan.

Northeast China's oil reserves are approaching uneconomic rates of return and soon will be virtually exhausted. Their high paraffin content adds a further complication by requiring special transportation facilities that consume additional energy to make the oil utilizable at the point of distribution.[14] Highly promising oil reserves in Xinjiang are nonetheless extremely remote from major consumption centers. Offshore oil has yet to realize the return anticipated from South China Sea exploration. The East China Sea potential remains unproven because conflicting claims between China and Japan inhibit foreign exploration. Meanwhile, the present and projected rate of growth in the Chinese economy together with the relatively low energy efficiency of industry makes continual energy bottlenecks inevitable in the absence of significant increases in supply. In this context Yakutiya natural gas can alleviate, albeit not solve, the problem.

Four-fifths of all power station capacity in the Russian Far East is thermal, drawing increasingly on imported fuel from as far distant as West Siberia.[15] Beyond supplementing existing supply, natural gas interested Soviet scholars in the potential gasification of coal in southern Yakutiya.[16] This would facilitate utilization of the vast Chulman coal reserves in south Yakutiya in support of an iron and steel complex based on nearby ore at Aldan. The total Yakut coal reserves constitute nearly one-fifth of the world's volume, with 11,000 million tons proved by 1980 (A + some B). Soviet and Japanese geologists estimated 40,000 million tons of hypothetical resources (A through D), of which two-thirds were within 300 m (972 feet) of the surface with one-fifth of coking variety.[17] The demands on Chulman forced reliance on adjacent Neryungri, where 500 million tons of proved reserves offer high-quality coking coal.

Unfortunately, the advantage of Chulman and Neryungri coal is offset by the pollution resulting from local conditions. Neryungri coal is high in ash, which contributes to pollution, as does burning the detritus (as steam coal) from the country's largest coal washery at the site, necessitated by the high mean volatility and high moisture content (Mote 1990:173). The pollution is worse in winter because of the temperature inversion and prolonged calm. Earlier Soviet experiments with coal gasification did not prove economical (Shabad 1969:277). However, rising energy costs resulting from recent economic reforms in Russia call for reassessment of this option. Gasification could offset other environmental concerns in Yakutiya over the possible impact of opening a massive gas field together with the associated facilities and pipeline.[18]

The Korean peninsula is primarily dependent on coal for an indigenous energy source. Both North and South Korea have relied on oil imports to date and are counting on nuclear power in the future. But whether separate or united, their energy needs are certain to grow and cannot be met locally. Moreover, the concentration of usage in the two main capitals makes pollution an increasing hazard to health as well as an unwelcome contribution to the atmosphere in Japan. This addresses the larger question of the growing buildup of CO_2 over the entire region. Access to natural gas by pipeline through the peninsula is the most efficient expedient.

Problems and Prospects

So far I have examined the political, economic, and environmental factors that favor the exploitation of Yakutiya gas to serve Northeast Asia. But this survey is incomplete on two counts. First, it needs to be weighed against the negative factors in all three categories. Second, it assumes rational and farsighted decision making among governmental and private interests. Such behavior cannot be confidently anticipated at this stage, given the problematic politics of virtually all five countries over the next decade. However, the more objectively determinable negative factors can be given careful consideration in a systematic feasibility study, an introduction to which is offered here.

Tokyo Gas estimates a necessary interval of ten years between inauguration of a feasibility study and the actual delivery of Yakutiya natural gas to Japan.[19] In part this is because of the formidable engineering obstacles to developing the necessary infrastructure in a region plagued with

daunting climatic and physical conditions that have frustrated exploitation of its abundant resources. Average January temperatures in Yakutsk,
the republic capital, at 62 degrees north latitude are –35°C to –40°C, with
the sun above the horizon less than six hours a day (Pryde and Mote
1990:38–39). The record minimum is –64°C. In addition to the problems of
human discomfort, transportation equipment must be warmed or kept
running, tires must be specially produced or they crack, and other measures are necessary to assure continuous performance. Ice fog builds up
from human breath and mechanical exhaust fumes, hampering transportation, especially at airfields. Winter temperature inversion exacerbates
the problem.

Permafrost covers most of Yakutiya at depths from 60 to 250 m, the latter dominating the large natural gas basin (Pryde and Mote 1990:41). Any
surface heat can cause shallow melting with upheaval of the ground; sum-
mer quagmires result from the inability of melted snow to be absorbed.
Roads must be elevated on protective berms or they break up and collapse. Buildings are elevated on pilings high above the ground to prevent
foundations from sinking. As a result, costs rise and construction sched-
ules are prolonged. To complicate planning further, the area across which
a Yakutiya gas pipeline must pass is among the more seismically active
zones in Russia. Although the gas field itself averages an intensity of under 5 on the Richter scale, this level rapidly increases southward to intensity ranges of 7 to 8 (Pryde and Mote 1990:44). Moreover, permafrost
worsens seismic disruption, threatening bridge supports and pilings.

Because of these conditions, the region lacks much of the necessary infrastructure for exploitation of its resources except in the southernmost
area. As a result Yakutiya is thinly inhabited. In 1989 the then Yakut ASSR
population totaled slightly over one million (Helgeson 1990:60–61). Declining productivity caused a net outflow in 1991–92 (see Chapters 3 and
4). Outside labor must be attracted by high wages and provided with
costly services if it is to remain. Virtually all supplies must be transported
from great distance. Eastern Siberian agriculture can supply one-third of
consumption needs; the rest must come from China, Vietnam, or remote
Russian and CIS sources. Only timber is readily available.

Formidable as these problems are, they are not unique. American and
Canadian pipeline construction encountered many of them to one extent
or another. Lessons learned there can benefit Yakutiyan engineering
through joint studies.[20] Nevertheless, the physical and technical problems
should not be underestimated.

Political problems will also require time for resolution. On 27 September 1990, the then titled Yakut-Sakha Soviet Socialist Republic declared its
sovereignty "as a member of the Russian Federation." Among its initial
assertions was ownership and control over the foreign trade of diamonds

on its territory (Mitchneck 1991:218–24). In January 1992 the republic changed its name to the Republic of Sakha to emphasize the local language terminology over that attributed to it by Moscow. The indigenous Yakuts, as they have been known in Western studies, suffered from Russian colonization mainly through decimation by diseases brought by the outsiders. The absence of brutal suppression and subsequent collectivization that left bitter legacies elsewhere in the Soviet Union facilitated cooperation between Yakuts and Russians. However, *glasnost'* released native feelings of resentment against Moscow's heavy-handed bureaucratic administration and local subordination to Russians. Thus the demand for self-determination and identity exists here as elsewhere in the former USSR, although to a less volatile degree.

The relationship between Moscow and Yakutsk remains to be determined. The republic can exercise control over its own resources, as shown by its closure of one of the four production works of the Yakut Diamond Association because of water pollution.[21] But it cannot conclude agreements for an international gas pipeline on its own. Both the Law of Underground Resources and the licensing regulations adopted in mid-June 1992 specify joint jurisdictions over resources by the federal and regional governments.[22] Draft versions of the pending Petroleum Law specify joint ownership and control over oil and gas reserves by the various levels of government. Not only will the route beyond Sakha need to be approved by some outside authority, but presumably the charges for its passage and perhaps a surcharge on the transported gas will have to be negotiated. As a final complication, the Khabarovsk and Maritime krais, sorely pressed for energy, are likely to demand a major share of Yakutiya gas and have the legal power to challenge Moscow as well as Yakutsk. It is impossible to know how much will be left for foreign consumption until domestic priorities have been established.

In addition to these problems of domestic politics, the aforementioned international political relationships have yet to become fully settled. The decades-old Kurile Islands dispute is relieved of Cold War political-military burdens that precluded a Soviet-Japanese peace treaty and inhibited Japanese investment in Siberia. But the newly established democracy in Russia requires two-thirds legislative approval of any territorial changes. This presents a double obstacle, first from the vocal lobby of Russian settlers on the southern Kurile Islands, small in number but large in television coverage. The second challenge comes from anti-Yeltsin politicians and Russian nationalists in Moscow. Basically the Russian Federation still lacks a viable and durable political system that can accommodate compromise, much less concession of the islands. Meanwhile Japanese politics, already hung up on the islands issue, became even more complicated with the defeat of the ruling LDP—so far as compromise is concerned. Although it is possible to envision eventual major Japanese investment in Yakutiya gas without resolution of the Kuriles dispute, this seems unlikely in the immediate future.

Passage of the pipeline through North and South Korea requires much more detente between the two governments than has occurred to date. They have not even been able to revive the former transpeninsular railroad to serve minimal economic exchange. There is no free movement of people or goods between the two Koreas. North Korean intransigence on inspection of its nuclear facilities has set back relations, albeit not to the pre-1989 depths. The succession beyond Kim Il Sung remains uncertain in stability, and the duration of communist rule is problematic. Pyongyang has yet to win diplomatic recognition from Tokyo, much less free itself from Washington's economic restrictions. Pyongyang and Seoul lack the mutual trust and confidence necessary to accept interdependence on energy supplied through a transpeninsular pipeline.

Equally daunting are the economic questions that remain unanswered as Russia and China attempt the transition from centralized socialist economies to privatized market economies. A complex of financial and monetary reforms is necessary to establish a reliable and predictable economic environment within which to invest so large a sum of capital for so critical a product with uncertain profit in the next century. With the major gas production and pipeline costs in Russia, Moscow's management of this economic transition is central to the project's viability. It is still too soon to forecast the outcome confidently, as evidenced by repeated delays in IMF funding and reservations among the Group of Seven on the magnitude of support to render Yeltsin's reform efforts.

Even the rough estimate of $15 billion for production and pipeline is dependent to some extent on how the Russian economy evolves. This estimate requires more careful and comprehensive calculation with possible ranges of variation dependent on intervening factors, some of which will be the availability, quality, and cost of materials in Russia.

Last but not least challenging is the assessment of alternate sources of energy for Northeast Asia, including natural gas, compared with the costs and risks of Yakutiya natural gas. Past projections of energy futures on both availability and price have been uncertain efforts at best, exemplified by the wide differences between anticipation and experience with oil. The definition of reserves is conservatively predicted on that which is known to be exploitable with available technology and prevailing cost-profit calculations. But critical components of this definition are subject to change over time, hence the difficulty of making confident projections over long futures. Yet this effort must be made to assess economic aspects of the Yakutiya venture.

In this regard, examination of the Sakhalin offshore gas project must assess its final promise either as a substitute or a supplement for Yakutiya. Years in negotiation, Sakhalin gas exploitation has yet to be wholly agreed upon by the relevant authorities in Russia and foreign firms. Technical obstacles to its success remain, notably the 1,800–2,800-m depth of reserves below the sea floor and the three-month limit to the drilling season. Platforms alone are estimated to cost $6 billion, with an anticipated delivery of only 4 million tons yearly.

Beyond these wider questions, more detailed matters remain to be addressed, such as the proportion of each national contribution to the consortium's financing of the Yakutiya project. At present, capital shortages plague the financing of energy development projects regionally as well as globally. The pricing of the final product must also be negotiated multilaterally. Outside agency financial support, necessary in any event, will be forthcoming only when the five countries have shown genuine interest and willingness to cooperate economically as well as politically.[23] Moreover, further geological surveys and well tests are required to determine the full amount of gas available and the costs of field development before private funding is likely on the necessary scale for this megaproject.[24] Environmental questions pose a third category of concern. At present Yakutiya is largely a virginal paradise of mountains, forests, and wildlife. The environmental movement is growing there as elsewhere, illustrated by the cutback in diamond production. Worst-case fears are likely to provoke protests against the pipeline. To some extent they can be answered by drawing on comparable American and Canadian experiences. Failures as well as successes can instruct the Yakutiya project, but an environmental impact study will be needed nonetheless.

Pre-Feasibility Study Steps

Conservative conventional wisdom argues for awaiting resolution of domestic and international political problems before attempting to answer the economic and technical ones. Against this approach stands the calculation of a necessary decade of delay between the start of a feasibility study and actual delivery of natural gas. This interval of time is a mixed blessing. On the negative side, it calls for uncertain risk taking without practical benefit over at least ten years. On the positive side, it permits a dual simultaneous approach rather than a singular sequential one. In the early period a feasibility study can be undertaken while the resolution of political problems proceeds apace, and economic calculations can gain greater confidence with accumulated data. The study need not start wholly anew because much of the 1970s work should be available from Japanese and Russian sources. The potential risk is loss of the feasibility study cost if the present favorable political trends are reversed or the problems remain unsolvable. The potential gain is acceleration of the process so as to bring the gas onstream to meet demand at an optimum future time, other obstacles having been overcome during the intervening period.

As a promising precedent, the Tumen River Basin Development Project presents most of the aforementioned political problems. Nevertheless, it has brought the participating players close enough to win $3 million UNDP funding for a feasibility study.[25] Estimates of the total cost range as high as $20 billion, with completion times of at least a decade or more. The specific challenges, while different from those of Yakutiya, are equally formidable. The necessary infrastructure must be developed to support a multipurpose coastal special economic zone in what is presently marshlands bordering three countries, two of which are virtually bankrupt. Though the climatic obstacles are absent, the political and economic problems rival those of a Yakutiya gas pipeline. Moreover, the practical benefits are predicated on the as yet undeveloped economic potential of linking western Japan with the opposite coast and beyond as a regional entity. These problems notwithstanding, UNDP sponsorship has carried the project through a succession of meetings and investigations.

So far there is no wholly accepted plan for the project or commitment of contribution by the participating countries, least of all from Japan as the key economic player. But two important accomplishments testify to the validity of moving ahead without waiting for the resolution of political and economic differences. First, the simple experience of multilateral dialogue has begun an unprecedented process of regional interaction. With UNDP sponsorship, national prejudices and suspicions have been somewhat allayed. Communication has progressed on an issue of potential mutual gain rather than on matters of zero-sum outcome. Second, professional expertise, sometimes recruited from outside the participating countries, has produced a growing body of knowledge that informs potential sources of funding on what can be expected as the project progresses, should in fact it continue to full realization.

Two factors argue for World Bank action as a catalyst to spark knowledge and interest in the Yakutiya pipeline. The contribution of natural gas to the global environment is undisputed. Pollution is a salient problem in Northeast Asia. The World Bank interest in development and energy is also served by this project. In addition, a World Bank aegis would desensitize the political relationships of the members of a Northeast Asia Energy Consortium while providing prima facie evidence of fiscal feasibility for other outside funding. Of course, the Bank's role would be limited by the fact that the Energy Consortium members would include only two bona fide recipients of Bank loans, Russia and China—North Korea not being in the Bank, South Korea approaching nonrecipient status, and Japan already being there. Nevertheless, the role of catalyst can be critical.

The East-West Center of Hawaii and the Asia-Pacific Research Institute of the Jilin Province of China started the Tumen project with a 1990 conference that eventually resulted in the Northeast Asia Economic Forum. The Forum's purpose is to encourage research on regional issues and facilitate continued consultation and discussions. This is the logical venue for exchanging views toward a feasibility study. Some of the individual participants might be drawn from the Tumen meetings on the basis of their personal experience in this type of multilateral dialogue. A wholly disinterested convener such as the East-West Center serves to provide an objective point of reference to assure that no special interest, national or commercial, is being served by the project. Other interested players, such as Tokyo Gas and Daewoo, might make practical contributions on the basis of prior study. Before convening such a conference, key interests, both favorable and opposed, should be interviewed in relevant governmental and private circles throughout the five prospective Energy Consortium members, with special attention to the Sakha Republic.

Conclusion

Multilateral economic gains cannot eliminate conflicting national interests. Northeast Asia's historical heritage is replete with war and political-military confrontation. Each country has experienced military conflict with or political oppression from each of the other countries. This heritage is not easily overcome. But multinational economic efforts can facilitate communication and compromise where national interests are not vital or mutually exclusive. Energy interdependence in the region can serve Russian, Chinese, Korean, and Japanese interests without threatening the political independence or economic development of any participant. A Northeast Asian Energy Consortium would appear to be a feasible vehicle for approaching the larger political objective of reducing tension and misperception in one of the more volatile regions of international relations.

Beyond regional security, environmental considerations are inextricably linked with energy consumption. The practical alternatives of coal, oil, and natural gas as sources of energy weigh overwhelmingly in favor of gas as the lowest producer of CO_2. Nuclear power is a better choice in this regard but poses other problems—political, technical, and environmental. Atmospheric degradation and the greenhouse effect remain the subjects of heated controversy, with doomsday projections being seriously disputed. On balance, however, the evidence to date argues in favor of reducing CO_2 emissions to the maximum extent possible.

The environmental impact factor gains added weight from the prospective economic development of Northeast Asia. Energy consumption in the region is certain to increase. In Japan rising standards of living are forecast with a greater use of electrical and electronic products. This will offset declining rates of energy consumption per unit of industrial output. Korean and Chinese industrial growth will compound an already existing energy problem. The consequent impact on the environment, global as well as regional, adds an admittedly intangible speculative factor to more immediately measurable economic considerations of cost calculation in a Yakutiya natural gas pipeline. But seen in this perspective, the whole is greater than the sum of its parts. As such the project deserves careful study and support by the prospective participants in a Northeast Asian Energy Consortium and the World Bank at the earliest opportunity.

Notes

1. Interview, Geological Institute, Academy of Science, USSR, Yakutsk, 3 October 1978.

2. "Interview with Hiroshi Anzai," *Business Japan*, February 1979, pp. 22–24.

3. The announcement was made by then deputy foreign minister Igor Rogachev, now ambassador in Beijing. Rogachev served as interpreter for the first Sino-Soviet Amur Basin survey in 1955–57. The author was privately informed by a Russian official that agreement on the channel had been reached by mid-1993.

4. *Izvestia*, 18 September 1992, in *The Current Digest of the Soviet Press* 44, no. 38 (1992):21.

5. *Far Eastern Economic Review*, 20 May 1993, p. 56. The reported cost of the pipeline is $1.2 billion. This is, however, very low, considering the much higher estimate of $10 billion for a shorter pipeline in 1979. Additional partners mentioned are Lucky-Goldstar Intl., Korean Petroleum Development Company, Korea Gas Co., Samsung, and Yukong; see Chapter 5 of this volume.

6. Interview with Tokyo Gas official, 17 January 1991.

7. Ibid. However, Mikio Nose, head of the Gas Resources Department at Tokyo Gas, said that if in addition Alaska (North Slope) and Oman start producing, there would be an oversupply; *Offshore/Oilman*, July 1992, p. 25.

8. *Offshore/Oilman*, July 1992, p. 25.

9. The Economic and Social Commission for Asia and the Pacific estimate, gratefully supplied by Professor Leslie Dienes in written comment to the author.

10. *Japan's Energy Position* (Tokyo: Foreign Press Center, 1992), pp. 53–54. Data from MITI, "Long-term Energy Demand and Supply Outlook," October 1990, and "Oil-Alternative Energy Supply Outlook," October 1990.

11. "Action Program to Arrest Global Warning," issued by the Council of Ministers in *Japan's Energy Position*, pp. 13, 39.

12. *China Talk*, July 1992, p. 6.

13. Ibid. The data do not discriminate between cancer possibly induced by cigarettes and by pollution.

14. The oil pipeline from Daqing requires gas heaters at regular intervals to keep the oil fluid at extremely cold winter temperatures. Railroad tank cars are double-walled so that high pressure steam can be applied in the terminal to restore fluidity. Interviews in Daqing, October 1975.

15. Leslie Dienes, personal communication.

16. Interview with A. G. Aganbegyan, 26 September 1979; also, interviews at the Siberian Energy Institute, Irkutsk, 29 September 1979.

17. Mote (1990:171). Mote cites British geographer Tony French as saying that once the earth's fossil fuels are used up, the last to go will be Yakutia coal.

18. "News Notes," *Soviet Geography,* November 1991.

19. Interview with Tokyo Gas official, 17 January 1991.

20. Interviews in Yakutsk, October 1978.

21. "New Notes," *Soviet Geography,* November 1991.

22. I am indebted to Leslie Dienes for calling this to my attention together with his critique of my paper.

23. See Appendix 1 for a World Bank perspective on this issue and for a review of Russian Federation joint petroleum ventures.

24. According to Leslie Dienes, the reserves are in two widely separated locations and 2,400–3,600 m deep, with well yields only 20–30 percent of those at Urengoy and Yamburg; personal communication. Intera Information Technologies has joined with the Ministry of Fuel and Energy for the Sakha Republic and Yakutgeophysika to prepare a regional data package by mid-1993.

25. Although somewhat out of date, the most convenient summary of the Tumen developments is Kim (1992). See also Chapter 5.

References

Conolly, Violet. 1976. *Siberia Today and Tomorrow.* New York: Taplinger.

Helgeson, Ann C. 1990. "Population and Labour Force." In Allen Rodgers (ed.), *The Soviet Far East: Geographical Perspectives on Development.* New York: Routledge.

Kim, Euikon. 1992. "Political Economy of the Tumen River Basin Development: Problems and Prospects." *Journal of Northeast Asian Studies* 11(2):35–48.

Mitchneck, Beth A. 1991. "Territoriality and Regional Economic Autonomy in the USSR." *Studies in Comparative Communism* 24(2):218–24.

Pryde, Philip R., and Victor L. Mote. 1990. "Environmental Constraints and Biosphere Protection." In Allan Rodgers (ed.), *The Soviet Far East: Geographical Perspectives on Development.* New York: Routledge.

Shabad, Theodore. 1969. *Basic Industrial Resources of the U.S.S.R.* New York: Columbia University Press.

Shabad, Theodore, and Victor L. Mote. 1977. *Gateway to Siberian Resources: The BAM.* Washington, D.C.: Scripta.

Williams, Robert H. 1991. "The Potential For Reducing CO_2 Emissions With Modern Energy Technology: An Illustrative Scenario for the Power Sector In China." Unpublished manuscript in author's possession.

ZumBrunnen, Craig. 1990. "Resources." In Allan Rodgers (ed.), *The Soviet Far East: Geographical Perspectives on Development*. New York: Routledge.

7

Transportation

Pamy J.S. Arora

In recent years, I have assisted governments in Latin America, Eastern Europe, and the former Soviet Union (FSU) to restructure and privatize their transportation infrastructure and institutions. In 1992, Booz Allen and other consultants helped the European Bank for Reconstruction and Development (EBRD) conduct an intensive sector-wide in-country survey of the transportation infrastructure of the FSU, to identify opportunities for investments that would support the government's efforts to transition to a market-driven economy. We developed restructuring and investment strategies for rail, water, air, and road transportation for Russia (including the Far East), Ukraine, Belarus, and Kazakhstan, and these are currently being selectively implemented. This chapter draws on these studies conducted for the EBRD and from my recent experience in Russia and the RFE, but also on work I have done in transportation privatization in other countries.

In identifying how the land, sea, and air infrastructure in Russia can be strengthened to support increased economic activity and human interaction between the RFE and its Pacific Rim neighbors, I attempt to answer three key questions: First, is the outlook for international trade and economic cooperation between the RFE and its Pacific neighbors favorable? Next, to what extent are the existing transportation infrastructures and institutions adequate and prepared to support the projected growth of trade and traffic in the RFE, and what infrastructural improvements are required? Finally, what will the necessary improvements cost, and how might they be financed? I address each of these issues in the following sections.

Outlook for Trade and Economic Cooperation

To investigate whether the outlook for trade and economic cooperation between the RFE and its Pacific neighbors is favorable, and if so, to determine the growth potential, I review three indicators: the historical trends

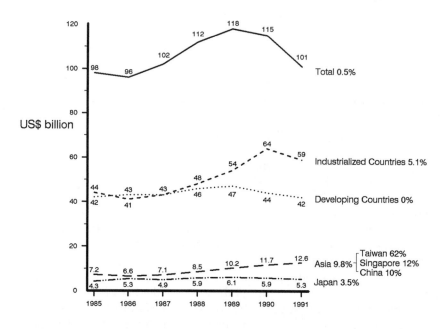

FIGURE 7.1 Soviet Union world trade (IMF, *World Trade Statistics*, various years).

in trade between Russia and the North Pacific; the potential for the growth of this trade; and any other synergies between the two regions that may promote trade.

Figure 7.1 depicts the level and direction of international trade of the FSU for the period 1985–91 and indicates that overall trade activity has been stagnant. But the FSU's trade activity with its Pacific neighbors, the majority of which occurs through the Russian Far East, presents a different picture. Trade with Asia, which is dominated primarily by China and India, almost doubled in this period, growing at an annual rate of 9.8 percent. Within Asia, other areas with smaller volumes of trade but with significant annual growth have been Singapore at 11.5 percent per year, Korea at 30 percent per year, and Taiwan, whose Russian trade grew by almost 62 percent per year in 1988–91. Trade with Japan (one of the "industrialized" countries) shows mixed results. Although there has been average growth in trade of 3.5 percent per year, it has been inconsistent, suggesting that all is not well, and future growth may be moderate.

A snapshot of the traffic patterns over the Trans-Siberian Railway (TSR) illustrates the dilemma facing Russia today. SeaLand Services, one of the world's largest ocean carriers, is operating a dedicated container train ser-

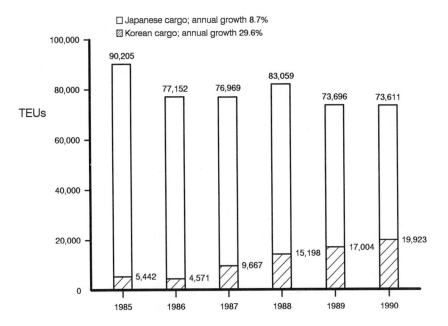

FIGURE 7.2 Container traffic on the Trans-Siberian Railway (data from Korean Motor Parts Association and Japan Automobile Manufacturing Research Institute files).

vice over the TSR for Europe-bound cargo between the RFE ports of Vostochniy/Nakhodka and Brest (Belarus), Chop (Ukraine), and Luzhaika (Finland). Set up as a joint venture between SeaLand and the Ministry of Railways (MPS) to provide an alternative to all-water service from the Pacific to Europe, the Trans-Siberian Express Service (TSES) has had mixed results, as shown in Figure 7.2. Whereas movement of containers from Korea to Europe across the TSES has gained strong momentum and increased fourfold since 1985, the traffic from Japan has actually declined by about 20 percent over the same period. This seems to be primarily because of the current unreliability of the TSES, possibly exacerbated by the logistical disruptions created by the breakup of the FSU. It is my opinion that, unless TSES addresses this problem, a lack of confidence in this service will limit the growth of trade at least from Japan through the RFE ports to Europe.

Let us now review the potential for growth of the RFE. The RFE is strategically located at the very center of economic activity in the Pacific. Over the past twenty years, while the world maritime trade for dry cargo grew by 3.7 percent per year, growth in East Asia was twice as high at 7.6 per-

TABLE 7.1 World Container Traffic: Top Ten Ports

| | 1988 | | 1991 | | |
Port	Rank	Million TEU	Rank	Million TEU	Average Annual Growth (%)
Far East/Asia					
Singapore	2	3.38	1	5.22	15.6
Hong Kong	1	4.03	2	5.10	8.2
Kaohsiung (T)	4	3.08	4	3.49	4.3
Kobe (J)	5	2.26	5	2.60	4.8
Busan (K)	7	2.07	6	2.35	4.3
Keelung (T)	8	1.71	10	1.81	1.9
Regional avg.					7.6
USA/Europe					
Rotterdam	3	3.29	3	3.67	3.7
Los Angeles	9	1.65	7	2.12	8.7
Hamburg	10	1.65	8	1.97	6.7
New York/N.J.	6	2.10	9	1.90	-3.3
Regional avg.					3.7

Source: Data from *Containerization International*, various issues.

cent per year (Wada 1992). The growth in air passenger traffic has been even greater. As an example, the number of air passengers from Seoul to other capital cities of East Asian countries has more than doubled since 1980 (Choe 1992).

Table 7.1 illustrates the recent growth in maritime activity at the world's major ports. The volume and growth of maritime container traffic handled at the world's top ten ports between 1988 and 1991 might be summarized this way:

- Six of the world's ten largest and busiest ports for the handling of maritime container traffic have consistently been from the Asia-Pacific region, all close neighbors of the RFE.
- These six ports have sustained an overall annual growth rate of 7.6 percent, or more than twice that of the remaining four ports in the top ten list, all of which are from the United States and northern Europe.
- For two of the RFE's closest neighbors, Japan and Korea, the growth rate has been more conservative, averaging about 4.5 percent per year.

A recent projection of growth in the ocean containerized traffic supports these findings (Table 7.2). Between 1990 and 1995, while the worldwide growth in maritime containerized traffic will be between 3.6 and 6.4

TABLE 7.2 Container Throughput Projections

	1990		Projected Annual Growth Rate to 1995	
	Million TEU	% of Total	Low (%)	High (%)
North Europe	14.1	18	2.5	3.6
North America	16.8	22	2.9	5.0
Latin America	3.2	4	4.0	7.5
Southeast Asia	7.4	10	6.0	10.0
East Asia	18.6	25	4.1	8.0
Other	15.8	21	3.5	6.2
World	75.9	100	3.6	6.4

Source: Data supplied by Ocean Shipping Consultants, United Kingdom.

percent per year, the growth in the RFE's neighboring regions of Southeast Asia will be 6–10 percent and in East Asia 4–8 percent per year. During this same period, the growth for the industrialized nations in North America and Europe will be 2.5–5 percent.

Just as important as the mature and established trading patterns between industrialized and developing nations are the consequences of a new world trading order. Driven by geographic proximity, cultural similarity, and, most important, lower transportation and labor costs, countries are rediscovering mutual synergies and the potential for incremental economic growth and multinational cooperation in trading with their regional neighbors (Cho 1994). The growth of regional free trade blocks represented by NAFTA in North America, the Andean Pact and the Mercosur agreements in South America, the European Union, and ASEAN in Asia suggests that future economic development and growth will be strongest intraregionally, with trade and traffic flowing in a north–south direction while knowledge and technology are transferred east–west between regions or interregionally. This is already clearly indicated in the automobile manufacturing industry, where assembly and manufacturing operations, and thus transportation flows, are moving increasingly north–south, such as between Canada, the United States, and Mexico. This projected world of large regional economic and trading blocs will result in a substantial restructuring of technology and transportation. For the RFE, this vision simply suggests that opportunities for growth in trade, transportation, and human interaction will be greatest intraregionally, or with its North Pacific neighbors.

A summary prognosis for the growth in trade and multilateral cooperation between the Russian Far East and its North Pacific neighbors is that, over the near term, growth will be strongest with China, South Korea, and

TABLE 7.3 Modal Shares of Soviet International Trade Tonnage

Mode of Transport	Foreign Trade Volume (million tons)			Modal Share of Total (%)	% Total without Pipelines
	Import	Export	Total		
Railway	25.6	78.7	104.3	20.0	26.5
Maritime	82.5	193.7	276.2	52.9	70.2
River	1.6	9.9	11.5	2.2	2.9
Automotive	0.5	1.0	1.5	0.3	0.4
Pipeline	1.2	127.5	128.7	24.6	—
Total	111.4	410.8	522.2		

Source: Data from Kazanskii (1987).

Taiwan, as these developing countries attempt to expand their export markets aggressively and are less discriminatory than Japan about the substandard operating conditions in Russia. Hong Kong and Singapore may become players later on as well. Trade growth with Japan will be conservative, at least until the infrastructure and reliability of the transportation infrastructure is improved sufficiently to restore Japanese confidence in the system. Over the near term, unless significant changes occur in the operations structure and privatization is accelerated, the overall international trade and economic growth of the RFE will be moderate (see Valencia 1992).

Adequacy of Existing Infrastructures and Institutions

The focus of this discussion is on the Russian Far East, but the transportation infrastructure and linkages that support the RFE extend across all of Russia. Without the extensive network of transportation infrastructure and institutions that connect the RFE with the rest of Russia and the other FSU states, as well as with Europe, opportunities for growth and market extension would be very limited. One might well say that "when Russia sneezes, the Russian Far East will catch a cold"; simply put, anything that affects Russia will greatly influence economic development in the RFE. Thus, although I pay specific attention to evaluating the ports and railroad systems of the RFE, this is done in the broader context of evaluating the entire FSU transportation infrastructure and institutions.

Present Capacity

The international trade of the Soviet Union was heavily dependent on the rail and maritime infrastructures. Table 7.3 shows its modal shares of international trade tonnage as of 1986. If pipeline commerce is excluded, 97

TABLE 7.4 Russia's Foreign Cargo Traffic, 1990

Major ports	Foreign cargo (million tons)	Containerized (million tons)	No. of vessel calls[a]
North			
St. Petersburg	10.6	1.2	1,776
Murmansk	5.2		578
Far East			
Vanino	2.0		na
Vostochniy	10.3	1.9	1,218
Nakhodka	6.3		1,901
Vladivostok	2.7		
Black Sea			
Novorossiysk	8.5	0.2	1,176
Total	45.6	3.5	

[a]Includes cabotage.
Source: Data from Maritime Transport Research Institute.

percent of all international trade for the FSU moved over maritime and rail systems, and of this 70 percent was maritime. The Russian Far East plays an important and key role in the international maritime trade of the FSU, as shown in Table 7.4. Of the seven major ports in Russia, the RFE ports handled 46 percent of all foreign cargo in 1990 and 54 percent of the high-value containerized cargo. Combined, the RFE ports of Vostochniy-Nakhodka are the single largest port system in Russia, and the largest for container cargo. Thus, the maritime ports of the Far East are a critically important gateway for international traffic to and from Russia. However, the key word is "gateway." Although international traffic will intensify at the RFE ports, the bulk of the cargo neither is destined for nor originates in the RFE. A relatively sparsely populated region with a scarcity of agricultural resources and a shortage of labor, the RFE is not a consumer of significant volumes of manufactured goods and consumer products. Thus, most international traffic moves through the RFE ports to and from either the densely populated western parts of Russia, Ukraine, and the Baltic states or the rest of Europe. And that is where railways become critical. The Russian railroad system is the only effective means of moving large volumes of goods through the RFE ports, both for distribution to domestic markets and across the Trans-Siberian Railway to Europe.

The importance of the Trans-Siberian Railway to the economic growth and well-being of the Russian Far East cannot be overemphasized: the TSR is the principal and very critical artery that links the RFE to the major markets in the West. The only limitation is the capacity of the rail lines that connect the RFE ports of Vostochniy-Nakhodka to the mainline TSR; this is no more than 30 million tons annually. However, the RFE ports combined currently handle less than 20 million tons per year, so the limitations of the rail connections are not likely to restrict the growth of these ports over the near term.

The road systems are less important in the macroeconomic sense that they are used mostly to feed and support the rail system. The air transportation systems, the other mode providing a link to the Pacific, are unimportant for freight traffic, somewhat important for international passenger traffic, and very important for domestic passenger traffic.

Ports and railway systems are, then, the most critical in determining the RFE's potential for greater interaction with its Pacific neighbors and indeed with the rest of the industrialized world. But do these systems have adequate capacity to handle growth in the future? Figure 7.3 shows the historical movement of general-purpose cargo over the period 1987–92, and Figure 7.4 presents the demand projections to 1995.

Even at the 1988 peak of 26 billion tons and 5 trillion ton-kilometers, the Russian transportation infrastructure was not fully utilized, except perhaps for the airline sector. Figure 7.3 shows that, since that time, traffic in all modes has declined at an overall annual rate of 3.6 percent per year. Based on Booz Allen's recent evaluation of economic conditions in the country, it is expected that this decline will continue at least until 1995, at an increased rate of around 5.6 percent per year. Thus, depending on the particular transportation sector, it is unlikely that demand for transportation services will approach the 1988 levels much earlier than ten years from now, suggesting that the transportation system in Russia has at least enough "raw" capacity for the next decade. This is particularly important for the railway sector, which was responsible for 54 percent of all transportation in Russia, and this will also decline at the rate of 4.1 percent per year until 1995. Table 7.5, another projection of rail traffic for Russia by regional railway area, indicates that through the year 2015 traffic on the system will decline across the country, and particularly in the RFE by about 35 percent. This suggests that new railroad capacity may not be required for at least twenty years.

The situation with the ports is similar. Table 7.6 analyzes the capacity of the three largest ports in Russia and shows that currently the ports are significantly underutilized. Each of the three ports has a potential throughput capacity of over 30 million tons per annum, but these are being utilized less than 50 percent. Again, the ports have enough "raw" capacity and are unlikely to require any significant addition of new capacity for the next five or ten years.

The air transportation system is another matter. The FSU's passenger airline system was the largest in the world, but with an overwhelming domestic focus (Figure 7.5). With highly subsidized fuel prices, Russian airlines have been able to offer airfares to passengers at as little as one-sev-

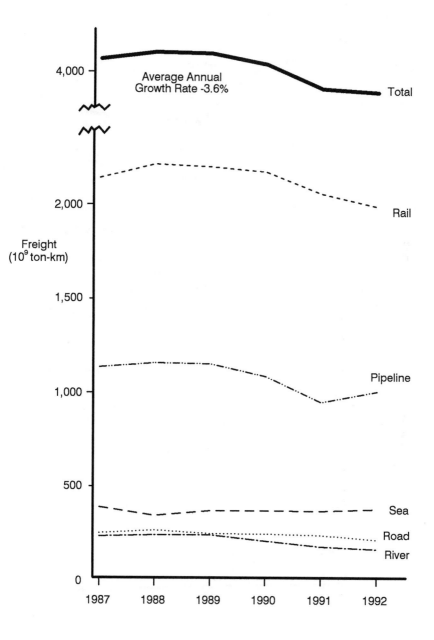

FIGURE 7.3 Russian freight transport, general-purpose cargo (data from Russian Ministry of Transport).

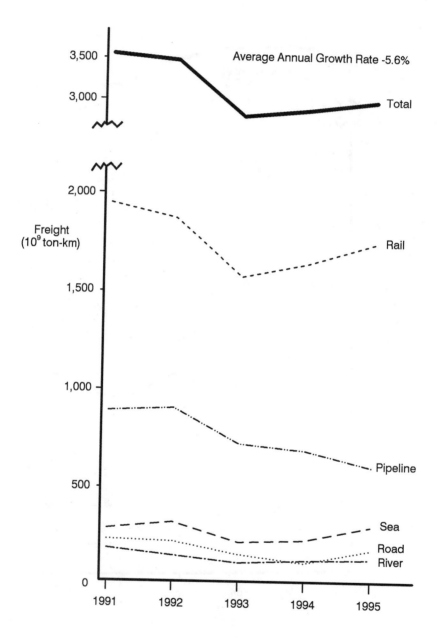

FIGURE 7.4 Russian freight transport, general-purpose cargo (data from Russian Ministry of Transport).

TABLE 7.5 Russian Freight Traffic, 1990 and 2015 Forecast (million tons)

Railway	1990 Actual	2015 Median	Railway	1990 Actual	2015 Median
Far East	109	72	N. Caucusus	162	90
Baikal-Amur	12	8	Kuibyshev	113	78
Transbaikal	47	27	Volgas	66	45
E. Siberia	84	55	Gorky	131	92
Krasnoyarsk	70	43	Northern	134	86
Kemerova	137	84	October	176	106
W. Siberia	116	75	Moscow	233	150
Tselinnaya	140	83	South East	103	72
Alma Ata	93	66	Southern	100	64
Sverdlovsk	214	118	Donetsk	292	124
Southern Urals	179	120	Dnepr	209	119
W. Kazakhstan	36	23	Odessa	110	84
Central Asia	160	102	South West	98	64
Azerbaijan	36	25	Belarus	125	71
Transcaucucus	66	47	Lvov	143	97

Source: Booz Allen analysis.

TABLE 7.6 Capacity of Russia's Ports

Port	Total Current Traffic (million tons)	Estimated Total Capacity (million tons)	Current Utilization (%) Berths	Current Utilization (%) Equipment
Vostochniy	11.4	>30.0	<50	<50
Novorossiysk	9.0	>30.0	<30	<50
St. Petersburg	10.8	>30.0	<40	<50

Source: EBRD surveys.

enth the cost of operating the services. With such cheap fares, and the great distances required for travel in Russia, air has become the favored mode of travel, and the airlines are heavily utilized. However, as the current reforms get under way and fuel prices are brought in line with market prices, passenger air travel will drop off significantly, freeing up capacity. Some prices have already been raised, and despite several flight cancellations airline load factors have dropped to around 80 percent in 1992 from 90 percent in previous years. With the continued tightening of the economy, it is not expected that this situation will improve for some years, suggesting that the air transport sector also has adequate "raw" capacity for the near future.

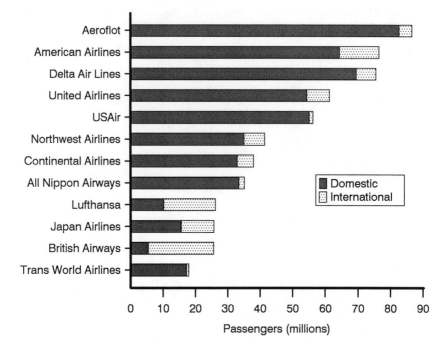

FIGURE 7.5 Air transport, scheduled passengers, 1991 (data supplied by the International Association of Travel Agents).

Thus, we can conclude that all modes of transportation have enough "raw" capacity and will likely not require additional capacity for five or ten years, and with proper operational improvements even for the next twenty years.

But, raw capacity notwithstanding, anyone who has visited ports in Russia or traveled there by rail, or has shipped cargo by rail, can narrate the horror stories of ships waiting for days at anchorage for a berth at a port, of excruciatingly slow loading and discharging rates, of containers getting lost or delayed for weeks in the maw of the Russian transportation system. So, if there is enough capacity, why is the Russian transportation infrastructure in such a state of chaos that the EBRD and other multilateral institutions have made its rehabilitation and improvement a primary investment priority?

The Russian transportation system is a series of subsystems, each dependent on another, linked across the country. Thus, as I attempt to identify the problems and deficiencies separately in the ports, rail, and air transportation systems, it should be noted that the problems are so interlinked that a defect in one system has a domino effect on the other systems, until the entire chain is affected.

Ports

While in the FSU in 1992, I was fortunate enough to visit several ports in Russia and the Ukraine, including most of the major sea ports discussed earlier in this chapter. These observations are based on those visits and on extensive analyses conducted on the productivity, operations, and institutional requirements of the ports. My conclusions are generalized for all ports in Russia, but with particular reference to the RFE ports as appropriate.

Although there is adequate raw capacity at the ports, these capacities are constrained by low productivity and operating problems. Berths are underutilized because aging, obsolete equipment sits idle awaiting spares and maintenance. Container cranes are broken down and awaiting spares—which may be a while in arriving since they have to be purchased with scarce foreign exchange. Cranes that work are more often than not continuing to cannibalize parts from those that are inoperable, further exacerbating the problems. Similarly, grain unloading equipment is aged and obsolete, has low productivity, and in many cases has to be supplemented by floating pneumatic unloaders.

Port capacity and productivity are also limited by landside bottlenecks—the railway and access roads. For one thing, the typical practice of direct unloading from the vessel to the rail wagon is the least productive manner in which to handle cargo. It not only slows down the handling of cargo but also ties up valuable dock space and terminal storage area, thus affecting cargo operations at adjacent terminals. Operations are also delayed during the harvest season, when transportation of agricultural goods throughout the country creates a shortage of rail cars and thus slows down vessel discharging activity at the port. Lack of appropriate gantry cranes to handle 40-foot containers at the rail yard requires the cargo to be restuffed into smaller 20-foot containers, further delaying vessel unloading. In addition, access roads to the ports are often the same as those serving the adjacent city—undersized, congested, and in poor physical condition.

Overall, poor planning has resulted in a counterproductive mix and layout of noncompatible cargo operations. Though the ports were designed to handle non-unitized breakbulk cargo and bulk cargo, they have not been flexible or quick enough to adjust their layout or operating practices to the changing nature of the cargo. Thus, coal or grain may be handled at terminals adjacent to container terminals, each with different cargo handling and transportation needs, resulting in operating ineffi-

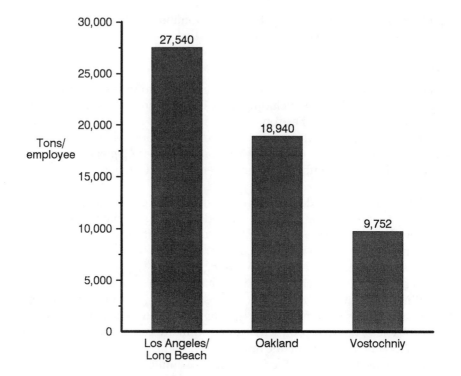

FIGURE 7.6 Port labor productivity (Booz Allen & Hamilton).

ciencies for all cargoes. Lack of on-terminal storage space has compounded this problem.

These operating problems have affected the productivity and hence the effective capacity at the ports. Figures 7.6 and 7.7 illustrate the deterioration in port productivity. Figure 7.6 compares the port labor productivity of the RFE port of Vostochniy with that of two major port systems in the United States: Vostochniy is only 35–50 percent as productive as its U.S. counterparts. Figure 7.7 shows that productivity at the RFE port of Nakhodka declined by about 25 percent from 1988 to 1990.

Railroads

Problems with the railway are related to deteriorating track quality, a lack of communication and management systems, and the inability to coordinate the conflicting parochial interests of the nineteen railroads of Russia. The difficulties experienced by the Trans-Siberian Express Service (TSES),

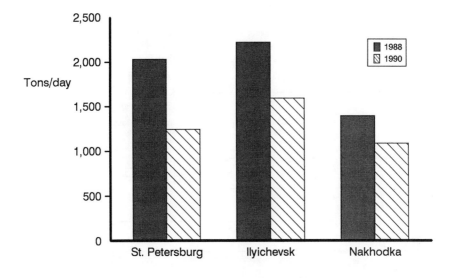

FIGURE 7.7 Cargo handling at three major CIS ports (data from various issues of *Seatrade*).

the fully containerized landbridge service between Vostochniy and Europe, highlight the problem of the Russian rail system.

The principal problem is that the TSES is unable to offer a competitive or reliable alternative to competing all-water services. Figure 7.8 compares the schedule of the landbridge with that of all-water services, and Figure 7.9 shows the cost of shipping cargo by the landbridge. As Figure 7.8 indicates, there is no significant difference in the transit time of a container of cargo via the landbridge compared to an all-water service, even when the service maintains its planned schedule and operates flawlessly. In addition, a delay at the RFE ports or overland on the Trans-Siberian Railway, not uncommon occurrences, can increase the landbridge transit time by five to seven days, making the service unacceptable and uncompetitive. Moreover, the landbridge service is an expensive alternative to all-water services, which are up to 30 percent less expensive.

A variety of factors make the Trans-Siberian landbridge uncompetitive. Containers arriving at the RFE ports are frequently held up for three to seven days while the unit train waits for enough cargo to make up a complete trainload for the trip to the West. Furthermore, lack of effective telecommunication and track management systems prevents the railway from accurately tracking and controlling the movement of the containers. Once cargo is in the system, the TSES usually cannot keep the customers accurately informed about its location. Finally, parochialism at each of the

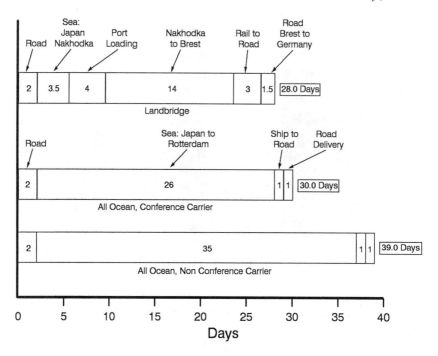

FIGURE 7.8 Landbridge and all-water transit times (Booz Allen & Hamilton).

different railroads the TSES passes through and a lack of incentive or interests results in containerized cargo being coupled with other, less time-sensitive and frequently incompatible cargoes, resulting in further delays to the containerized cargo. The end result is that the landbridge container service may not compete with the all-water services in either transit time, price, or service. Unless addressed, this situation will seriously inhibit the growth of the TSES.

In addition to these organizational problems, track quality is deteriorating and requires rehabilitation. One indication of this is the steady increase over the past several years of speed-restricted track, reviewed in Figure 7.10.

Air Traffic

Because the air transportation system is focused more on domestic transport and less on international transport, deficiencies in this system have less impact on the international trade and human interaction of the RFE with its Pacific neighbors. The condition of the airports and traffic systems

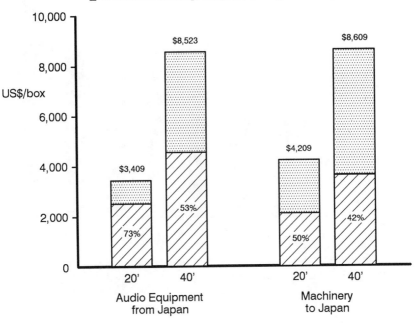

FIGURE 7.9 Freight rates by Trans-Siberian landbridge (Booz Allen & Hamilton).

is nevertheless important to the growth of multilateral cooperation in the RFE and the North Pacific.

The problems with the air transportation system are much like those of the port and railway system. Put simply, modernization is needed throughout the air transportation subsystems. There is presently only an ineffective air traffic control system, for example. Passenger reservation systems are remedial as well. And airport facilities and equipment—terminals, communications, maintenance, and runways—need rehabilitation and modernization. Additionally, the chipping away of the mammoth state carrier Aeroflot to form smaller regional airlines is creating significant safety problems. Strapped for cash, many of these start-ups attempt to increase revenues by overloading the planes and to reduce costs by skimping on maintenance. This has resulted in several fatal accidents in 1993 and 1994 and has earned Russian air carriers the dubious distinction of being the most unsafe in the world by an international air safety organization in Europe.

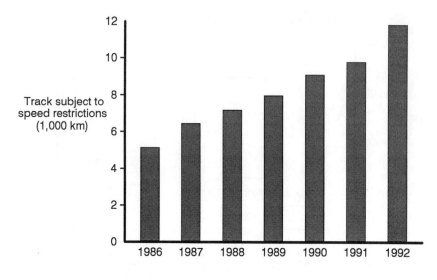

FIGURE 7.10 Rail capital maintenance and repair indicators (EBRD files).

Institutional Organization

Prior to 1991, all the major transportation enterprises of the FSU were vertically integrated megabusinesses, responsible not only for operating the core business of transportation but also for managing ancillary and support businesses and social services, much like a benevolent but all powerful "big brother." A shipping enterprise, for example, might control not only ocean shipping but also all port and shipyard activities. Not only that, the enterprise also provided health care facilities, food markets, entertainment, and communications for all those workers involved in these activities.

Privatization, particularly in the maritime and trucking sectors, is the first step in the transition of these industries toward a market-based economy. The trucking sector is mostly privatized and deregulated. The ports sector has also been privatized but has not severed all ties with Moscow. Port prices and operating conditions are still regulated by the Department of Marine Transport through Sea Port Authorities, while port services are offered by private entities under a single joint stock company that is still under the management of those who ran the ports when they were state-owned. However, competition and market pressures are already forcing these large joint stock companies to restructure and split up into smaller competing entities, resulting in higher productivity, lower prices, and a greater choice for the end user. As these companies restructure and become independent of Moscow in setting prices and reducing labor costs, foreign capital investment will quickly follow. With reduced costs and increased productivity, trade will grow and benefit the region and the Russian economy as a whole.

Infrastructural Improvements: Cost and Finance

During Booz Allen's own survey of the waterborne and rail transport sector surveys of the FSU for the EBRD, we evaluated the infrastructural improvement investments proposed by the officials and bureaucrats of the various enterprises in Russia and the Ukraine. Invariably, our conclusion was that these investments were simply plans to further increase capacity, were significant in size of investment, and often had little relation to the ability of the enterprise to recover a return on the investments. Two examples were a plan to build a new Russian port in the Baltic to compete with Talinn, for a cost exceeding $1 billion, and another plan to build a high-speed passenger rail between Moscow and St. Petersburg. In neither of these projects would the projected volume of traffic generate enough business revenue to recover the cost of investments—if tariffs were to be maintained at competitive market levels.

I have already shown that additional capacity is not required now and will not be required over the next decade. As the next step in the infrastructure investment survey of the transportation sector in Russia and the RFE, we reevaluated each of the investment proposals presented by the enterprises, as well as other necessary investments we identified, against two key criteria: the investments must be targeted to rectify the specific operational and infrastructural deficiencies identified during the assignment; and they must be accompanied by a plan to recover the cost of the investments over a reasonable business time frame. Table 7.7 delineates those investments that both (1) were considered essential for rectifying the operational and infrastructural shortcomings identified earlier for each transportation sector, and (2) passed the test for an acceptable return on investment as suggested by the two screening criteria.

The table is by no means a complete list of all investments required to fix the ills of the transportation infrastructure in Russia and the RFE. However, it does provide a list of the critical near- and medium-term investments required for the ports and rail sectors, and the proposed investments for the air transport sector are for a longer term, with a time frame of around twenty years. In most cases these investments could be financed through privatization and recovered through user charges and commercialization. In some cases, like rail track rehabilitation and purchase of essential spare parts for port equipment, where the linkage between the investments and commercialization cost recovery is less clear,

TABLE 7.7 Investment Requirements for Upgrading Russia's
Transportation Infrastructure

Sector Critical Investments[a]	Financed by	Estimated Cost ($ million)
Ports		
Vostochniy: grain terminal	Privatization	92
St. Petersburg: grain terminal	Privatization	36
Novorossiysk: storage area	Privatization	45
Spare parts/port design	EBRD/World Bank	150
Technical operations training	EBRD	30
Ports sector subtotal		353
Railways		
Telecommunications	Privatization	192
Transport mgmt. info. systems	Privatization	146
Track maintenance	EBRD/World Bank	900
Railways sector subtotal		1,238
Air		
Air traffic control systems	Privatization	10,000
Rehabilitation of airports	EBRD/Privatization	700
Passenger reservation system	Privatization	150
Air sector subtotal		10,850
Total, all sectors		12,441

[a]Near to medium term for ports and railways; medium to long term for air.
Source: EBRD surveys.

the financing may have to come from multilateral agencies such as the
World Bank and the EBRD. The total cost of these improvements would be
around $1.5 billion for ports and railways and $11 billion for the air transport system.

Notes

References

Cho, Lee-Jay. 1994. "Culture, Institutions, and Economic Development in East
Asia." In Lee-Jay Cho and Y. H. Kim (eds.), *Korea's Political Economy: An Institutional Perspective*. Boulder, Colo.: Westview.

Choe, Sang-Chuel. 1992. "Transportation Problems and Policies in Northeast Asia." In Won Bae Kim et al. (eds.), *Regional Economic Cooperation in Northeast Asia*. Honolulu: Northeast Asia Economic Forum.

International Monetary Fund (IMF). Various years. *Trade Statistics Yearbook*. Washington, D.C.

Kazanskii, Nikolai. 1987. *Geografiia putei soobshcheniia* (The economic geography of transport). Moscow: Transport.

Valencia, Mark J., ed. 1992. *The Russian Far East and the North Pacific Region: Emerging Issues in International Relations*. Honolulu: East-West Center.

Wada, Zenkichi. 1992. "Summary of Regional Infrastructure: Ports and Harbors." In Won Bae Kim and Burnham O. Campbell (eds.), *Proceedings of the Conference on Economic Development in the Coastal Area of Northeast Asia*. Honolulu: East-West Center.

Choe, Sang-Chuel. 1992. "Transportation Problems and Policies in Northeast Asia." In Won Bae Kim et al. (eds.), *Regional Economic Cooperation in Northeast Asia*. Honolulu: Northeast Asia Economic Forum.

International Monetary Fund (IMF). Various years. *Trade Statistics Yearbook*. Washington, D.C.

Kazanskii, Nikolai. 1987. *Geografiia putei soobshcheniia* (The economic geography of transport). Moscow: Transport.

Valencia, Mark J., ed. 1992. *The Russian Far East and the North Pacific Region: Emerging Issues in International Relations*. Honolulu: East-West Center.

Wada, Zenkichi. 1992. "Summary of Regional Infrastructure: Ports and Harbors." In Won Bae Kim and Burnham O. Campbell (eds.), *Proceedings of the Conference on Economic Development in the Coastal Area of Northeast Asia*. Honolulu: East-West Center.

8

Fisheries

Douglas M. Johnston and Mark J. Valencia

Since the late 1960s an immense amount of diplomatic energy has been devoted to restructuring the law of the sea. Between 1973 and 1982 especially, virtually all states were directly involved in the Third United Nations Conference on the Law of the Sea (UNCLOS III). The complex lawmaking process required not only a sophisticated analysis of *national* ocean interest on the part of all delegations but also a collective effort to develop a *global* outlook on almost all ocean policy and management issues, including those in the fisheries sector. In most of these contexts, coastal states have had to balance out the costs and benefits associated with competitive, cooperative, and autonomous behavior. In contexts where cooperative interest outweighs competition or autonomy, most states have been willing to adopt a policy favoring at least consultation at the regional level.[1]

The regional approach might be appropriate for fisheries in the Sea of Japan and the extreme southern Sea of Okhotsk. These fisheries are among the most productive and intensively utilized in the world. Some of the harvesting states, such as Japan and South Korea, have highly advanced fishing industries. Elsewhere, including the Russian Far East, the fishing industry needs technical upgrading, better management, higher quality products, and improved domestic and external marketing. Joint ventures with foreigners could satisfy these needs. Japanese and South Korean fishing companies are interested in joint ventures in Russian waters because of the decline of stocks in their own zones and their exclusion from former fishing grounds in distant waters now under the jurisdiction of other countries. U.S. companies have also expressed an interest in similar joint ventures in the region. The Soviet Union had bilateral fishery agreements with Japan, North Korea, and the United States in the RFE. Several existing private joint fishing and processing ventures focus on herring, pollock, and salmon. Many others are proposed. But if the North Pacific fishery resources are to be sustained, there must be careful assessment of the stocks, identification of areas and species that can support continued fishing, and consideration of appropriate regional management measures.

Common recognition that even a poor regime is better than no regime compels nations to collaborate in the search for at least a minimally satisfying mode of cooperation. A functionalist, regime-oriented approach to fishery development and management is likely to achieve this objective if it is based on common habits and interests within the North Pacific region. Such an approach depends on the willingness of the national governments in the region to downplay the quasi-territorial significance of ocean boundaries and to give less weight to the certainty of linear settlements than to the flexibility of cooperative arrangements (see Johnston and Valencia 1991).

The 1920s witnessed the introduction of the world's first international fishery management authority, the International Pacific Halibut Commission, which was created by Canada and the United States in 1924. Between then and the mid-1960s over twenty bilateral or regional high seas fishery commissions were established around the world with varying degrees of managerial authority. In most of these treaties the commission's authority was limited to the power of *recommending* management or conservation measures to the member governments (Koers 1973:80–82).

The concept of a multilateral regional approach to ocean management issues has evolved considerably since World War II. There are currently more than twenty regional fishery organizations with three or more states. However, a new era of intergovernmental fishery cooperation was born in the circumstances of UNCLOS III, which endorsed the African proposal for a 200-nautical mile exclusive economic zone (EEZ) extending from the baseline of the territorial sea. The vesting of the coastal state's sovereign rights to all living and nonliving resources within these extended limits meant that over 95 percent of the world's (then existing) commercial fishery stocks were brought under national jurisdiction and thus removed from the jurisidiction of these international commissions in areas that no longer possessed the legal status of high seas. UNCLOS III made no attempt to prescribe mechanisms for the international management of shared or shareable stocks, although numerous provisions in the 1982 Convention emphasize the need for cooperation. Most of the regional commissions have survived, but with greatly diminished geographic scope and significantly reduced control (Carroz 1984). In addition to these post-UNCLOS adjustments of existing arrangements, new kinds of regional fishery organizations with new mandates have emerged, such as the Forum Fisheries Agency (FFA) in the South Pacific region (Doulman 1988; Cicin-Sain et al. 1989).

In the late stages of UNCLOS III it was believed that a new international legal "system" for ocean fisheries would emerge from the bilateral agreements negotiated between EEZ and non-EEZ states, and some thought was given to the range of "competent international organizations" required at the global level to implement the 1982 Convention. What could not be envisaged, much less designed, in the global arena was the diversity of ocean development and management arrangements that would have to be negotiated at the regional level. There is still no blueprint. Each marine region is virtually free to find its own way of building a bridge between the aspirations of national autonomy and the responsibilities of the world community.

Formal Coastal Fishery Diplomacy in the Northwest Pacific

There are five bilateral fishery agreements in force covering fishing in the Sea of Japan, the Sea of Okhotsk, and "coastal" adjacent areas; of these, three involve Russia. Japan is, by cultural tradition and technical mastery, the most important fishing nation in the North Pacific. It has the biggest total annual catch and maintains bilateral agreements with all the other countries in the region. Because of the tenuous diplomatic relationship between Japan and several of its neighbors up to the end of the 1980s, these agreements are largely among fishermen and their organizations rather than between governments, and they apply more to bottom (demersal) fisheries than to pelagic species, which normally migrate and occupy different areas for spawning and feeding. Such accommodations have been successful for the most part.

One agreement between Japan and Russia establishes reciprocal fishing rights and conditions for each country, including fishing grounds, number of vessels to be licensed, total allowable catch, and catch quotas for major species. The areas covered by this agreement include five fishing grounds in the Russian EEZ. Japanese fishing rights in Russian waters under this agreement are subdivided into two categories: fishing free of charge and fee fishing. Bilateral consultation among scientists and fisheries experts has become a prominent feature of the Japan–Russia fishery regime. This agreement also makes provision for several private-level arrangements: (1) for Japanese crab fishing off Sakhalin, in the Sea of Okhotsk, and in the Sea of Japan; (2) for Japanese kelp and sea urchin fisheries around Russian-controlled Kaigara Island, east of Hokkaido; (3) for Japanese purchase at sea of Alaska pollock and Pacific herring; and (4) for Pacific cod dragnet fishing in the Russian EEZ.

There is also an agreement between Russia and Japan which regulates Japanese fishing on the high seas for salmon of Russian origin. Such fishing has declined in recent years because of severe restrictions imposed by Russia in conformity with the provisions on anadromous species contained in the 1982 UN Convention on the Law of the Sea.

An agreement between North Korea and Russia establishes reciprocal fishing rights, with catch quotas for each in the other's waters to be decided at regular meetings of the Joint Fisheries Committee organized by the two countries. Scientific and technical cooperation has also been discussed in detail at these committee meetings. Large North Korean trawlers have been reported fishing in both the Sea of Japan and the Sea of Okhotsk.

A North Korea–Japan agreement established on a nongovernmental basis is overseen by the North Korea–Japan Joint Fisheries Cooperative Committee. This agreement defines the conditions of Japanese fishing in the EEZ and North Korea, including squid jigging, salmon gillnet, salmon longline, and crab pot fisheries. Fishing fees have been required for these fisheries since 1988.

A Japan–Republic of Korea agreement was reached shortly after normalization of relations between the two countries in 1965. Each has a 12-nm-wide exclusive fishing zone around its territories. The Korean exclusive zone is surrounded by a joint regulatory zone, inside which conditions for both parties are prescribed, related to number of boats, size of boats, type of gear, dates of operation, and catch. There are also two types of subdivision within the joint regulatory zone: trawlers of more than 50 tons are not allowed to operate east of the meridian 128° E, and mackerel fishing from boats of less than 60 tons is restricted to a zone south of 35°30′N to the east of the peninsula and south of 33°30′N west of Cheju-Do. Only fifteen such mackerel boats are allowed to fish. Beyond the joint regulatory zone, there is provision for a joint fishery resources zone defined by the Joint Fisheries Commission created under the agreement. In 1983, Japan and the Republic of Korea also established a separate domestic, self-regulatory scheme for their fishermen operating in the other's coastal waters beyond the joint regulatory zone. The reason for the establishment of such a scheme is that the Republic of Korea has not yet extended its jurisdiction, and Japanese extended jurisdiction has not yet applied to the Republic of Korea fishery. The scheme covers the Japanese trawl and purse seine fisheries operating along the Korean coast, particularly south and west of Cheju-Do, and trawl, squid jigging, and pot fishing by the Republic of Korea along the Japanese coast, particularly around Hokkaido.

In both the Japan–Republic of Korea and Japan–Russia agreements, the construction of a bilateral fishery regime took place within the context of the normalization of bilateral diplomatic relations. In both cases, the fishery talks affected, and were affected by, the negotiation of overall diplomatic relations. The fishery interests of Japan, Russia, North Korea, and the Republic of Korea are not always mutually exclusive. Complementary issues can be found. A good example is the balance between Russian reliance on herring, which is not so highly valued in Japan, and Japanese appreciation of Alaska pollock, which Russians tend to undervalue.

Despite their overall shortcomings, the Japan–Russia and Japan–Republic of Korea fishery regimes have provided a modicum of stability and predictability to fishery relations in the postwar period. The annual technical meetings under the two regimes have allowed experts from the countries involved to exchange their assessments of the stocks concerned and to recommend to their governments acceptable, if not optimal, levels of fishing effort and regulatory measures necessary to achieve those levels. Negotiations between government representatives, occasionally including cabinet ministers, have managed to produce mutually beneficial agreements. The whole process has forced the governments to coordinate their respective policies.

Once the governments agreed to limits on their fishermen's activities, however painful those limits may have been, the latter knew how much "return on investment" they could expect from their fishing operations. Drastic reductions in fishing efforts forced many fishermen to give up fishing, temporarily or permanently. Many surplus boats also had to be scrapped or transferred to other areas or uses. These measures affected the livelihood of many fishermen. However, at least in Japan, since continual reductions in Japanese fishing efforts in Russian and Republic of Korea waters had become expected, the bilateral fishery arrangements provided a degree of stability and predictability. Moreover, under pressure from well-organized Japanese fishing interests, the Japanese government has established a now familiar array of relief measures for those affected.

The Japan–Russia and Japan–Republic of Korea fishery arrangements have shown a remarkable degree of adaptability to the changing needs of the countries involved. Probably the single most important development affecting the bilateral fishery relations between these countries has been the expansion of the fishing industries in Russia and the Republic of Korea since the 1970s. The existing bilateral agreements have shown enough flexibility to accommodate these trends, but the South Korea–Japan agreement is a seriously flawed compromise of its fishery interests. Provisions of the South Korea–Japan agreement are outmoded under the new framework negotiated at UNCLOS III. At the time it was signed, their bilateral agreement meant that South Korea limited its claim to 12 nm despite the emergence of the 200-nm EEZ concept around the world. The agreement makes no provision for reviewing the annual allocation in light of the "official," globally approved objective of "maximum sustainable yield." It also appears to make South Korean delineation of its straight baselines contingent upon agreement by Japan, despite the apparent guarantees provided by the 1982 UN Convention. Another South Korean concern is flag-state enforcement of fishing regulations in the area covered by joint fisheries regulations, which is scarcely compatible with the EEZ provisions in the 1982 Convention.[2]

The current regime for fishery management is thus a delicate balance of multiple and competing interests within the fishing sector as well as in regional and global political relationships. Conflict, more than cooperation, has historically been characteristic of fishery relationships in the Northwest Pacific. Even the current balance, despite its apparent stability, is subject to the willingness of states to maintain compromises of questionable economic merit. Geographically, none of the bilateral agreements take into account the whole region. The lack of overt conflict does not mean that nations in the area are, or will remain, totally satisfied with the compromises that sustain the stability of the fishery regime. Nor does the status quo mean that nations do not perceive gains in fishery policy and management which could be obtained at acceptable costs.

There is, however, no forum wherein all Japan Sea fishing nations meet to discuss the distribution of catches. Coastal states have made some attempts to reserve coastal fisheries for their own fishing interests. International agreements make some modest attempts to provide for the sharing of catches within jointly regulated areas or for limiting effort within catch quotas for designated areas. But even the concept of allocations remains unexplored until other questions are settled.

Despite its advantages, the present system of bilateral arrangements is fundamentally flawed. Although the stocks are often multinational in distribution, there is no corresponding multinational body to manage them. The result is a fishery hegemon—Japan—with a virtual monopoly of information. Theoretically this system—an interlocking web of bilateral agreements dominated by one nation—could remain the framework for fishery management in the Northwest Pacific, even if it is deemed inequitable. The fact that many species are overfished indicates that the system is not working and suggests the need for multinational monitoring and regulation of this multispecies fishery, and ultimately for a more equitable allocation of the resource.

Formal High Seas Fishery Diplomacy in the North Pacific

One of the consequences of UNCLOS III has been to create a formal legal distinction between EEZ (and other "coastal") waters within 200-nm limits and high seas waters beyond. Most of the Sea of Japan and the Sea of Okhotsk falls within such limits. However, in an age of ecological awareness it has become widely evident that this is an arbitrary distinction, aggravating the problems of fishery management, which is notoriously difficult to execute on a scientific basis even in the absence of such artificialities. Many species or stocks of major commercial importance simply cannot be wholly contained within "coastal" regimes such as those of the Northwest Pacific described above, or wholly within high seas regimes for distant-water areas outside EEZ limits in regions such as the North Pacific.

The arbitrariness of 200-nm limits from the fishery management perspective was acknowledged by the delegations at UNCLOS III, and special provisions were adopted to combat the unnatural disjunctiveness of ocean fishery management systems. The need for cooperative management across 200-nm limits was conceded for four categories of fisheries: (1) those involving highly migratory species, such as tuna; (2) those involving anadromous species, such as salmon; (3) those involving catadromous species, such as certain kinds of eels; and (4) those consisting of straddling stocks, which swim, and are subject to harvesting, in adjacent areas on both sides of 200-nm limits, as in the case of many kinds of (demersal) groundfish as well as of pelagic species. On the other hand, while a great effort was made at UNCLOS III to establish new ground rules for fishery management and conservation within 200-nm limits under the EEZ regime, no comparable effort was made to develop meaningful norms and procedures for high seas fisheries beyond these limits.

Since the conclusion of UNCLOS III, the deficiencies of the bifurcated framework for ocean fishery management have been the target of mounting criticism, both privately within the established field of professional fisheries management and publicly from the increasingly influential environmental movement. In the mid-1980s environmental attacks on the world fishing industry, somewhat comparable to those on forestry and other extractive industries, were directed chiefly by U.S. environmentalists. But in recent years environmental campaigns against certain high seas fishing practices have extended beyond North America into other regions, including the North Pacific. The first environmental issue of this kind was generated at the end of the 1980s by the harvesting of targeted species such as squid by large-scale driftnets in the North Pacific and the Southwest Pacific, but the nature of this criticism ensured that it would extend to other modes of fishery both inside and outside 200-nm limits (Gurish 1992; Wright and Doulman 1991; Johnston 1990).

For ideological, political, and economic reasons, it has not been possible for the North Pacific to coordinate high seas fisheries management policies and practices within a single, comprehensive, macroregional framework such as those serving the North Atlantic: the Northwest Atlantic Fisheries Commission (NAFO), succeeding ICNAF, and the Northeast Atlantic Fisheries Commission (NEAFC). In the pre–UNCLOS III period of regulated high seas fishing (1924–74), the closest approximation to a macroregional commission in the North Pacific was the North Pacific Fur Seal Commission, involving the four relevant harvesting states: Canada, Japan, the Soviet Union, and the United States (Johnston 1987:205–12, 264–69). Only three of these states—Canada, Japan, and the United States—belong to the International North Pacific Fisheries Commission, and only Canada and the United States were parties to the International Pacific Halibut Commission (IPHC) and the International Pacific Salmon Fisheries Commission (IPSFC), both of which had strictly limited purposes that could not have been achieved by a more widely based organization.

Since the establishment of the EEZ regime, all these organizations have been replaced or substantially modified. Russia has joined Canada, Japan, and the United States as a party to the new Anadromous Species Commission, which has replaced the old IPSFC. Meanwhile, a new marine science organization has been created with special responsibilities for the promotion and coordination of fishery science investigations in the North Pacific—known as PICES, because it represents a Pacific counterpart to ICES (the International Council for the Exploration of the Sea), which has served the Atlantic Ocean in that capacity since 1902. In 1994, Russia joined Canada, China, Japan, and the United States as a member of PICES. It is uncertain how PICES and the Anadromous Species Commission will divide their scientific research responsibilities, whether other fishing states of (or in) the region (e.g., South Korea, Taiwan, Poland, and North Korea) will be invited to join one or more of these organizations, and what impact these efforts at coordinated research will have on the management of fisheries inside as well as outside EEZ limits in the North Pacific.

Special Problems of Fishery Development and Management in the Russian Far East

The next decade will pose daunting problems for Russians in the field of fishery development and management. Some of the difficulties now experienced extend throughout all Russian coastal areas, but some are of particular concern in the Russian Far East. In Russia, as in some other countries, media reports of the collapse of certain stocks may be exaggerated. Most salmon stocks are in good condition generally throughout the North Pacific, perhaps reflecting the peak of a 30-year cycle according to some scientists. On the other hand, herring stocks are down, and the pollock population in the Okhotsk Sea is in trouble. Despite the high standard of Russian fishery science, the prospect for sustainable development and effective management of ocean fisheries is fairly bleak, especially in remote areas. Some of the obvious reasons are economic and political:

1. The grave run-down of the Russian economy has resulted in critical deficiencies throughout the public sector. The fishing fleet is old and inefficient, and Russian shipyards do not have the capacity to rebuild it.[3] Laboratory facilities have deteriorated, key personnel have been forced to look for a better livelihood in other occupations, and it is difficult to envisage how professional standards can survive without the assistance of other advanced fishing states with expert knowledge of the region's fishery resource. In the meantime, however, the Russian fishery science community has found a way to conduct on-board research under joint fishing ventures with foreign enterprises, which provide better salaries than Russian research institutions. Russian fishery data are no longer classified as secret information, and although the high cost of publication has the effect of limiting the availability of reliable data, Russian scientists are beginning to publish English-language journals in certain fishery-related fields and hope to generate dollar income in this way. Some Russian fishery research findings may also soon appear in foreign journals for the first time.

2. Even if substantial external assistance were forthcoming, it is not clear where it should be directed. Formal authority over Russian fishery development and management still resides mainly in the central government, but as the Russian government's effective control over remote areas such as the Russian Far East continues to decline, questions of constitutional authority and legislative responsibility become less and less meaningful. The problem of governance between the core and the periphery in Russia has become more critical than in any other huge country such as Canada, China, or the United States, and even though it may never deteriorate to the level that occurred in China in the 1930s and 1940s, the trend to further de facto decentralization in the fisheries sector is certain to continue as a controlling reality throughout the foreseeable future.

Under the Soviet system, the Russian fishing industry was administered by the Ministry of Fisheries in Moscow through five regional agencies, each controlling its own fleet. The most important of these commercially was Dalryba, which was responsible for operations in the Bering and Okhotsk Seas and other areas in the Pacific Ocean.[4] It still has offices in Vladivostok, Nakhodka, Khabarovsk, and other ports in Kamchatka and Sakhalin, but apparently there are plans to replace Dalryba with a regional fisheries committee that would be based in Khabarovsk with a view, it seems, to reducing the leverage commercial interests in Vladivostok now have on fishery policy and management.

3. The downscaling and restructuring of the industry are certain to have a profound effect on its long-term performance in the Russian Far East. The vastness of the Russian industry at the end of the Soviet period is re-

flected in FAO figures for 1991: a labor force of 800,000, a fleet of 6.8 million metric tons, and an earning capacity of US$6,132 million, which was more than 1.5 percent of the GNP that year.[5] The latest estimate for the labor force engaged in the industry is just over 500,000. The national catch has fallen from the record level of 11.2 million metric tons in 1986 to 10.4 million in 1990 and is expected to fall much farther through the early 1990s.[6] Much of this decline was due initially to the loss of about one-fifth of the industry to other republics on the dissolution of the Soviet Union. By the end of 1991 the staff of the Ministry of Fisheries was halved, and the mandate of the ministry was greatly reduced as a result of the new policy whereby the state-owned fleets, combines, cooperatives, and joint ventures were required to assume responsibility for their own day-to-day operations.[7] The effort to incorporate this reduced agency into the Ministry of Agriculture was fiercely resisted, and in October 1992 it resumed its autonomous career as the Russian Federation Committee of Fishery Management, thereby releasing both ministries to devote their depleted energies to the solution of Russia's food production problems.

In the view of many observers, the new ministry is unlikely to function effectively since its mandate is still too broad for the resources committed to it,[8] and, like all central government agencies, it suffers from Russia's notoriously poor communications infrastructure and from a tradition of bureaucratic rigidity and indifference. It can be hoped that the new and relatively young minister, Vladimir Korelsky, who is also vice-minister of agriculture, has the vision and ability to raise the Russian fishing industry from its present travail,[9] but the prevailing mood in Moscow and Vladivostok is one of pessimism, at least for the short term.

4. The state of the fishing industry in the Russian Far East is greatly affected by political tensions and realignments between Moscow, Vladivostok, Khabarovsk, Nakhodka, and other centers of local power. The old and much weakened Communist Party still operates as the principal nationwide network of power and influence, in the absence of any alternative, but unprecedented weakness at the party center and in the parliamentary system has created innumerable opportunities for political advancement at three subnational levels: the regional level such as that of the RFE; the provincial level such as that of Primorski, Khabarovsk, Amur, Yakut ASSR, Magadan, and Kamchatka, which together constitute the Far Eastern Region; and the municipal level such as that of the greater Vladivostok area in the Primorski Krai.

In the present period of political realignment it is difficult, if not impossible, for an outsider to discern a clear pattern of political development. But most observers attach significance to the emergence of local politicians and entrepreneurs, many of whom are seen to be working in collusion with one another to exploit the opportunities for personal gain which have arisen from the new ethic favoring local initiatives in both the economic and governmental spheres. The new minister, Korelsky, assigns much of the blame for the decline of the fishing industry on local politicians who focus on personal "allotment" deals with Russian entrepreneurs and foreign joint enterprise operators without regard to the public interest or, specifically, to the need for national conservation and management of the fisheries, some of which are believed to be seriously, or even critically, overexploited.[10] The Ministry of Fisheries and other central government agencies in Moscow have very little control over these deals, or indeed over the pace of decentralization, deregulation, and privatization in fishery-dependent areas as remote as Primorski and Kamchatka.[11] Because so many of the local people in these areas are Russians resettled there several generations ago, there is no immediate prospect of a formal secessionist movement, but there is no doubting the destabilizing effect of the trend to regional, provincial, and municipal autonomy and of its tendency to undermine long-term management considerations in the fishing industry.

International Issues

Anadromous Species Management

One consequence of the spread of 200-nm EEZs is increasing pressure on anadromous species (mostly salmon), which usually migrate from coastal waters to the open sea beyond 200 nm. The North Pacific region is the world's largest dispersion area for anadromous species, and about 90 percent of the world's stocks are concentrated there. Due to their high consumer quality, anadromous species such as salmon are the major targets, and in the late 1980s the salmon catch exceeded 600,000 tons (Mirovitskaya and Haney 1992:247). The states of origin have responsibility for the protection and improvement of hatcheries and bear the lost opportunity cost of alternative uses of spawning rivers. These investments are lost when salmon are intercepted on the high seas or in the EEZ of other countries. States of origin contend that they are entitled to a volume of salmon catch proportional to their national investment or, in the case of resources used by other countries, for compensation of expenses minus the money expended by the user to help restore or maintain the resources. The participants should ensure not just compensation for the catch but optimal stocking of spawning sites for the population fished. But in contemporary practice, the revenue derived from programs of salmon restoration does not exceed 15–20 percent of total management costs. In high seas fisheries, the total loss of salmon biomass sometimes exceeds the volume of catches. Due to the inability to regulate fishing pressure, there is a high risk of overfishing the population essential to the total structure of the stocks, and a risk of total collapse.

Contemporary international law does not empower coastal states to impose their national legislation on foreign fishing vessels operating outside EEZs, even to regulate anadromous species exploitation. Thus the only viable way of solving the problem seems to be through regional regulatory agreements. The participation of all states concerned in these agreements is, however, crucial to their effectiveness (Saguirian 1992:2).

In the current international practice, there are two major regional options. The first is to formulate regional agreements prohibiting any fishing activities for anadromous species outside EEZs. This would reflect the relevant provisions of the 1982 UN Convention on the Law of the Sea. The North Atlantic Salmon Conservation organization (NASCO), which was established pursuant to the Convention for the Conservation of Salmon in the North Atlantic Region, is using this approach, but this approach is feasible only when there is no substantial fishing effort outside EEZs and when the number of states interested in fishing for salmon is limited to the states of origin.

The other, more moderate, approach is an international agreement on joint management and conservation of anadromous stocks in a particular geographic area without an immediate ban on high seas fisheries for these stocks. This is the approach of the 1952 Convention for the High Seas Fisheries of the North Pacific Ocean (INPFC), signed by Canada, the United States, and Japan in its latest amended version. The Convention's key feature was the principle of "abstention," under which noncoastal states are required to refrain from fishing stocks already at the level of maximum sustainable yield.

Until very recently there was no evidence of Japan's readiness to support either of these approaches in its salmon-related bilateral relations with the USSR. The Soviet Union had repeatedly stressed its intention to phase out all fishing for salmon of Soviet origin by 1992 in the high seas area adjacent to its EEZ. In an effort to curb high seas salmon fishing, Russia suggested in October 1992 that Russian supervisors should be allowed to board Japanese vessels operating in Japan's EEZ. In the past, Japan had objected on the basis that such activity would infringe upon its sovereignty.[12] Japan and Russia did, however, reach broad agreement on a fishery joint venture in the North Pacific and a salmon catch quota for 1992. The agreement calls for a salmon catch by Japanese boats of some 14,000 tons for this year's joint venture. The negotiators also agreed that Japan should pay 450 million yen in fisheries cooperation fees to Russia for a catch of 2,800 tons of salmon in Japanese waters, because the salmon spawn in Russian waters.[13]

In light of subsequent discussions within the Soviet-American Intergovernmental Consultative Committee on Fisheries, it has become evident that Japan and Russia also agreed to refrain from unilateralism and put a stronger emphasis on international cooperation between the states concerned, and to approach the problem of anadromous species in the North Pacific areas outside the coastal states EEZs in a single package incorporating straddling stocks between EEZs and the open sea in the same geographic area. Presently, the Committee is preparing a draft International Convention for the Conservation and Management of Fishery Resources in the Central Bering Sea, which is to be submitted shortly for the consideration of the states concerned with fishing for either salmon or straddling stocks, or both.

Nevertheless, the problem of high seas fishing for salmon in the North Pacific remains unsolved. Past difficulties encountered, mainly by the Soviet Union, in dealing with anadromous species conservation and management can be explained by the ineffectiveness of global legal instruments for the regulation of high seas fisheries, a lack of political will, and the unwillingness of distant-water fishing nations to adapt their national fishery policies to the realities of today's world by creating new regional and subregional fishery institutions.

In accordance with the 1982 UN Convention's provisions, states of origin for North Pacific salmon are obligated to establish conservation measures (including maximum sustainable yield and terms and methods of fishing) for species originating in their rivers. Arguably, they are also entitled to insist, even before the entry into force of the Convention, on the complete cessation of high seas fishing for salmon by every fishing state except Japan; to demand that Japan exercise high seas fishing in strict correspondence with agreements, giving due regard to the conservation requirements and needs of the states of origin; to define appropriate enforcement measures; and to cooperate in conserving and managing those states in whose EEZs anadromous stocks migrate. In case of disagreements, the states involved might use the Convention's dispute settlement procedures.[14]

Even when the 1982 UN Convention comes into force on 16 November 1994, it might be argued that non-ratifiers should not be entitled to partake of rights and privileges that arise from the Convention. The most appropriate options are either to conclude a multilateral convention on the conservation of North Pacific anadromous species, elaborated with due regard to the 1982 U.N. Convention's provisions and international salmon management practice, or to solve this issue within the framework of a regional agreement on the conservation of all the living resources of the high seas. To confirm and develop corresponding Convention provisions, it would be useful in any international agreement to outline the aims and applicable principles of anadromous species management, including the duties of parties to prevent stock depletion and to promote optimal exploitation; the vesting of primary interest in and responsibility for salmon stocks with the state of origin, if its stocks are used by other countries; the necessity to use ecologically optimal fishing gear; and compulsory coordination of large-scale programs of artificial reproduction (Mirovitskaya and Haney 1992:254).

Driftnetting and Poaching

Russia also faces problems of poaching and driftnetting. The environmental impact of driftnetting in the North Pacific cannot be measured with any precision. However, there is reason to fear it causes disruption of the age structure and genetic composition of the stock and has a deleterious effect on marine ecosystems (Mirovitskaya and Haney 1992:252). Recent efforts to control driftnetting involve the appointment of former KGB officer Evgheni Slavksy to the Russian team responsible for high seas fishery patrols. Slavsky has said that patrols will be almost trebled in 1993 to stop salmon pirating in violation of the international prohibition of driftnetting. The captain of a vessel seized for alleged violations may be fined 100,000 rubles under new Russian legislation, and he could be held in prison until the fine is paid. Some Japanese fishermen were held for nine months in 1992.[15]

Uncontrolled high seas fishing has continued even after depletion of the resource. Recent investigations by Russian scientists demonstrate an inverse correlation between high seas fishing efforts and the number of spawning salmon. Extrapolation of these data gives an estimate of the scale of coastal states' losses from the high seas fisheries as 100,000 tons of possible catch. Ministry officials in Moscow say Russia is losing an estimated $100 million worth of fish a year to large-scale poaching operations in the waters of the Russian Far East. Thus Russia plans to intensify its efforts to control poaching. For example, in February 1993 Russian Minister Korelsky asked the Ministry of Foreign Affairs to protest against what he said were unlawful activities by an American stern trawler in the Bering Sea. As the United States increases its efforts to curtail pollock fishing in the Bering Sea's "Doughnut Hole," Russia naturally wants to do the same.[16] In 1992, Akio Kyoya, Japan's vice minister of Agriculture, Forestry, and Fisheries, told reporters that he had asked the Fisheries Agency if it was possible to make changes in the catch monitoring system for 1993. The changes he is seeking include requiring salmon fishing boats to be equipped with transponders to prevent their operating illegally and transferring the catch checking process to the agency from the Hokkaido government. Several salmon boats are suspected of operating illegally in

Russian waters, and the Hokkaido government has allegedly submitted a false report understating their catches, which are supposedly considerably higher than their acceptable quotas.[17]

The "Peanut Hole" Controversy

The controvery over the so-far unsuccessful attempt by Russia to impose a regime for pollock fisheries in the "Peanut Hole" in the Sea of Okhotsk is instructive because it involves most Northeast Asian governments. The Peanut Hole is an oblong, 35-by-300-mile window in the central Sea of Okhotsk lying outside—but completely surrounded by—the 200 nm EEZs of Russia and Japan's Hokkaido. The Sea of Okhotsk as a whole contains perhaps the richest Alaskan pollock fishery in the world. It is fished by Russia, South Korea, China, Taiwan, and North Korea as well as Poland, Panama, and Bulgaria, and Japan fishes there for other species but not for pollock. The importance of the Peanut Hole to South Korea is extreme. South Korea's pollock catch there of 200,000 metric tons in 1993 was almost twice as much as its catch in the surrounding Russian EEZ for the same period—107,000 tons. Together these catches supplied half its domestic demand. During this period, Poland also caught 200,000 tons of pollock in the Peanut Hole, and China 170,000 tons. By 1991 it was apparent to Russia that pollock stocks in the Sea of Okhotsk were rapidly diminishing, and it requested the fishing countries to voluntarily limit their catches in the Peanut Hole. Some Russian administrators even called for making the entire Sea of Okhotsk an internal sea.[18]

In May 1992, South Korea concluded an agreement with Russia for acquisition of 155,400 tons of pollock in the Peanut Hole for 1993, a reduction of nearly 25 percent from 1992. But in January 1993, a price dispute arose between the two over Alaskan pollock. Seoul proposed US$470 per ton for oviferous pollock but Moscow demanded $530—*in advance*. Talks broke down and Seoul feared cancellation of its 150,000-ton annual fishing quota for pollock. In mid-February, Russia barred not only South Korea but all other countries as well from catching Alaskan pollock in the Peanut Hole. At the same time, the "Russian Fisheries Committee" submitted a proclamation to parliament proposing that it declare the entire Sea of Okhotsk an ecological disaster area—barring even Russians from fishing there. South Korea protested that Russia could not unilaterally make such a declaration, since the area was high seas and thus such a ban required agreement through multilateral negotiations. South Korea argued further that a unilateral ban would be a violation of the Law of the Sea.[19]

In early March, Russia reversed its position and stated its readiness to hold multilateral negotiations on the issue with South Korea, Japan, China, Poland, and other relevant countries. South Korea held unofficial talks with other countries to prepare for the negotiations and to formulate a proposal for safe fishing operations and conservation of fishery resources in the area. At the time, South Korea still had 31 fishing boats in the Sea of Okhotsk, six *more* than even their previous bilateral agreement allowed. However, South Korea announced that it would voluntarily remove all the boats in order to smooth negotiations.[20]

On April 16, the Russian parliament again reversed its position, adopting a resolution banning all fishing inside Russia's EEZ in the Sea of Okhotsk starting in mid-June and lasting until an acceptable agreement could be reached among the countries concerned. Russia also called on Japan, South Korea, Poland, and China to join in a three-year moratorium on fishing in the Peanut Hole. Russian deputy prime minister Alexandr Shokhin said that Russia would use naval vessels to reinforce the ban in Russia's EEZ. Labeling all foreign fishing vessels in the area as poachers, he added that his government would deal sternly with any fishing vessels caught in the area. The fine for poaching in Russian waters is 200,000 rubles (then US$400,000).[21]

South Korean Foreign Ministry officials, after consulting with other involved countries, stated that any such moratorium should be based on scientific evidence, which Russia did not present. On April 18 all of South Korea's vessels were still in the Sea of Okhotsk. An administration official asserted that those ships operating within the Russian EEZ would continue fishing under a contract signed previously with Russia.[22]

Multilateral talks in late May and early June between South Korea, China, and Poland produced an agreement to resume fishing in the Peanut Hole but to voluntarily reduce their pollock catches by 25 percent until talks with Russia were held in October. This would be a 25 percent reduction of South Korea's 1993 quota, which was already a 25 percent reduction of its quota from the previous year. Nevertheless, the agreement among the distant-water fishing nations was protested by Russia. In a letter to Kim Yong Sam dated June 29, Boris Yeltsin asked him to stop South Korea's fishing in the area, since Russian fishermen had by then turned the dispute into a domestic political issue. In an attempt to be conciliatory, Russia told South Korea that it would allow South Korean fishing companies to purchase Russian catch quotas in compensation.[23]

Japan did not participate in the debate because it has not engaged in pollock fishing in the area since 1990. Nevertheless, Japan did sign an agreement with Russia in early June which kept unchanged the terms of Japanese flatfish fishing in the Peanut Hole. The two countries also agreed at the flatfish negotiations to hold a bilateral conference of scientists that autumn on marine resources in the Sea of Okhotsk.[24]

In early 1993, Russia began arresting foreign fishing vessels in the Peanut Hole in earnest. In March, for example, a Chinese trawler was detained near Kamchatka and its gear and catch confiscated. In mid-June, China retaliated by boarding or attempting to board at least 14 Russian fishing vessels. In early July, Russian radio reported that 50 fishing vessels flying Korean and Taiwanese flags were still poaching pollock in the Sea of Okhotsk, taking fry as well as food fish and thereby undermining the stocks of several species. Russian vessels had left the area in April to allow renewal of the stocks, but the poachers took their place and sold the fish on the world market. Later in July, a Polish trawler was detained by a Russian patrol vessel and escorted to Magadan, where charges against it were considered. Nevertheless, more than 20 Polish and Chinese trawlers continued to fish in the Peanut Hole.[25]

Meanwhile, the UN conference on migratory fish stocks was under way. At this first effort since 1982 to regulate global fishing, Russia and the United States issued a joint statement calling for conservation measures to prevent fish stocks in both the Sea of Okhotsk and the Bering Sea from dwindling further. The statement added that the two states would take all necessary steps to protect their interests and those of future generations in the region, by conserving and replenishing fish stocks in strict accordance with international law. Satya Nandan, the conference chairman, worried that an accumulation of similar disputes could even threaten the regime of the Law of the Sea.[26]

On 6 August 1993, South Korea announced that losses by its fishermen had forced it to resume fishing in the Peanut Hole—despite threats of retaliation and despite uncertainty as to whether its operations there had ever even ceased. A South Korean Foreign Ministry official stated at the time, "We will stick by last May's agreement with other countries to reduce our catch by 25 percent, but Russia has no right to declare a unilateral ban because the area is outside its economic zone. We repeat that South Korea and other countries should make an objective joint survey to see how serious the depletion is and decide on further actions." Russia then responded by declaring that it would withhold the repayment of a $1.47 billion loan from the South Korean government.[27]

Later in August, South Korea announced that it would resume fishing in the Sea in mid-September, since its quota in the Bering Sea of 70,000 tons would be exhausted by then. South Korea then suggested that it would be willing to accept only 40,000 tons of pollock taken from anywhere in the Russian EEZ, but this offer was also turned down. The sense of urgency was heightened by the fact that August–September is the height of the pollock season.[28]

A scientific conference was then scheduled in Vladivostok for September 21–23, to reach agreements on stock levels prior to a diplomatic summit between at least Russia and South Korea to be held in mid-October. South Korean fisheries administration officials announced that they planned to send a large number of marine scientists and fisheries experts to the conference to present evidence that fishery resources in the sea were not as depleted as claimed by Russia. Officials from the South Korean Fisheries Administration, the Foreign Ministry, and the National Fisheries Promotion Corporation also held a meeting to consolidate their plans and policies. The diplomatic talks ended in deadlock, as did a second round which concluded on October 27. South Korea asserted that its ships had not been fishing in the area since April, and that it had lost around $100 million as a result. Meanwhile, Russia claimed that foreign poaching in all its waters cost it $700 million annually, a figure which may be a conservative estimate. A third round of talks concluded about November 20 also proved fruitless.[29]

By the end of November 1993, Russia had reinforced its Okhotsk fleet of one aging patrol boat with at least five more boats, four of them just built. Russia's total fish inspection fleet for its entire EEZ at this time consisted of only 19 vessels, which were chronically short of fuel and spare parts. The inadequacy of this fleet may be seen by comparison with Japan's inspection fleet of 160 ships, plus airplanes and helicopters. The weakness of Russia's enforcement capabilities was noted by a Russian fishery official who stated that, when his ship detained a Chinese trawler in the Peanut Hole in March 1993, they had to wait two days for the Russian patrol boat to arrive. The official went on to state that Russian fish inspectors had even been killed.[30]

In mid-December 1993, Russia reduced North Korea's 1994 fishery quota to 50 percent of its 1993 quota of 60,000 tons, due partly to depletion of stocks in the Sea of Okhotsk.[31] On 10 January 1994, South Korean pollock fishing finally resumed legally within the Russian EEZ, with 32 vessels from 16 companies taking part. The Russian government allowed the vessels to begin fishing in order to avoid missing the pollock season entirely, and both sides agreed that the price of the fish would be set at a later date. However, no agreement has yet been reached over the Peanut Hole, and Russia continues to protest foreign "poaching" in the area.

This episode leads to several conclusions relevant to this study. First, in the absence of adequate scientific information or agreement on the status of the stocks, Northeast Asian fishing nations will assume that the stocks can withstand more fishing. Indeed the size of the quotas may be more a factor of political bargaining than scientific knowledge. Also, with valuable fish stocks like pollock, value is an important factor in allocating catch quotas.

Second, if an area falls outside an EEZ or, as in Northeast Asia, where EEZs have not yet been universally declared, countries will continue to fish and cite the regime of the Law of the Sea as their justification for doing so. In Northeast Asia, such areas include the East China Sea and parts of the Yellow and Japan Seas. Indeed, China and South Korea could find themselves in a similar position to Russia if they do not soon declare EEZs.

Third, a united front by noncomplying fishing nations, including retaliation, may successfully pressure a coastal state—even a strong and tough-talking coastal state like Russia—into a compromise, despite the backing in principle by a hegemon like the United States. Persistence, as by South Korea, even in overfishing, appears to have paid off. Finally, in fisheries, the influence of domestic pressures is a paramount driving force both in Russia and in South Korea.

Transboundary and Straddling Stocks

Another international legal problem affecting Russia's interests in the North Pacific is the problem of fishing for transboundary and straddling stocks, that is, stocks occurring within the EEZs of two or more coastal states or both within the EEZ and in an area beyond and adjacent to it. Here again the issue of conservation and management of such resources is a major difficulty for Russia (Saguirian 1992:5).

In the aftermath of widespread extension of EEZs, the central high seas part of the Bering Sea is one of the few regions of the world ocean where the problem of fishing for straddling stocks has become acute. There are serious concerns within both the United States and Russia about the growing fishing activities there of noncoastal fishing nations—Japan, South Korea, Poland, Taiwan, and China—which threaten to undermine certain fish populations. As in the case of salmon fishing, the problem of fishing for straddling stocks has been exacerbated by the exclusion of distant-water states from waters encompassed by EEZs in which they had fished for decades. This has led the distant-water states to concentrate their efforts outside these zones, often in areas where fish stocks move between EEZs and the high seas.

In a legal sense, anadromous stocks are a special instance of straddling stocks. But due to their unique biological characteristics, the primary interest and responsibility for the conservation and management of anadromous stocks should lie with the coastal states in whose rivers they originate. In both legal and practical terms, however, it is much more difficult to prove the "exclusivity" of coastal states' rights over straddling stocks. The reasoning seems to be at least twofold. First, neither existing customary international law nor the 1982 Convention provides coastal states with preferential rights to straddling stocks seaward of EEZs. On the high seas all nations are equal in their exercise of the freedom to fish. Conservation is not a sufficient reason for claiming the unilateral right to control fishery resources. Second, there is a lack of relevant scientific knowledge concerning straddling fish stocks. Japan, for example, has claimed that the Alaskan pollock they harvest in the central part of the Bering Sea is a completely different fish stock that does not depend on similar stocks found in coastal waters. If so, the argument goes, conservation measures taken by coastal states in respect to the living resources of their respective EEZs should not extend to the stocks found on the high seas.

As in the case of transboundary stocks overlapping the EEZs of two or more states, the 1982 Convention calls only for cooperation between the coastal state and other states fishing the stocks in areas adjacent to the EEZ. Regarding the regulation of high seas fisheries, the 1982 Convention stipulates in Article 117 that fishing nations are obliged only to "cooperate" and to "enter into negotiations." Obviously this is not enough to force distant-water fishing nations to become legally bound by conservation and management measures taken by coastal states, or even to agree on a common fishery conservation policy. Noncoastal countries like Japan usually blame coastal states for constantly decreasing foreign countries' fish catch quotas in their EEZs, and this provides them with strong arguments when discussing the straddling stock issue.[32]

Under Article 123 of the 1982 Convention, the states bordering closed or semiclosed seas should cooperate in the exercise of their rights and in the performance of their duties. To this end they shall endeavour, directly or though an appropriate regional organization, to invite other interested states to cooperate with them in furtherance of the article's provisions. But coastal states do not have the right to impose measures of fish conservation and management upon foreign vessels operating in the high seas portions of enclosed and semienclosed seas, and even less so to enforce compliance with such measures unless the involved noncoastal states agree to be so bound. It follows that the general provisions on high seas fisheries in the 1982 Convention apply to the regulation of high seas enclave fisheries in semienclosed seas such as the Bering Sea.

Recent developments toward regional cooperation in conservation and management of straddling stocks in the Bering Sea are somewhat encouraging. Six states, both coastal (United States, USSR, Canada) and the most interested noncoastal (Japan, Poland, South Korea), met in Washington, D.C., in February 1990 to discuss current fishery problems in the Bering Sea. Serious difficulties were created by the position of Poland, whose fishing in the Bering Sea is substantial. The major item of discussion was the management of straddling stocks, mainly high seas fishing for pollock. Japan promised not to increase its fish harvest and not to modernize its fishing vessels while the negotiations were under way. The second part of this conference was held in July 1991.

Constraints on Russian Fishery Diplomacy
in the North and Northwest Pacific

Russia has inherited twelve international fishery "conventions" and eighty-four intergovernmental fishery agreements signed by the former Soviet Union. The new State Committee for Fisheries under Minister Korelsky has accepted responsibility for the implementation of these numerous arrangements and pledged to cooperate with the Ministry of Foreign Affairs in the negotiation of further fishery agreements. Doubts arise, however, about the ability of the Russian central government to develop further such a vast network of treaty commitments around the world, and in particular to hold the balance between domestic interests and international responsibilities within the framework of fishery regimes emerging in the North Pacific.

There are several obvious constraints. Factors discussed in the previous sections serve to weaken the effectiveness and even the credibility of the central government in the eyes of local politicians who have acquired a large degree of control over the operations of the fishing industry in remote provinces like Primorski and Kamchatka. Authority shared among four levels of government is authority diffused, and the central government agencies responsible for the conduct of formal fishery diplomacy may be losing the capability to guarantee compliance with its negotiated instruments on the part of an industry that is passing out of its control.

Russian fishery diplomacy is also weakened by inconsistencies in legal policy. Like most of the other states originally opposed to the EEZ concept in the global law-of-the-sea negotiations, the Soviet Union was never enthusiastic about the outcome of UNCLOS III. Both before and after the demise of the Soviet system, Russian attitudes toward the outcome of UNCLOS III have been ambivalent, for a variety of reasons, and somewhat similar to those of the United States and the UNCLOS III "allies" such as Japan, Germany, and the United Kingdom. As one of the ambivalent states, Russia may continue to decline to ratify the 1982 UN Convention on the Law of the Sea in its present form. At the same time it is obliged to participate in global fishery diplomacy such as the UN Conference on High Seas Fishing, which began in July 1993 and is purported to represent an extension of the 1982 Convention. Ambivalence of this kind weakens a state's resolve to take a leading role in regional fishery negotiations that pivot on legal issues.

The weakening of central government influence in remote areas like Primorski and Kamchatka seems to reinforce the need for provincial or local involvement in fishery diplomacy as well as fishery management. It is not new for representatives of Dalryba to serve on Russian delegations and negotiating teams, but in the past they have usually played a subsidiary or supportive role. It seems likely that provincial and local agencies and enterprises will be able to cope effectively with central roles in international negotiations if officials and diplomats with national experience are made available to them through secondment or other modes of recruitment.

In the Russian Far East, as in most other regions around the world, nongovernmental organizations (NGOs) have emerged as significant and sometimes unwelcome political influences. Most of the Russian NGOs active in a province like Primorski have American and other foreign advisers, and these organizations are mostly funded externally. Given the low level of income for many educated Russians, these NGOs offer a fairly attractive part-time, if not full-time, occupation in fields of expertise such as environmental protection and natural resource management. It is highly probable that the 1990s will witness the growing influence of NGOs of this kind in Russia, perhaps along the lines of North America, Western Europe, and elsewhere. But it remains to be seen whether this is likely to serve as a constraint on formal fishery diplomacy in the Far East. Special interest and other lobbying traditions were never highly institutionalized in Russia during the Soviet period, at least until its final years. But lobbying, community action, and related activities are spreading rapidly through the country, and in the present conditions of widely diffused power and authority, especially in remote areas such as the Far Eastern Region, it seems likely that NGOs will play an increasingly significant role at the periphery of formal Russian fishery policymaking and diplomacy. Indeed they may eventually present a more direct challenge to government authority by conducting an effective campaign of informal diplomacy over certain environmentally sensitive issues, such as choice of gear.

The trend to rapprochement in Northeast Asia and the special problems of the RFE have, in combination, attracted the sympathetic attention of the international community. This has given rise to new, hybrid forms of macroregional networking designed to stimulate ideas for regional cooperation in various sectors, including that of fisheries. It remains to be seen what kind of impact this informal cross-national networking of academics, scientists, and officials will have on formal fishery diplomacy in the North or Northwest Pacific, but it is unlikely to be entirely inconsequential. Normally, the intervention of international groups in an area of diplomatic concern would be perceived as a threat to a foreign ministry's monopoly on such issues, but it is possible that in the decentralized circumstances of fishery management in the RFE, these visitations might be characterized as less a constraint than an opportunity for leverage in the central government.

Finally, formal Russian fishery diplomacy in the Northwest Pacific is seriously constrained by the dispute with Japan over the Kurile Islands, and, of course, by related ocean boundary issues in adjacent waters (Johnston and Valencia 1991:118–21, 172–75). Although Japanese business executives are still the most numerous of all visitors to the cities of the RFE, it appears that this dispute has contributed to the reluctance of the Japanese government to commit itself to large-scale investment in the region and in Siberia farther west.[33]

The problem has not only affected the potential for joint ventures between the two countries but also spilled over to Russia's joint efforts with other states in the region. For example, Japan asked South Korea not to fish in the area under the Korea–Russia fisheries accord. A group of private companies entered into a subsidiary accord opening the zone around the Kurile Islands to Korean fishing vessels for a set fee. Japan has its own accord with Russia under which it pays for fishing rights in the same disputed zone, but the Japanese agreement has a special clause that automatically nullifies it when the four islands are turned over to Japan. Tokyo has asked Seoul to refrain from fishing near the islands, but Seoul government officials have responded negatively, stating that "economics and politics should be treated separately." The three countries eventually reached a basic agreement that Japan would transfer the fishing rights it obtained from Russia in a triangular area southeast of the northern Kurile Islands to South Korea, and that South Korea would give up fishing around the four islands.[34]

Prospects for Regional Cooperation

Objectives

Several kinds of goals might be pursued through regional cooperation, and each has its own precedents and organizational requirements.[35]

To exchange and disseminate scientific and technical information within the region. Data exchange is a task frequently assigned to regional organizations. PICES has a direct concern with research data, since this is the service it was designed to provide to other bodies charged with the responsibility for fishery policy, development, and management. Of the Northeast Asian fishing states, only three—China, Japan, and Russia— were involved in the negotiation of the PICES treaty along with Canada and the United States. One option for data-sharing arrangements in Northeast Asia is to expand PICES to include all the countries that conduct fishing operations in the North Pacific, perhaps including even the extraregional fishing state of Poland. But arguments can be made against creating an unwieldy, pan-regional scientific organization of this kind. Interpersonal trust and professional credibility may be the most important ingredients in a successful data-sharing arrangement, and the nongovernmental network approach may be more beneficial than an all-inclusive PICES forum.[36]

To promote, coordinate, and conduct cooperative research within Northeast Asia and to facilitate research with adjacent and other relevant regions. One of the features of the 1982 UN Convention on the Law of the Sea is the regulatory system for marine scientific research contained in Part XIII. After much controversy, the delegations agreed that research in the EEZ and on the continental shelf may be conducted only with the consent of the coastal state. In these areas adjacent to its coastline, a coastal state may withhold consent to the conduct of a research project of another state or "competent international organization" if that project "is of direct significance for the exploration and exploitation of natural resources." This language reflects and indeed reinforces the reluctance of many countries, especially developing coastal states, to permit foreign research in their offshore waters that might put them at a knowledge disadvantage in the development and management of fishery resources in these areas. Thus one incentive for regional cooperative research arrangements is the existence of high seas (or "commons") areas of unknown resource potential. Although there are still considerable high seas areas in Northeast Asia beyond the limits of national jurisdiction, this may not remain so for long. Nevertheless, most states of the region have an interest in cooperative research as a basis for effective high seas fishery management, particularly of straddling stocks. It is expected that the present limited-membership version of PICES will facilitate experiments in cooperative research within the region. It might also be expected that the nongovernmental Pacific Economic Cooperation Council (PECC) Fisheries Task Force will create research-related linkages between Northeast Asia (or the North Pacific) and adjacent Southeast Asia.[37]

To exchange views on current fishery policy and management issues and developments within Northeast Asia, and to promote and conduct such consultations with adjacent and other relevant regions. Most major marine fisheries are part of a larger marine ecosystem, and thus international in scope, and almost all are international in significance from legal, political, diplomatic, and commercial perspectives. Few of the fundamental issues in fishery policy and management can be confined to the national level of analysis without the risk of serious lacunae and distortions. Even in the age of extended coastal state jurisdiction, most questions of fishery policy and management have an international dimension. And the regional level of consultation is the most convenient level for the exchange of policy and management ideas and proposals.

Since the end of UNCLOS III, most opportunities for relevant "back-channel diplomacy" have been provided by nongovernmental organizations and networks. Given the difficulties of promoting intergovernmental cooperation in Northeast Asia for the fisheries sector, it might be wise for the governments of this region to follow the same course, at least initially, and encourage institutions such as the East-West Center, the United Nations University, and the PECC Fisheries Task Force to organize regular consultative meetings and to coordinate linkages with counterpart officials and specialists in adjacent and other relevant regions, perhaps in cooperation with extraregional networks.[38]

An agenda for such meetings might include such topics as the conditions of access to the EEZ of another state, high seas fishery management issues (such as those affecting driftnetting and straddling stocks), problems associated with joint ventures, opportunities for cooperative management, allegations of illegal fishing and enforcement issues, relevant GATT issues and rulings, and the extraterritorial application of national environmental standards to fishing practices.

To provide fishery development and management assistance within Northeast Asia and to coordinate such assistance to adjacent and other relevant regions. In the context of fishery development and management assistance, the Northeast Asian (or North Pacific) region consists of both contributor and recipient states. Training programs are expensive undertakings, and although private foundations might be expected to provide some support, most funding for this purpose in Northeast Asia will have to come, directly or indirectly, from the governments of the region. Only a small fraction of regional fishery training requirements can be met through long-term academic degree and diploma programs conducted by universities and major oceanographic institutions. Most training of this kind must depend on short-term, intensive, certificate courses of not more than three months.

At present, Northeast Asian trainees participate with trainees from other regions in fishery-related programs offered by institutions as diverse as ESCAP, FAO, International Center for Living Aquatic Resources Management (ICLARM), the International Oceans Institute (IOI), and PECC, and interregional training courses of this kind might be developed further in the coming years through cooperation among other institutions such as the Asian Institute of Technology (AIT), East-West Center, the Southeast Asia Fisheries Development Council (SEAFDEC), the Southeast Asian Program on Ocean Law, Policy and Management, and the United Nations University.

A case could, of course, be made for creating a new, wholly Northeast Asian organization for regional training in the fisheries sector, given the insufficiency of existing training courses, both short-term and long-term, elsewhere in the world. The fact is, however, that training requirements are a "bottomless pit," and training resources are always scarce. It might be more cost-effective for the governments and other institutions of Northeast Asia to avoid the costs of establishing their own institution and to invest instead in the strengthening of existing arrangements.

To harmonize national fishery development and management policies and practices within Northeast Asia. Policy harmonization is, of course, a principal function of an organization committed to regional integration such as the European Union. In rhetoric, if not in substance, it is also an objective of continental organizations such as the Organization of American States and the Organization of African Unity. However, no such regional organization is immediately in prospect for Northeast Asia. Nevertheless, intraregional harmonization of national policy and legislation in selected sectors can be undertaken by less ambitious, consultative networks, such as has been accomplished by the Association of Southeast Asian Nations (ASEAN) for certain states in Southeast Asia and the Nordic Council in Scandinavia and neighboring countries (Denmark, Finland, Iceland, Norway, and Sweden). A similar consultative mechanism for fisheries for the Northeast Asian (or North Pacific) countries is a possibility in the 1990s, given the conflict potential of fishery issues in the post-UNCLOS era (Johnston 1992). Such an initiative would presumably have to be taken by the governments themselves, not least to ensure the effective participation of all relevant ministries and agencies.

To negotiate and conduct cooperative fishery management activities within Northeast Asia (or the North Pacific). "Cooperative fishery management" is a concept that could include virtually every facet of fishery development, management, and conservation: exchange of data, research, surveillance, enforcement, entry limitation policymaking, quota allocation, gear regulation, vessel inspection, joint ventures, and marketing. Intergovernmental cooperation is, of course, more difficult to promote in some of these areas, such as surveillance and enforcement, than in others.

General Options

There are three basic stances available on Northwest Pacific regional cooperation: maintenance of the status quo, acceptance of international trends, and design of a new approach.

Maintenance of the status quo. The existing mix of national regulations and international agreements has survived with minor changes for more than two decades. The lack of diplomatic relations among all fishing nations in the region makes the ambiguity of regulations in the central portions of the seas and the relative certainty of coastal regulations a positive circumstance rather than a negative one. Considerable voluntary restraint is required by all nations fishing in the region for this arrangement to exist, and unquestionably the agreements in the seas impose compromises on all parties which remain irritants of some significance. Further, the status quo may result in resource depletion.

Two factors could destabilize this regime. Probably most important is the question of whether the coastal states in the region desire to develop fisheries beyond current levels. This would entail a reduction of fishing by Japan. A decision to demand exclusive fishing rights for coastal states would involve economic and political relations between themselves and Japan and would not be taken lightly. Furthermore, a coastal state's demand for extended jurisdiction would necessitate either direct negotiations to establish fishing zone boundaries and agreement on regulations or indirect recognition of respective claims. A second destabilizing factor could be entry of another fishing nation such as Hong Kong or Taiwan into the region. Without further definition of national jurisdiction in the area, new entry is possible outside, and even within, the negotiated boundaries.

Acceptance of international trends. Accepting international trends means implementing the fishery provisions of the 1982 UN Convention on the Law of the Sea. The major features of these fishery regulations are that coastal states may establish a 12-nm territorial sea and a 200-nm EEZ within which they regulate fisheries subject to a variety of responsibilities, and that they shall seek to agree with adjacent states on the regulations of shared stocks.

The four major fishing nations in the Northwest Pacific (Russia, North Korea, South Korea, and Japan) are signatories to the Convention. Although none has yet ratified it, their signature is substantial evidence that there is agreement, in principle, on the text. All four have been observed to respect the EEZ claims of other nations outside the region. All have joint ventures or fishing access agreements with other states that attest to this.

Why has there not been a move to implement the Convention in the Sea of Japan? One reason is that the Convention does not *require* states to claim EEZs; it only establishes some parameters to follow for those that wish to do so. Second, declarations would disrupt a delicately balanced fishery regime and replace it with a sensitive and unsteady coastal state relationship. Third, as long as diplomatic relations do not exist between some coastal states, it would be difficult to implement a more satisfactory regulatory regime. Fourth, EEZ declarations, even if limited to the Sea of Japan, would pose substantial problems of precedent for other issues and negotiations in fishery and broader economic and political arenas.

What would coastal states gain from the establishment of EEZs? Extended jurisdiction holds the promise of marginally more catch for Russia and South Korea to be taken from the current harvests by Japan. Japan, however, might institute restrictions on imports, or it might engage in a "fish war" by increasing harvests in the Northwest Pacific or in its own zone which would affect harvests in the Sea of Japan and Sea of Okhotsk. In sum, the benefits to be gained by extended jurisdiction come only through the ability to improve regulatory measures over a much wider area than previously administered. Extended jurisdiction is no panacea for improvement in management.

Design of a Northwest Pacific approach. The Sea of Japan is unique, and the political, economic, and social relationships of the coastal countries are also unique. Possible management responses that move incrementally from the status quo and do not require extension of jurisdiction include modification of the existing arrangements, creation of quadrapartite nongovernmental arrangements, and establishment of a scientific organization.

The present bilateral agreements could be used as a basis for discussing coastal state/distant-water fishing concerns as well as for developing a coordinated approach to improving the scientific basis for regulation. The key element in this arrangement would be the extent to which Japan is willing to accept the role as a "hinge" state on what is likely to be a closing door for its fisheries. Japan would assume the role of information broker and analyst in coordinating international scientific studies. If coastal states with which Japan has fishery agreements agree that Japan should play this role, there can be relatively direct communication concerning all aspects of fishery science and regulation. By providing the hinge-state function, Japan ensures itself continued access to fisheries as compensation for invaluable mediation services. Such a service by Japan could stave off coastal state demands for EEZs. It would also permit communication on fishery regulation matters to be systematic regarding standardization of statistics, coordination of scientific research, delineation of shared stocks, or evaluation of overfishing. Japan could perform a similar hinge-state function with nongovernmental arrangements with a willing North Korea. In the event that Japan is unwilling to perform this role, or this arrangement is unacceptable to any party, another third-party state or entity (e.g., the Indo-Pacific Fisheries Commission, FAO) could be asked to undertake it. Nongovernmental fishery arrangements were instrumental in the development of the China–Japan fishery agreements and have been used with some success by Japan with North Korea and South Korea. They have the advantage of avoiding problems associated with direct government-to-government negotiation, but their ability to foster serious discussions of fishery regulation problems is likely to be limited. In each of the region's fishing nations, there seems to be a dichotomy between the government scientific establishment and academic scientists. This means that those who have the best access to fishery resource data would be least able to divorce themselves from a fixed government position, while those able to maintain an independent posture would have less access to data. In addition, the motivation of representatives of the fishing industry may be difficult to anticipate or control.

Is an organization consisting of the fishing nations in the area a possibility, if its sole function is scientific research? There does not seem to be adequate access of national researchers to the published literature of colleagues within the region. It should be feasible to organize at least an exchange of publications among the principal researchers around the Sea of Japan. The level of scientific capacity in the coastal states is strong and growing. With a comprehensive, focused set of surveys and analyses, much could be learned. FAO regional fishery bodies have done extensive scientific work in areas where international cooperation is difficult. Another approach could be the establishment of a Sea of Japan working group through existing international organizations like the International Oceanographic Commission's WESTPAC. Sea of Japan fishing nations are already members. One advantage of such an arrangement would be the useful collaboration and the addition of capabilities from outside the region to augment existing expertise. It is, however, doubtful that national decisions would be taken based on research only by an outside scientific organization. Nevertheless, fishery resource management requires reliable information on the status of the resources in demand. Moreover, an analysis of the postwar bilateral fishery regimes makes it clear that the parties to those regimes often came up with different and competing resource assessments. This fact alone argues strongly for coordinated efforts at resource studies.

First Steps

Many models of cooperation are available, ranging from the most formal organizations and commissions to hybrids of nongovernmental forums or networks, which offer the advantages of informal back-channel diplomacy. Because of the history of conflict in Northeast Asia, the first stage of Northwest Pacific fishery cooperation might be expected to emerge not directly from formal intergovernmental initiatives, such as treaty negotiations, but from a common willingness to participate in regular informal meetings, which would be, at least initially, the responsibility of a coalition of respected nongovernmental institutions, such as KORDI, the East-West Center, and appropriate universities. Regular meetings of this kind would facilitate the establishment of a network of government officials, scientists, and other experts and eventually provide the opportunity for the governments of the region to proceed to the negotiation of more for-

mal cooperative arrangements and the building of a well-designed regime. Given the socioeconomic dimensions of fishery policy and management (see Glantz 1986), it might be wise to extend the suggested regional
network to representatives of the various sectors of the fishing industry,
the relevant trade unions, and the fishing communities, as well as to academic specialists in the field of ocean development and management, including the law of the sea. Such a network might either be limited to the
four "coastal" fishing states of the Northwest Pacific (Japan, Russia, and
the two Koreas) or extend to all states with fishery interests in the North
Pacific, thus including Canada, China, Poland, Taiwan, and the United
States. Ideally the network should be broadly conceived, so that high seas
as well as EEZ fishery issues of the day can become a regular focus of discussion. In fact, an informal North Pacific forum for these nine fishing
states would represent a "regularization" of the two private meetings
held in Victoria, B.C., Canada in 1990 and 1993, organized and hosted by
the Centre for Asia-Pacific Initiatives of the University of Victoria in partnership with the School for Marine Affairs of the University of Washington. The problems of the North Pacific region would be open for much
more specific analysis and back-channel diplomacy than is possible in
more broadly based forums such as the PECC Fisheries Task Force, which
encompasses four marine regions: the Southwest Pacific, the Latin American Pacific region, and Southeast Asia as well as the North Pacific. The
uniregional focus of the suggested network would make it more similar to
SEAPOL, which has served Southeast Asia for over a decade.

The comparison with SEAPOL raises the question whether it would be
a mistake in the 1990s, in the age of integrated ocean or coastal management,[39] to establish for the North Pacific a network limited to the fisheries
sector. In its early years SEAPOL was dominated by law-of-the-sea specialists, consistent with SEAPOL's original purpose of examining the
problems associated with the implementation of the UN Convention on
the Law of the Sea in the ASEAN region. In recent years SEAPOL's mandate has expanded functionally (as well as geographically) beyond the
various areas that make up the modern law of the sea to include cognate
fields such as coastal management, maritime security, and relevant aspects of trade and environmental diplomacy (e.g., GATT, UNCED). Given
the widely accepted need for an integrative approach to ocean and coastal
management, it might be anomalous to bring together North Pacific individuals who share a common expertise in fishery development, management, and diplomacy but may lack specialized knowledge in cognate
fields such as marine pollution, wetlands management, mangrove protection, maritime security, international environmental law and diplomacy,
international trade law and policy, and the law of the sea.

Perhaps the most obvious beneficiary of such a network, especially if it encompassed the larger North Pacific region, would be the Russian Far East. An informal forum of the kind envisaged would offer maximum flexibility for RFE specialists who have to contend with severe constraints on fishery development, management, and diplomacy. The informality of the proposed network—the "North Pacific Forum for Fishery and Ocean Management" (NORPOM?)—should also appeal to North Koreans and Taiwanese, who have often found themselves excluded from formal talks and negotiations for political or diplomatic reasons and yet have an important role to play in fishery-related matters.

At first impression, Japan might be likely to hesitate before becoming involved in a North Pacific network, even an informal one. It might seem to threaten their informational hegemony in the Northwest Pacific. Yet many Japanese may now be ready to accept that the days of wholly bilateral fishery diplomacy in the Northwest Pacific are numbered, as the pressures mount for negotiated linkages between EEZ and high seas fishery management and for the integration of fishery and other facets of coastal management. The old stability derived from the system of bilateral fishing arrangements for the Northwest Pacific may have to be replaced by a new stability offered by a realignment of long-term fishery and related ocean management interests in the larger region of the North Pacific. After all, Japanese scientists participating in PICES will be pressed to make more of their fishery research data available to other members of that North Pacific organization. With an eye on long-term advantage for a country required to plan for a downscaling of its fishing industry, the Japanese may be attracted to the prospect of acquiring a leadership role in the development of an ocean regime in the North Pacific. They too may accept a NORPOM-type initiative as an acceptable first step toward that end.

Notes

1. For a detailed study of regional arrangements negotiated up to the end of the 1970s in fishery management and cognate fields, see Johnston and Enomoto (1981).

2. "The exercise of flag-stage enforcement jurisdiction by non-coastal states in the EEZ is compatible with the vesting of "sovereign" rights for the purpose of ... managing the natural resources" of the area, as prescribed in Article 56(1)(a) of the Convention.

3. "Soviet Union: Raising Standards to Forge Trading Links," *Fishing News International* 30 (August 1991):8. The industry fought a long battle with the government to retain hard currency earnings to pay for the modernization of its operations. It was recently rewarded by a decree signed by President Yeltsin allowing companies to retain 90 percent of proceeds from exports, but since the state no longer pays for overseas fishing licences, which are required to enable the Russian fleet to operate in foreign fishing zones, this costly burden falls on each enterprise. In Au-

gust 1991 the Russian industry faced a choice between seeking huge state subsidies or writing off one-third of its fishing vessels, 90 percent of its factory ships, 60 percent of its refrigerated carriers, and over 50 percent of its salvage tugboats. Over 1.2 billion rubles was needed for repairs, and national credit allowances had been exhausted. Correspondence from Peter Christiansen to Peter Bird Martin, Institute of Current World Affairs (hereafter "Christiansen Letters"), 10 Nov. 1992, p. 4. When devalued rubles could no longer buy ships built in other countries, Russia turned to the West for assistance to finance the construction of vessels in Western shipyards; "First Ships in L360 m. Contract—as Russia Turns to the West," *Fishing News International* 30 (November 1991):30. Russia continues to seek foreign investment and technology to its fishing industry; "Show to Help Russian Processors," *Fishing News International* 31 (March 1992):4.

4. Dalryba's fleet includes crab processing factories and transport and factory ships as well as fishing vessels; see "Soviet Union: Raising Standards."

5. Christiansen Letters, 10 Nov. 1992, p. 5.

6. "Soviet Union: Raising Standards."

7. "Russia Frees Fleet," *Fishing News International* 30 (October 1991):1.

8. On the new agency's functions, see Christiansen Letters, 10 Nov. 1992.

9. Korelsky believes that without state support progress for the industry is not very hopeful because of the debt burden accumulated over the years. Since state loans are no longer easily available, it must be hoped that the new "free market" policy will motivate the industry to find new credit lines to finance future operations and fleet modernization. See "Russia Frees Fleet."

10. It is difficult to judge which institutions and levels of authority have effective control over fishery policy and management. The situation seems to be in flux. Dalryba may be gaining in influence by reason of revenues that can be generated out of joint ventures negotiated under its auspices, but local "mafias" are powerful both inside and outside the official political system. Everyone, it seems, is making deals, with few if any constraints. Christiansen Letters, 5 Oct. 1992, p. 2.

11. The situation in Kamchatka is a good example of the situation in Far East fisheries as a whole. Kamchatka now has more political autonomy, freedom of economic action, and control over regional natural resources than ever before, but these freedoms are a result of degeneration of central authority and are not particularly well organized. There is a workmanlike group of administrators laboring in Petrapavlovsk-Kamchatsky for local political autonomy, economic freedom, and control over resources. There are now 4,000 registered private enterprises in the Kamchatka region which employ roughly 17 percent of Kamchatka's workforce. The changes due to privatization are enormous and show no signs of slowing down. Christiansen Letters, 5 Nov. 1992, p. 8. Kamchatrybprom's remaining industrial assets are being privatized, including the Tin Can Factory, the Fish Cannery, and many of the distribution networks, shops and material bases Kamchatrybprom once controlled. Unfortunately, for some of Kamchatrybprom's fishing collectives in the more remote regions of Kamchatka, privatization is harder than expected. In Ossora, a one-factory town on the Bering Sea coast, nobody has worked for over four months.

In Petropavlovsk there were five major fishing enterprises: Okeanribflot, Rybkholodflot, Tralflot, the Lenin Kolkhoz, and UPF-KMPO. However, with privatization, change is rapid and there are only three left intact. JPF-KMPO has been replaced by AO (Aktsionernoye Ob'yedineniye, or Stock Company), one of the economic structures permitted under the new system). Tralflot recently privatized and will become a "federal trust" with 25 percent of its shares to be distributed free to its workers. Lenin Kolkhoz may privatize in the near future. Christensen Letters, 5 Oct. 1992, p. 2. Ruble vouchers are being issued to citizens to allow them the opportunity to become stockholders in fisheries. Also, private citizens can form their own fisheries companies by investing the ten-thousand ruble vouchers. Although the actual cash value of the vouchers is about 233 rubles—roughly 2 percent of their declared value—the hope is that once private persons combine their capital, small businesses can get a start. One official in the Kamchatka Regional Anti-Monopoly Committee believes that the vouchers will especially help the salmon industry in Kamchatka, which consists mostly of small producers.

There are now more than fifty foreign vessels in Kamchatka's waters. Christiansen Letters, 20 Jan. 1993, p. 1. Unofficial estimates put the cost of fish sold out of the RFE at one-third the world market price. Kamchatka fishing enterprises produce substandard products in outdated processing plants, hence the low market price; ibid. p. 4. Because the RFE does not have modern processing plants, fish caught there are shipped elsewhere for processing. The deep-water fishing branch of Kamchatrybprom ships the cod it catches to Thailand for processing. The finished product, labeled "Product of Thailand," is then sold in North America. Arctic Alaska Fisheries Corporation, the largest U.S. fishing and at-sea processing company operating in the U.S. Northwest, is expanding its fishing and fish processing operations into the RFE. It purchases fish in Russia and ships it to China, where it is filleted and frozen before being transported to the United States; "Arctic Alaska Looks to New Waters," *Fishing News International* 31 (April 1992):32. For the people of Kamchatka, this means they cannot purchase fresh, high-quality fish, despite their fishery-oriented economy. There have been recent hopes that this situation might change. A fish processing plant designed to produce high-quality value-added products from Russian-caught groundfish and crab was proposed in Kamchatka by a U.S. company. Production of filleted products from white fish such as pollock and canned products from crab were under discussion. The president of the Kamchatka Trawling and Refrigerated Fish Co. (VTRF) planned to have the shore-based plant ready for operations by the end of 1993.

Rybkholodflot is a deep-water fishing enterprise, which, like other fishing enterprises in Kamchatka, assumes an entire range of "social services" such as housing and medical care for its workers. Unfortunately, the percentage of privatized housing in Petropavlovsk-Kamchatsky is minimal, and while the workers' salaries doubled, it was at the expense of housing. In 1991 there were 1,200 people in line for housing, which represents one-fifth of the entire collective; Christiansen Letters, 10 Nov. 1992, p. 7. The solution has been to allocate money into a fund for construction of housing near the city air-transit station. Any worker who lives in that building will have ten years to pay off the cost of his or her apartment to the fleet.

12. FBIS-EAS, 29 October 1992, p. 10.

13. FBIS-EAS, 16 March 1992, p. 3.

14. For a development of these views, see Saguirian (1992).

15. "Drift-net Pirates Could Face Jail," *Fishing News International* 31 (July 1992):4.

16. "Russia Says U.S. Ships Poaching," *Fishing News International* 32 (February 1993):48.

17. FBIS-EAS, 26 October 1992, p. 5.

18. FBIS-EAS, 21 April 1993, p. 21, and 26 April 1993, p. 39; *RFE Update,* August 1993, p. 3; *IBRU Boundary and Security Bulletin,* April 1992, p. 63.

19. FBIS-EAS, 24 February 1993, p. 26, and 26 August 1993, p. 19.

20. FBIS-EAS, 9 March 1993, pp. 24–25.

21. *New York Times,* 1 August 1993, p. 9; FBIS-EAS, 21 April 1993, p. 26.

22. FBIS-EAS, 21 April 1993, p. 26, and 26 April 1993, p. 39; *RFE Update,* August 1993, p. 3.

23. FBIS-EAS, 6 August 1993, p. 19, and 26 August 1993, p. 19.

24. FBIS-EAS, 14 June 1993, p. 8.

25. *RFE Update,* August 1993, p. 3; *IBRU Boundary and Security Bulletin,* October 1993, p. 46.

26. *IBRU Boundary and Security Bulletin,* October 1993, p. 46; *New York Times,* 1 August 1993, p. 9.

27. FBIS-EAS, 6 August 1993, p. 19, and 10 August 1993, p. 23.

28. FBIS-EAS, 6 August 1993, p. 19, and 10 September 1993, p. 33.

29. FBIS-EAS, 29 October 1993, pp. 21–22, and 16 November 1993, pp. 30–31; *Greenwire,* 7 December 1993, p. 11.

30. FBIS-USR, 1 December 1993, p. 92.

31. FBIS-EAS, 22 December 1993, p 33.

32. For discussion and further development of this argument, see Saguirian (1992:5–7).

33. A Japanese fishing firm recently suffered the negative consequences of rejecting a government request to reconsider its plans for a tuna joint fishing venture with a Russian partner in waters within 200 nm of the disputed islands. The Japanese Fisheries Agency wanted Etorofu Fisheries to scrap the project and insisted it would be politically undesirable for the joint venture to operate in waters around the islands. Etorofu Fisheries declared it would go ahead with the project, claiming the joint venture had been approved by Sakhalin provincial authorities, which administer the disputed islets. Etorofu Fisheries planned to remit its $30,000 contribution to the joint venture through its ventures in China or Malaysia and procure fishing boats in Sakhalin to engage in operations in waters around the islands. In response, the Fisheries Agency warned that remittance through an overseas joint venture without government permission would constitute a violation of Japan's Foreign Exchange Control Law. See FBIS-EAS, 23 September 1992, p. 9.

34. FBIS-EAS, 10 April 1992, p. 24, and 1 June 1992, p. 4.

35. For an elaboration of the following points, see Johnston (1993).

36. The PICES treaty, negotiated in 1991, creates a forum for scientists and technical experts to meet on a regular basis for the exchange and evaluation of fishery and related data and for the promotion and coordination of cooperative research. It is expected that PICES experts will participate in a technical, as distinct from representative, capacity.

37. PECC has recently concluded a preliminary cooperative research project between Southeast Asia and the South Pacific, which seems to have established that the tuna resources of these two regions belong to the same biological population.

38. Interregional networking has been the purpose of several programs such as the PECC Fisheries Task Force, which provides a linkage among the fishery specialists in Northeast Asia, Southeast Asia, the South Pacific, and the Central Eastern Pacific. Interregional networking is now about to be attempted across a much broader spectrum of ocean affairs, under the auspices of the Southeast Asian Program on Ocean Law, Policy and Management (SEAPOL). In December 1994, SEAPOL will be organizing a triregional conference designed to bring together the ocean law, policy, and management specialists of Northeast Asia, Southeast Asia, and the South Pacific.

39. For a discussion of these and other cognate terms, see Lévy (1993).

References

Carroz, Jean E. 1984. "Institutional Aspects of Fishery Management under the New Regime of the Oceans." *San Diego Law Review* 21.

Cicin-Sain, Bilancia, and Robert W. Knecht. 1989. "The Emergence of a Regional Ocean Regime in the South Pacific." *Ecology Law Quarterly* 16.

Doulman, David J. 1988. "In Pursuit of Fisheries Cooperation: The South Pacific Forum Fisheries Agency." *University of Hawaii Law Review* 10.

Glantz, Michael H. 1986. "Man, State, and Fisheries: An Inquiry into Some Societal Constraints that Affect Fisheries Management." *Ocean Development and International Law* 17.

Gurish, J. A. 1992. "Pressure to Reduce Bycatch on the High Seas: An Emerging International Norm." *Tulane Environmental Law Journal* 5.

Johnston, Douglas M. 1965. *International Law of Fisheries: A Framework for Policy-Oriented Inquiries.* New Haven: Yale University Press.

Johnston, Douglas M. 1990. "The Driftnetting Problems in the Pacific Ocean: Legal Considerations and Diplomatic Options." *Ocean Development International Law* 21.

Johnston, Douglas M. 1992. *Fishery Politics and Diplomacy in the North Pacific: New Sources of Instability.* York University, Centre for International and Strategic Studies, Working Paper no. 7.

Johnston, Douglas M. 1993. "Regional Fishery Arrangements: Options for Northeast Asia." In Hyung Tack Huh, Chang Il Zhang, and Mark J. Valencia, eds., *Proceedings of the International Conference on East Asian Seas: Cooperative Solutions to Transnational Issues.* Korea Ocean Research Institute and the East-West Center.

Johnston, Douglas M., and Larry Enomoto. 1981. "Regional Approaches to the Protection and Conservation of the Marine Environment." In Douglas M. Johnston, ed., *The Environmental Law of the Sea.* Gland, Switzerland: International Union for Conservation of Nature and Natural Resources.

Johnston, Douglas M., and Mark J. Valencia. 1991. *Pacific Ocean Boundary Problems: Status and Solutions.* Dordrecht: Martinus Nijhoff.

Koers, Albert W. 1973. *International Regulation of Marine Fisheries: A Study of Regional Fisheries Organizations*. Surrey: Fishing News Books.

Lévy, Jean-Pierre. 1993. "A National Ocean Policy: An Elusive Quest?" *Marine Policy* 17.

Mirovitskaya, Natalia S., and J. Christopher Haney. 1992. "Fisheries Exploitation as a Threat to Environmental Security." *Marine Policy* 16.

Saguirian, Artemy A. 1992. "Russia and Some Pending Law of the Sea Issues in the North Pacific: Controversies over High Seas Fisheries Regulation and Delimitation of Marine Space." *Ocean Development and International Law* 23.

Wright, Andrew, and David J. Doulman. 1991. "Drift-net Fishing in the South Pacific: From Controversy to Management." *Marine Policy* 15.

Appendix 1: World Bank Loan Policy and Russian Federation Petroleum

William T. Onorato

In March 1993 the World Bank's Executive Directors approved a new policy under which qualified countries in transition to a market economy may be granted a waiver for up to five years of the Bank's standard negative pledge provision, thereby making investment in Russian resource development more attractive to both the Bank and international investors. The first document in this appendix in an extract from the statement of the Bank's negative pledge policy. The second document is an extract from an internal Bank memorandum, prepared as part of the evaluation of an application for such a waiver from the Russian Federation, which reviews current and projected petroleum exploration, development, and production arrangements with international oil companies.

World Bank Negative Pledge Policy (December 1993)

Loan and Guarantee Agreements of the International Bank for Reconstruction and Development (the Bank) include a provision on negative pledge, which is contained in Section 9.03 of the Bank's "General Conditions Applicable to Loan and Guarantee Agreements Dated January 1, 1985" (the General Conditions).

This provision provides very important protection both to member countries and to the Bank. It is clearly not in the long-term interests of member countries that their critical export earnings be mortgaged for extended periods in order to meet current needs. For its part, the Bank cannot accept that public resources potentially essential to the servicing of its external debt be exclusively mortgaged to other lenders, thereby relegating the Bank to a secondary level of preference. The negative pledge provision thus plays a vital role in protecting both member countries and the Bank against the commitment of governmental resources, or the use of governmental authority to mobilize resources, which result in creditors having direct and preferential access to export earnings set aside in off-shore escrow accounts, or any other form of lien which enables such creditors to obtain foreign exchange to service their loans in preference to the Bank. The Bank strongly adheres to this fundamental policy.

Nonetheless, the Bank recognizes the special, albeit temporary, dilemma faced by countries which are in active throes of transition to market economies but are currently in a situation where the vast majority of their economically significant assets are still owned directly by the government, political or administrative subdivisions of the government, or entities controlled by or operating for the account or benefit of the government, all of which fall under the purview of the Bank's negative pledge clause. At this time, the perception is that foreign investment, and particularly loans from private sources to enterprises in countries in transition, may be difficult to attract on an unsecured basis. To the extent that this perception is accurate, it is clear that member countries which borrow from the Bank may find it extremely difficult to enter into financial transactions with other foreign lenders, particularly private sources, if they grant the Bank equal and ratable security.

The Bank remains firmly committed to the view that the medium/long term solution to the investment problem being faced by countries in transition lies in the strenuous implementation of a program of structural change, including satisfactory macroeconomic policies, supported by the Bank, along with the establishment of an appropriate legal framework and stable investment conditions.

However, in order to address, during the temporary period of time lag referred to above, the critical need for an immediate stimulus to private investment/lending, the Bank's Executive Directors have decided to grant to eligible countries a waiver of the Bank's negative pledge clause in respect of specific investment projects based on the following criteria:

Country Eligibility. In response to a request from a member, a waiver would be granted in respect of loans to borrowers within a country where income producing public assets constitute a predominant share of total assets, provided that a program of structural change described below has been decided upon by the country and is supported by the Bank. The eligibility of a country for the wavier would be subject to approval of the Executive Directors following a recommendation by Management. The waive would be given legal effect by an exchange of letters between the member and the Bank. Country eligibility will be assessed on the following basis:

(a) Share of Income Producing Assets. A country would be considered eligible for the waiver provided that at least 75 percent of income producing assets are in the public sector. The estimation of the share of income producing assets in the public sector would be based on the best available information and would include all segments of the economy.

(b) Program of Structural Change. The key elements of structural change that would be expected to characterize the economies in transition are: (i) diversification from the public to the private sector including an appropriate privatization program; and (ii) a shift from an administered system to a market economy. Bank staff would make an assessment that a program is in place to achieve structural change, including in the key sectors of the economy that would underpin long-term creditworthiness. The country assistance strategy and lending program would be geared to support such a program of structural change. In addition, to benefit from the waiver the country should, in the judgment of the Bank, be experiencing improvement in its macroeconomic situation and the waiver of the negative pledge would be deemed to further contribute to the accomplishment of the above goals.

Time Period. Eligible countries would be granted a waiver under the proposed policy for an initial period of 2 years. Subject to review by the Executive Directors at the end of the first year, the waiver could be extended for a further period of 2 years This would provide potential lenders reasonable assurance that the waiver would be available after completing the lengthy process of developing and negotiating a complex project, while affording the Bank the opportunity to reassess whether the country's economic policies and circumstances remain consistent with the objectives of the waiver. All eligible transactions signed during the waiver period would be covered for the full maturity of the liens established. The review would focus on whether the implementation of the program of structural change, including the foreign investment framework and the privatization of the economy, is broadly appropriate, as well as the use of waivers to date.

Coverage. The waiver would be granted with respect to any lien to secure repayment of external debt incurred in connection with the financing of the acquisition, construction or development of any properties related to a project (a "project financing"), provided that (a) the public assets to which such lien applies are (i) properties which are the subject of such project financing,[1] (ii) revenues or claims which arise from the operation, exploitation, failure to meet specifications, failure to complete, sale or loss of, or damage to, such properties, or (iii) shares of a special purpose project entity established for the purpose of carrying out the project in question; and (b) the project financing is supported by a feasibility study prepared by competent independent experts which concludes that the project would generate foreign exchange in excess of the amount necessary to service the external debt incurred in connection with the project; provided in all cases that the original maturity of the loan is not less than 5 years, and that the lien does not permit the accumulation of more than 12 months' projected debt service obligations in any related escrow accounts. The lenders may also require reserve accounts to be established to sequester appropriate amounts of project revenues as provision for future operating expenditures, and other project contingencies. This would be limited to the equivalent of an additional 6 months' projected debt service obligations, consistent with normal commercial practices. The five year floor on loan maturities would enable a wide range of project finance to be covered by the waiver. In addition, the following conditions must be met:

(a) the lender does not have alternative recourse[2] for repayment of the loan, interest and other charges through (i) the guarantee or any other form of full faith and credit backing of the country of the borrower or of any of its sub-divisions or of any public authority, institution or company therein, or (ii) investment insurance or any form of third party indemnity, undertaking or guarantee, excepting that provided by a private source or by an official agency which requires the establishment of the lien as a condition of its support;

(b) the lender is private in character, i.e., an individual, a privately owned corporation or a publicly owned corporation which operates for a commercial purpose such as publicly owned commercial banks and investment companies. Liens created in favor of public policy agencies such as official bilateral aid agencies, official agencies and multilateral development finance institutions are therefore excluded from the scope of this waiver, except that (i) the waiver would also extend to liens created in respect of loans made by a multilateral development finance institution which is unable to obtain a government guarantee in respect of the loan due to legal restrictions or the unavailability of such guarantee for reasons beyond its control; (ii) an official agency which has guaranteed a loan by a private lender may benefit under a lien in favor of the latter by subrogation of rights; and (iii) the waiver would also extend to liens created in respect of direct lending, informal cofinancing arrangements with private lenders, of an official agency which shall not obtain a government guarantee, provided that such private lenders are contributing the majority of the total funds provided under such cofinancing arrangements; and

(c) the Bank is not a cofinancier of the investment project concerned. Where the Bank is cofinancing an investment project it is generally its practice to share, equally and ratably, in any escrow or other security arrangements, so that the Bank is not in a subordinated position relative to such debt.

Notes

Copyright to this policy statement and the following background note is retained by the World Bank.

1. Section 9.03(c)i of the General Conditions already permits liens to be created on property at the time of purchase thereof solely as security for payment of the purchase price of such property or as security for payment of debt incurred for the purpose of financing the purchase price of such property.

2. Where the lender does have recourse to another source but this is limited as to the amount recoverable or as to the risks or period of activity covered, the waiver would be applicable with respect to any claim not covered thereby.

Background Note on Russian Federation Joint Ventures with International Oil Companies (extract, July 1993)

Inherent in exploration, development, and production arrangements between host countries and international oil companies (IOCs) are the latter's requirement for and opportunity to supply significant quantities of petroleum exploration and production hardware, equipment, technical services and expertise to these new operations. Under the proposed negative pledge waiver for Russia, it should be considerably easier and more economically attractive to supply such goods and services, taking adequate security for same, insofar as such operations produce incremental extra production to service the supply debt.

In addition to such new exploration and development opportunities, there are currently in Russia more than 25,000 idle oil wells, accounting for 15% of the total, which have been shut-in due to lack of equipment, spares and other technical reasons. Concurrently, there is also the problem of significant numbers of underperforming wells due to outdated equipment and lack of spare parts for routine maintenance of enhanced recovery facilities, such as gas lift compressor stations. Thus there are also significant needs and opportunities for supply of goods and services to upgrade oil production facilities with modern oilfield technology and hardware so as to generate significant quantities of incremental extra oil, both for domestic consumption and for export.

To underscore the increasing number of such opportunities, it appears from data collected from available Industry sources and publications (principally *Petroconsultants International Oil Letter*) that, in 1993 alone, the following new petroleum arrangements have been negotiated/concluded/ commenced and the following new exploration/development acreage has been offered by organizations/units of the Russian Federation:

1. Symskaya Exploration has signed a joint venture (JV) production-sharing agreement (PSA) with regional authorities Yeniseyneftegasgeologia and Yeniseygeophysica for rights to explore, develop and produce hydrocarbons over a 4,500 km^2 tract in Krasnoyarsk Krai. The acreage is located in easternmost Western Siberia. Subject to approval of Russian and regional authorities, the license agreements calls for Symskaya to in-

vest \$12 million over five years, to include \$1 million during the first twelve months. Full term of the PSA is 25 years. Symskaya will be allowed to recover costs from an 80% share of production after payment of an 8% royalty. The remaining 20% of production will be split on a sliding scale tied to output levels. Symskaya Exploration is 80% owned by Equity Oil Co. of Salt Lake City, U.S., and 20% by Coastline Exploration Inc;

2. The administration of Tomsk Oblast and Tomskneftegazgeologia have extended the bid deadline for 20 exploration blocks in the Tomsk region. The 20 blocks in the Tomsk bid round range in size from 2,000 to 6,000 km^2. Contracts specify an initial five-year exploration period and a 20-year exploitation term. Royalty has been set at 12.5% with a 32% profits tax. Tomskneftegazgeologia will be allowed to associate as a JV partner, taking up to a maximum 25% interest;

3. Russian authorities have released details from a recently completed feasibility study by a five-company IOC consortium on development of the Pil'tun-Astokh and Lun'skoye fields, offshore Sakhalin Island. The study proposes production start-up during 4th Qtr. 1995. Peak output from the two fields is forecast at some 200,000 BOPD oil/liquids and 1.55 BCFD gas. Construction of a 4–6 million tonnes/yr LNG plant is recommended to handle exports. Regional domestic demand is expected to require 175–300 BCF/yr from 1996, with much of the gas piped from Sakhalin to Khabarovsk. Partners in the consortium are Marathon (operator), Mitsui, McDermott, Mitsubishi and Shell;

4. Saudi-based Nimir Petroleum has acquired an unspecified interest in the Petrosakh JV which is undertaking development of the Okruzhnoye oilfield, onshore eastern Sakhalin Island. Original Petrosakh partners included Sakhalin industry group Sameko, Smith Energy of the U.S., Labrador Oil and other smaller interests. Prior to Nimir's participation, Petrosakh was capitalized at \$46 million. Sakhalin sources report Okruzhnoye reserves at 58–73 million bbl. Development plans call for plateau production of 20,000 BOPD beginning in 1994. Construction of a 4,000 BOPD mini-refinery is reportedly planned, and work on a topping plant at Okruzhnoye has already begun;

5. Privately held Israeli consulting group Geos Ltd. will proceed with formation of a JV with the Tatarstan State company, Tatneft, to delineate and develop nine select oil fields within a 7,000 km^2 area in the northwest part of the republic, near Kazan. The Geos/Tatneft JV will presumably also have exploration rights over the area. Twelve months earlier, Geos reached agreement with Tatneft to undertake a development feasibility study over an 11,800 km^2 area. The study area was said to encompass 57 small fields/oil pools with an aggregate reserve base reported to total 330 million bbl recoverable. The nine fields targeted for joint venture development are said to hold reserves of 250 million bbl of recoverable oil;

6. Shell will reportedly join Saga Petroleum in an agreement of intention with proposed Russian JV partners Severgazprom, Arkhangelskgeologia and Ukhtaneftegasgeologia to develop known fields in the Timan-Pechora Basin, Nenets Okrug, Arkhangelsk Oblast. Saga's earlier negotiated preliminary agreement called for equal interest participation between foreign and domestic firms. Fields targeted by Saga/Shell and the Russian partners include the Mid and North Kharlaga oil accumulations and the Layavosh, Vasilkov, Kumzha and Korovin gas/condensate plays. Plans call for the completion of feasibility studies, an environmental impact assessment and formal agreement on JV terms during 1993. As part of that effort, a delineating well is planned on the Mid Kharlaga field;

7. A number of large IOCs are expected to submit applications in a competitive bid round covering at least six known fields and one exploration area in the Khanty-Mansiysk region of Western Siberia. In-place oil in the six nominated fields is estimated at 33 billion bbl. A preliminary tender call was issued in Moscow; an official call followed during presentations in Houston and London. Among the approximately 40 companies which have expressed serious interest are Amoco, British Gas, BP, Exxon, OMV, Occidental, Repsol and Shell. The inventory of Khanty-Mansiysk area fields includes Khulturskoye, Polun'yakh, Priobskoye, the southern portion of Prirazlomnoye, Salym Yu, Slavinskoye, Symor'yakh, Tal'nikovoye, Taylakovskoye, Verkhiviy Salym, and Zapadnyy Salym, encompassing the Vadelyp sector. Several Western oil companies known to have undertaken feasibility studies on certain of these fields are likely to be well-placed for eventual award. The formal tender process is intended to formalize the assignment of development rights;

8. "Blue Kama," an equal interest JV between Swiss-based Panoco and the Tatarstan State enterprise, Tatneft, began first oil production from a 3,175 km² area near the city of Nurlat during April 1993. Phase 1 operations involve 35 well completions on one or more of seven known fields within the southern Tatarstan contract area. Operating with a reported charter capital of $112 million, Blue Kama is expected to invest up to $1.2 billion over the next 10–14 years for full-scale development of the Aksubayevo-Mokshinskoye, Cheremusha, Kiyazli, Kutush, Mel'nikovskoye, Starokadeyevskoye and Yenoruskin heavy oil fields. Up to 2,770 wells are proposed to raise output to an average 150,000 BOPD. Blue Kama will export its share of production through cost recovery; thereafter each partner will be free to market its net share of crude produced. Blue Kama expects that a portion of near-term capital expenditures will be used to fund construction of a 93-km pipeline from the fields to an oil treatment center at Almatyevsk. Tentative future plans may also include construction of a small refinery to meet domestic demand for products in Tatarstan;

9. Novosibgeolkom, the regional oil and gas enterprise of Novosibirsk Oblast in Western Siberia, is proposing to offer the Verkhne-Tarskoye oil field for international tender. Originally discovered in 1971, the field is located in the Mezhovskiy High area of the Western Siberia Basin some 400 km west of Tomsk town. Only limited test production has ever been attempted. Based on seismic evaluations and a minimum of 23 known wells on the structure, productive limits are estimated at 44 km^2 with recoverable reserves of about 180 million bbl. Novosibgeolkom is apparently planning to undertake the tender without external assistance. Details of the offering are awaited;

10. The "Komi Quest" joint venture has boosted incremental oil production from the Vozey field complex in the Komi Republic from 1,500 BOPD at year-end 1992 to some 3,000 BOPD currently. Plans call for workover and recompletion of 62 additional wells during 1993, allowing production to rise to some 20,000–30,000 BOPD by year-end. Plans also call for Komi Quest to begin delineation drilling during 4th Qtr. 1993; the number of wells has not been reported. Average well workover costs are put at $80,000–$100,000 each. Cost per bbl of incremental oil produced is estimated at $12.10; the figure include $3/bbl production costs, $2/bbl to cover a 10% royalty, $5/bbl in oil export taxes and $1.60/bbl for pipeline tariffs. Quest Petroleum, a 50% partner in the joint venture, is a German-based consortium which includes Mannai Corp. of Qatar (62.5%), Callina of Australia (22.9%) and Star Valley Resources of Canada (9.2%); remaining shareholders are unknown. The Russian partners in the Komi Quest JV include Komineft and Usinsk NDOU (25% each);

11. Texaco has firmed up its first production venture in the Russian Federation. A recently concluded agreement with the Western Siberian operating association Sutorminskneft involves a risk/service contract on the Sutormin field in the northern Tyumen region. Two rigs will be utilized for workover and reactivation of up to 143 wells on the one billion bbl (recoverable) field. According to Texaco, Sutormin output is currently averaging about 140,000 BOPD of 35° API sweet crude despite the fact that some 40% of the wells on the field are idle. Texaco expects to boost output by some 15,000–20,000 BOPD over the next two years. Texaco indicates it will receive dollar payments to cover project costs/expenses. Texaco has also secured oil export guarantees from the government and "will receive a share of the earnings from the project that will be calculated separately from Russian taxes, tariffs and other duties." Sutorminskneft will presumably be responsible for payment of all royalties, taxes and tariffs including those on exports;

12. Texaco continues to negotiate for exploration and production rights in the Timan-Pechora Basin, west of the Yamal Peninsula, in Western Siberia. In addition, the U.S.-based IOC also awaits final government approval

for a JV PSA with Arkhangelskgeologia for separate operations elsewhere in northern Timan-Pechora. Additional Western partners are sought for the latter project, details of which remain sketchy. Identified but as yet undeveloped oil fields are thought to be involved;

13. Calgary Overseas Development Company of Canada reports that its Western Siberia operating unit, Neft Services Ltd., is achieving notable success with a well workover program on the Vat'yegan field in the Tyumen region. Through year-end 1992, 250 wells on the field had been reworked, increasing Vat'yegan production from 43,000 to 210,000 BOPD. Four rigs remain active, servicing an average 35–40 wells per month. Plans call for reworking up to 500 wells on Vat'yegan. Neft Services' success at Vat'yegan has prompted an expansion of workover operations to the Povkhovskoye field, where 1,000 of 2,200 wells are idle. One rig has been activated and a second is mobilizing from Canada to Kogolym. Once both rigs are active, an average of 15–20 well workovers are planned per month. Several service companies have been subcontracted by Neft Services for work on the two fields, including Atlas Wireline Services, Baker Hughes Tubular Services, Beta Well Services and Reda Pump;

14. A recently established private Russian stock company identified as "Shelf" and based in Okha, Sakhalin Island, is prepared to become a new regional operator. Near-term operations by the company will reportedly include the development of three marginal oil discoveries onshore Sakhalin Island which are estimated capable of producing a combined 6,000 BOPD. One of the projects will involve development of a deeper oil pool beneath the largely depleted Okha field; efforts will be undertaken in conjunction with state enterprise Okhaneftegaz. Shelf has also identified four undrilled onshore prospects it would like to test in the current year;

15. Snyder Oil Corporation affiliate Lomax Petroleum, Snyder's SOCO International unit, and Territorial Resources Inc. have joined forces with an unnamed foreign oil company and regional Russian operator Permneft to establish the "New Horizon" joint venture. New Horizon has executed a letter of intent to develop the shut-in Kustovsk field located west of the Ural Mountains near the city of Perm. Sixteen delineation wells have been drilled on Kustovsk to date, establishing the existence of some 40 million bbl of recoverable reserves. The field is located less than 4 km from a major oil pipeline; no specific development plans have yet been announced;

16. Total and regional JV partner Komineft report "encouraging results" from ongoing tests on the Khar'yaga field. Current plants call for Total and Komineft to develop two of seven known "sectors" of the Khar'yaga field complex in Nenets Okrug. In the present Khar'yaga draft agreement, the royalty would be set at 5% until cumulative production exceeds 10 million tons; 7% for cumulative production of 10–20 million tons; 9% for 20–30 million tons; and 11% when cumulative output exceeds 30

million tons (220.5 million bbl). Taxes are to be calculated at 25% on profit oil plus a profit repatriation tax not to exceed 15% of the value of Total's share of exported oil. Total's feasibility study puts the estimated recoverable reserves of two of the sectors at about 248 million bbl, whereas internal Russian estimates put reserves at 387 million bbl;

17. The North East Petroleum Operating Agency (NEPO) and Dalmorneftegeofizika Trust (DMNG) have announced plans to hold a series of international exploration licensing rounds over the next four years. Sixteen tracts located largely offshore Khabarovsk Krai, Magadan Oblast and the Koryak and Chukotka regions have been nominated for licensing beginning in 1993 and extending through 1996. Halliburton Geophysical Services (HGS) has been selected by NEPO and DMNG to assist and advise in preparation and promotion of these various offshore tracts in the Russian Far East. Three blocks, identified as Primagadan and located offshore Magadan Oblast, and East Kahtyrka and Anadyr in the Bering Sea off the Chukotka region, have been nominated for the initial bid round. A 1994 international tender call will cover four blocks: Pyagin-Utkholok off Magadan Oblast, Shantar off Khabarovsk Krai, South Chukchi Sea off northeast Chukotka, and West Kahtyrka off the northeast coast of the Koryak region. Four additional blocks will be opened for licensing in 1995: Gizhiga-Shelikhov located offshore between Magadan and the southern Koryak region (Kamchatka peninsula); Kukhtui, sited off northeastern Khabarovsk Krai; East Siberian Sea off northern Chukotka; and Olyutor off eastern Koryak. A 1996 tender call will cover the North Shelikhov block off Magadan and the adjacent Mamet block off western Koryak, the Ilpin block off eastern Koryak and including the island of Ostrov, the Southern block off the northwestern tip of Sakhalin Island and extending along the Khabarovsk coast, and the North Chukchi Sea block located north of 72° north. The full Far East licensing inventory has been approved by the Russian Committee for Geology and Use of the Subsurface and Roscomnedra (formerly Rossgeolcom);

18. Neft Services Ltd. and Canadian subcontractor Beta Well Services have been contracted by the Tyumer production company Chernogorneft for workover operations involving 268 wells on the Nizhnevartovsk field in Western Siberia. Four rigs are being mobilized from Canada to handle operations; work is expected to begin during April. Nizhnevartovsk and a separate parallel structure identified as Sovetsk together constitute the multizone Vartov-Sovetskoye complex, with productive limits of some 390 km^2. Discovered in 1962, the field was brought into production in 1966; cumulative output through year-end 1989 had totaled 151.6 million bbl oil and about 48 BCF associated gas;

19. "Polar Lights," Conoco's JV with the Russian production association Arkhangelskgeologia, has contracted Halliburton Geophysical to under-

take a detailed 3-D seismic survey over the Ardalin field complex in Nenets Autonomous District. The 1,100-km survey will be carried out with focus on a 100-km² area encompassing the Ardalin field. HGS will subcontract much of the work to Russian geophysical operator Pechorageofizika. Polar Lights' American JV partner, Conoco, announced that a $50 million loan commitment has been secured from the U.S. government's Overseas Private Investment Corporation (OPIC) to underwrite Phase I development of the Ardalin field complex. Conoco and Arkhangelskgeologia expect to invest more than $300 million to bring the northern Timan-Pechora Basin field onstream over the next two years. Remaining funds will source from the European Bank for Reconstruction and Development ($50 million thus far secured) and from the World Bank's International Finance Corporation. Polar Lights is concluding the first of a two-year winter season construction project to build a 60-km oil pipeline from the Ardalin field to existing facilities at the Kharyaga field complex. Phase I development, to include drilling 24 wells, is expected to begin soon. Production start-up from the 100 million bbl Ardalin field is planned during the second half of 1994. According to Conoco, Ardalin marks the first new field JV development between Russian and U.S. partners to move forward in Western Siberia;

20. A senior delegation representing the Sakhalin Island Tender Committee, regional production association Sakhalinmorneftegaz and Dalmorneftegeofizika will travel to Denver during the week of 12–16 July to announce the formal opening of a competitive offshore Far East bid round. The offering will cover some 20,000 km² on the northeastern Sakhalin continental shelf, designated the East Odoptu block, which has been subdivided into four separate areas for bid purposes. According to Denver-based Wavetech Geophysical, technical advisor for the North Sakhalin Basin offering, the area being opened for bidding includes a large number of highly prospective structures which are "analogous in areal extent, relief and reserve potential to previously discovered fields" including Pil'tun Astokh, Lun'skoye, Odoptu and Chaivo. These four fields all lie within the overall limits of the East Odoptu block but are excluded from the planned offering;

21. Intera Information Technologies has been contracted by Vostokgeologia to prepare and promote regional data packages for three separate areas of the Russian Far East. Packages covering the Khaborvsk region and onshore Kamchatka peninsula have been completed and the Russian Federation Geological Committee has authorized their release. A third package covering Sakhalin Island is scheduled for release soon. Separately, Intera has joined with the Ministry of Fuel and Energy for the Sakha (Yakutia) Republic and Yakutgeophysika to prepare a regional data package. To be made available by mid-1993, the package will include

some 8,000 km of existing seismic lines, which will be integrated with results from some 80 exploratory wells;

22. Occidental Petroleum has already begun production and export of oil by its enhanced oil recovery JV company, "Vanyoganneft," of Western Siberia. Occidental's partner in the JV is the Russian production association Chernogorneft. Production commenced at 40,000 bbls/day from 100 wells in the partially developed Vanyogan and Ayogan fields and is expected to reach 65,000 bbls/day by 1994. It is estimated that there are 320 million recoverable barrels of oil in place. Occidental is contributing technical expertise, providing access to Western contractors and staffing the joint venture with its share of onsite management, engineering and technical personnel. The investment program includes modifying and replacing existing facilities, reactivating approximately 150 shut-in wells, drilling production and water-injection wells and constructing facilities to handle increased production and to provide an efficient water-injection system. Programs will also be implemented to provide worker safety and environmental protection. Total capital investment by the joint venture over the 25-year life of the fields is expected to exceed $800 million. In addition, Vanyoganneft will pursue methods to produce undeveloped, shallow, heavy-oil zones containing large potential reserves;

23. The Russian government has approved a proposal to invite IOCs to bid for rights to explore and develop offshore oil and gas deposits in the Sea of Okhotsk and the Bering Sea. The proposal was made by the State Committee for Geology and the Use of Underground Resources and the governments of the Magadan region and the Chukotka Autonomous District in the Far East. The auction will cover 10,000 square miles of the Magadan section in the Sea of Okhotsk and 8,000 square miles in the Vostochno-Khatyrsk section of the Bering Sea. Western IOCs have already been offered packages of geological information on these sections and sample license agreements. They have also been given details of royalties for the use of underground resources. Exxon Corp. and Unocal Corp. had requested more information on the Magadan section, while Occidental Petroleum Corp. sought information on both of the sections.

Appendix 2: Greater Vladivostok: A Concept for the Economic Development of South Primorie

Robert B. Krueger and Leon A. Polott[1]

Russian reform efforts have resulted in remarkable progress. A new Constitution has been adopted. New political institutions function. "Most of the Russian economy, measured by either employment of output, has been privatized in just two years. Russia has already become a market economy, but one in the midst of a long-overdue and massive restructuring. In short, Russia has undergone fundamental changes and appears to be on the right track."[2]

The early stages of Russian reforms were characterized by a rancorous struggle between regional and federal authorities. The gradual stabilization of political institutions has resulted in the redistribution of much of the economic power from the center to the regions. The new tax system, introduced in early 1994, is based on the ideas of fiscal federalism. Consequently, the acrimony between the federal and regional authorities appears to be subsiding.

The cities and regions, the new centers of economic power, are emerging as the true catalysts for market reform. In an effort to stimulate economic growth, the regions are competing for foreign and domestic investment capital and trade. In the course of these efforts, free market and democratic reforms are advanced.

Local business circles have lent their active support to the improvement of the market in which they operate and to the creation of mechanisms that ensure the market's long-term growth and stability. In some cities, including Vladivostok, economic development corporations, styled on the American non-profit model, have been created to serve as clearinghouses for regional promotional information and to develop contacts with potential investors and trading partners.

In Primorski Krai (the southernmost region of Russia's Pacific coast, which includes Vladivostok) regional efforts to devise a long-term development strategy materialized in a collaborative effort between local authorities, academics, industry, and business. The result, the Concept for the Economic Development of South Primorie (hereafter "Primorie Concept"), was a creative and comprehensive approach to long-term regional economic development, planning, and policymaking.

The Primorie Concept, presented below, is a unique example of a region's efforts to develop a long-term strategy of growth under free market conditions. It is the product of the Primorie Economic Development Task Force (hereafter "Task Force") created in 1992 by the City of Vladivostok (hereafter "City" or "Vladivostok") and Primorski Krai (hereafter "Krai" or "Primorie") through their Executive and representative (Soviet) branches. The purpose of the Task Force was to identify goals and the means of implementing privatization, establishing free market mechanisms, governmental reforms, and development projects in the South Primorie region (hereafter the "Greater Vladivostok Project" or the "Project"). Southern Primorie—which includes the Southern and Coastal zones of the Primorski Krai and the ports Posyet, Vladivostok, and Nakhodka— is economically the most important region in the Russian Far East.

The Task Force's goal of regional economic development and growth was guided by concern for South Primorie's long-term needs. The Primorie Concept identified the necessity of economic, social, technological, administrative, regulatory, and legal transformation to accommodate long-term market and democratic reforms.

The process through which the Primorie Concept was developed may be as important as the ambitious, comprehensive reforms it proposes. The work of the Task Force represented the active, democratic involvement of the private sector with local authorities in the formulation of long-term social and economic policy goals. The Task Force's meetings were open to the general public, which was encouraged to participate. Local business leaders contributed significantly to the formulation of the plan.

The scope and sophistication of the Task Force's approach is evidenced by the work undertaken by its action committees and by the expertise of the individuals involved. The chairman of the Primorie Task Force and the originator of the Primorie Concept was Yuri A. Avdeev, vice chairman of the City Soviet. The Primorie Concept report was coedited by Chairman Avdeev and Professor V. V. Savaley of the Pacific Center of Economic Cooperation and Development. Nine action committees were created to study key socioeconomic issues. The Land Use Policy Committee analyzed land management and zoning and evaluated anticipated structural changes in the economy. The Financial Resources Policy Development Committee evaluated the assets and financial potential of the Krai. It studied the conditions necessary to attract foreign and domestic venture capital and investment to the region. The Energy Supply Policy Development Committee studied the systems of generating, transmitting, and distributing energy and heat to the City and Region. It focused on the feasibility of developing and implementing efficient and ecologically sound energy alternatives. The Social Support Policy Development Committee examined methods of providing necessary support to the disadvantaged and dislocated sectors of the society within the context of a free market system. The Automation and Information Policy Development Committee studied methods of improvement, automation, and systemization of information-gathering mechanisms to facilitate City and Regional management capabilities, financial planning, and decision making. The Island Territories Development Committee analyzed environmentally sound means of economic development for the territories. The Transportation and Industry Policy Development Committee analyzed the impact of regional growth and improvements necessary in marine, rail, road, and air transportation systems to accommodate the increase in regional and international trade. The City Planning and Construction Policy Development Committee focused on the City's infrastructure needs. The Ecological Policy Development Committee considered measures for the improvement of the region's environment and preservation of resources.[3]

The Task Force's efforts were a unique example of collaboration between the local authorities, business, industry, and the academic community in developing a comprehensive, studied method for regional development, planning, and policymaking. This effort was undertaken by and received the support of several successive City administrations.

Despite the comprehensive approach to regional problem solving and development represented by the Primorie Concept, it has received inadequate attention and support from the international community. Former President Nixon recognized the importance of regional development in the evolution of Russian reform. He stated that "the most stable arrangement for Russia is a genuine federation as set forth in the New Russian Constitution, under which the republics and regions have considerable control over their own affairs and a meaningful voice in central government."[4] It is implicit that the only way for regions to achieve "control over their own affairs" is through independent economic viability. Western private and governmental assistance programs, which seek to promote Russian reforms, should focus more attention at the City and Regional level. Comprehensive programs for regional privatization and reform, such as the Primorie Concept, and private and public sector collaboration in the formulation of long-term policy objectives should be encouraged.

The Primorie Concept

I. General Statements
The Primorie Concept is taken from local, regional and foreign program experiences and is based upon the ideals embodied in Russia's reform programs.[5] The Primorie Concept has evolved as a result of the economic and political situation facing Russia and particularly the RFE today, as well as from the complex levels of the Krai's economic development, existing structures, current relationships and the specific problems that exist in Vladivostok. It recognizes and seeks to draw on the significant economic and political changes have occurred in the interregional and the international relationships of the Russian Federation, the Krai, and the City.

The economic, social and political crises facing Russia today require a choice between one of two strategies of regional management: either return to the former centralization characteristic of the economy of the former Soviet Union or establish a local and regional economic independence and determine regional priorities.

With due regard to the economic reform program developed by the federal government which is supported by the region, the second option has been chosen. This option allows the krais and oblasts of Russia many more management rights than they had previously—rights similar to those enjoyed by American states or the German Lander. Consequently, the City and the Krai have been given the opportunity to analyze the structures of regional processes, to assess the equality of interchange between regions and to evaluate and compare the macroeconomic relationships the region has with neighboring countries and territories in such areas as national income, gross output, finance and security.

The more freedom that the City and the Krai establish in management prerogatives, the wider the range of potential territorial economic development trajectories. As a result, prerogatives in analyses and forecasts, strategic planning and program regulation—in short the role of responsible governmental management—are strengthened.

The Primorie Concept encompasses social and economic development for the South Primorie for the next 10–15 years. It includes goals and stages of territorial and economic development. It sets objectives for structure and investment policy, and it proposes the mechanisms and methods necessary to implement the Concept. Given these parameters, it has been necessary to develop standards for economic, social, technological, organizational and legal transformation both for the region as a whole and for its most active economic centers.

It is hoped that the Primorie Concept will become the model for designing local development programs, projects and schemes throughout the Krai. The focus of these programs must be on solving such problems as attracting capital and financial resources, achieving effective economic specialization, accelerating needed social adaptation to a free-market economy, planning, coordinating and achieving infrastructural construction and maintenance and planning the region's urban development—in short, improving the economic, social and natural environment of our lives.

The Primorie Concept is openly submitted and is subject to open critique and change as the Primorie Task Force advances in the planning and implementation of the Greater Vladivostok Project.

II. Original Terms for Primorski Krai Development
A. Characteristics of the Region
This review of the region details its available natural resources, the level and structure of its industrial development and its social, political, financial and economic environment. There is significant natural resource potential in the Krai, primarily in mineral, timber and marine and fishery resources. Population density is the highest in the RFE. It is, however, lower than that found in neighboring countries, such as China and the Koreas. Nonetheless, the people of the Krai possess the capacity to accomplish almost any project that is economically feasible.

As for industrial development, South Primorie is far and away the most important region in the RFE. Our primary economic activities are fishing (40 percent of the RFE volume), sea transport (80 percent of the RFE volume), heavy equipment production, mining and forestry. In 1990 figures, industrial output accounted for 64.5 percent of the region's economic activity, transport for 14.6 percent, construction for 9 percent, agriculture for 6.2 percent, and other for 5.7 percent. The region's social and political dynamics are volatile and unstable—the Krai is part and parcel of the fast-changing environment that characterizes Russia as a whole.

Some elements of partnership between the territories and the federal government do exist, yet a certain degree of independence from the control of the Russian Federation can be observed, singularly in financial and economic areas. Here, a set of problems common to the entire country can be found—stagflation, a decrease in the level of production and civil construction, late payments or defaults on business debts, a decrease in stock prices and increases in unemployment.

Relatively speaking, however, when the political and economic chaos characteristic of life in much of the former Soviet Union is taken into account, the social, political and economic situation in the City and the Krai can be considered more stable, with governmental and economic reforms proceeding without extreme conflict or opposition.

B. Economic Structure, Reproduction Reserves

For many years, the Krai was the site of two strategic functions that significantly influenced its pattern of development. First, it was home to the Soviet Union's Pacific Navy Fleet and provided relatively cheap raw materials (e.g., lumber, fish, and minerals) to the area. These materials were obtained by order of the central government, rather than as a result of market demand, for both domestic and foreign consumption. The economic impact of this factor cannot be overestimated.

One long-lasting effect of this system was that certain types of more expensive production facilities that were mandated by the central government of the Soviet Union were financed by underinvesting both in other industries considered strategically less important and in the social and service sectors of the economy. The result of this policy can be seen throughout the Krai—an economy with an overreliance on raw materials, military establishments and military traditions—and a crumbling social and physical infrastructure.

The need to reduce the region's reliance on natural resource usage is dictated not only by the limits of its environment to reproduce itself but by other economic imperatives as well. Under current circumstances, capital expenses per unit of mined raw materials are increasing at a faster rate than the price they can command on the open world market, which is set by real consumer demand. Clearly, continuing our traditional predisposition to exploit our natural resources for economic survival is counterproductive. Yet, especially in the beginning stage of our structural economic redevelopment, our natural resource potential is most capable of leading the Krai's economic revival. As quickly as practicable, however, it is imperative to begin the transition to a more balanced and integrated economic mix.

The industrial sector of the Krai is strongest in machine building, ship repairing and shipbuilding, tool construction, aircraft construction and machine tool production and repair. Thirty-seven percent of the population works in one of these industries. Practically all of the Krai's large heavy equipment plants are involved in the military-industrial complex— an industrial sector already suffering a severe slump. Other sectors in the manufacturing complex most susceptible to the changing economy are the food industry (primarily fish processing), light industry and wood processing. It should be noted, however, that these industries face stiff competition, not only nationally but internationally as well.

The secondary economic sectors of the Krai are not in a position to play any immediate role in its transition—either in terms of financial resources or in an effort to fill gaps in the local market. These sectors must be technologically reconstructed and readjusted to global standards before they can be expected to take a role in transforming the region's economy. Two other important economic sectors, construction and agriculture, face similar basic problems that have resulted from indefinitely postponing necessary reorganization and from the failure to develop strong ties with foreign partners or investors. As a result, they suffer from low profitability, outdated technology, price disparities and inadequately trained staffs. Largely due to this, the region relies upon imports for food and has been increasingly using foreign (Chinese) labor in major construction projects.

One of the unique characteristics of Primorski Krai's economy is its industrial/transportation specialization. Due in large measure to its geographic location, transportation plays a key role in the Krai's economic mix; its proportion in the economic structure is almost twice that of the average industrialized Russian norm. Altogether, the Krai boasts four deepwater ports, several smaller ports, three railroad stations with ocean access and two railroad connections with China and North Korea. This transportation network represents a powerful asset which is capable of energizing the Krai's economic redevelopment.

In order to mobilize the Krai's production capabilities, a consistent and substantial inflow of capital into its industries without a concomitant increase in the number of employees is necessary. In addition, its service industries need a significant boost—in terms of both financing and trained personnel. Nothing less than structural transformation is needed if it expects to create a stable environment to which foreign investment would be attracted. Practically speaking, there is very little hope for any large injection of capital from the federal government. In fact, indirect financial support from the federal government, coupled with a greater degree of economic independence for the Krai, appears to be the most favorable situation.

Given this scenario, three distinct patterns of possible social and economic policy development for the region emerge:

1. *Status Quo.* With no new policy direction, financial intervention, social mobilization or political imperative, the economy will continue to function much as it has in the past. The only likely movement will be toward more contact with neighboring Asian countries. The probability of realizing this scenario is relatively high simply because it would be a product of the inertia of current policies.

2. *Independence.* In this model, the Krai economically separates from the Russian Federation, promptly allows wide access to its economic frontiers and focuses on the Northeast Asia market. The key component in

this pattern is an economic reorientation to the Tumen River Basin Project, with the goal of creating an economic ring circling the sea of Japan. In order to bring about this model, the governments of China, North Korea and Russia would have to work in close cooperation, a condition that would necessitate the construction of completely new economic and political structures and a reorientation of national psychologies, cultures and traditions.

3. *Integrated.* This scenario would develop on the basis of economic cooperation and increased trade with neighboring territories of the RFE, Siberia, the Urals and the European portion of the Russian Federation. Realization of this ideal would demand significant investment in basic infrastructure: redesigned and expanded ports, office facilities, warehouses, executive housing, recreation and resort construction, and creation of an efficient private service sector. Under this scenario, the Krai would become an essential link between Russia and the Asia-Pacific region.

In choosing the third model, the Krai would not merely advance ahead of the economic reforms evolving in the rest of the Russian Federation, but would be among the first to reap the economic rewards of those reforms. Clearly, this course would be difficult and could be achieved only through the concerted dedication and commitment of the citizens, the business sector and the political establishments of the City and the Krai.

III. Objectives, Prerequisites and Stages of Development

A. Objectives and Conditions of Development

The only goal that makes these difficult economic, social and political reforms worthwhile is a significant improvement in the social, environmental, and labor conditions throughout the Krai—an improvement to a level that would correspond to that enjoyed in other developed industrial countries. In general, the standard of living in terms of per capita income can be measured.

There is little disagreement that the only way to realize a long-term advanced standard of living is through the development of a highly productive, efficient market economy with appropriate environmental constraints. The degree and intensity of economic productivity necessary in the Krai can best be achieved on the basis of a regional structure.

To establish a workable regional economic structure, the following problems must be addressed:

1. Political and economic stability must be achieved and maintained. A stable and convertible currency, low inflation rate and prices set in concert with world demand must be established.

2. Basic infrastructure, transportation, communications, electricity, water and sewer, housing, and storage and office facilities must be constructed or upgraded to international standards.

3. A well-trained and motivated labor force is essential and must be established.

4. A business service sector must be cultivated and established. At the minimum it must include banks, insurance companies, stock, bond, monetary and commodity exchanges, consultation and information services, and customs and visa assistance equal to world standards.

5. Positive, progressive governmental economic policies, especially in the area of investment stimulation, must be in place. Policy formulation and implementation, especially as it relates to taxation, real property entitlement and rights, intellectual property rights, interest rates, and export/import regulations must be rational and stable.

The optimum functioning of this model can be realized only when:

(a) economic borders between the regions of the Russian Federation are abolished and the regulations relating to trade across the borders of the regions and the republics are reduced to a minimum;

(b) international rules of accounting, auditing and investment valuation and of management standards and certification are adopted;

(c) the maximum use of the advantages of national and regional economic associations in interregional and external trade, such as corporations/joint stock corporations, cooperative partnerships, and joint ventures are adopted;

(d) equality of rights, based upon law, for all forms of private business activity, except monopoly, are established;

(e) entrepreneurs are allowed a full range of capital investment options;

(f) strict delineation of management authority between the central state structures, regional structures and structures of the local administrations in regulating economic activity on the territory, as well as in owning and using land and natural resources, is established and observed; and

(g) local social and governmental resources are mobilized and utilized at their maximum levels.

B. Economic Factors in Development

1. Positive Factors for Economic Growth

Primorski Krai possesses several unique characteristics that are conducive to future economic growth, including:

(a) vast reserves of biological, marine/fishery and mineral resources;

(b) an advantageous economic and geographic position, which has only increased in value as a result of the strengthening economic role of the

Asia-Pacific area and its eastern Asian subregions in the international arena due primarily to the loss of the Baltic and Black Sea ports of the former Soviet Union;

(c) a new state policy with the goal of constructing an open economy in the Krai and Russia as a whole—in combination with the substantially high level of productivity in the Krai, this policy provides an excellent basis for capital generation and investment, both foreign and domestic;

(d) existing significant scientific and technical abilities and even greater potential for the immediate future, as evidenced by Vladivostok University, the Polytechnic Institute, seven institutes associated with the National Academy of Sciences and the Maritime Institute; and

(e) large tracts of undeveloped territory, especially when compared with the densely populated territories found in neighboring countries.

2. Negative Factors for Economic Growth

The factors which are impediments to the speed and direction of economic development of the region include:

(a) unique and vulnerable natural environment, including the Taiga (pine forests), as well as our agricultural, coastal and aquatoreal landscapes, all of which have great intrinsic ecological and aesthetic values independent of their potential developmental use;

(b) an ecological crisis in a number of the Krai's cities, rivers and marine/aquatic areas;

(c) historically intensive, ecologically unsound harvest of fish, mineral and timber resources with a potential for exhaustion of stocks;

(d) infrastructure neglect;

(e) lack of well-trained, available labor force, in spite of apparent unemployment;

(f) outmoded production equipment at many plants; and

(g) increased expense of acquiring and supporting new technologies of all kinds.

Any industrial growth called for in the Primorie Concept must be accomplished with the greatest attention to its environmental impact. Only carefully and strategically planned economic development can create the prerequisites necessary for technological reconstruction, modernization of production facilities and a decrease in the current negative impact on the environment, as well as an increase in the financial resources necessary for environmental protection.

C. Determination of Economic Direction for the Region

Prioritizing the Krai's economic development program was done by comparing development prerequisites and the factors currently limiting development with the needs and interests of those who own necessary financial, property and natural resources.

1. Perspective of the Federal Government

Four governmental elements in the Krai's economic development were identified: the government of the Russian Federation, local government as it reflects the interests of the people, local business interests and foreign business interests. Each element has its own perspective on the ultimate goals of the program and the tasks necessary to attract capital investments. From the perspective of the Russian Federation, the Krai is:

(a) a region that contains strategically important raw materials (timber, fish, polymetallic concentrated products) necessary in both domestic and international markets;

(b) a nexus of transportation facilities capable of sending and receiving export/import and strategic goods; and

(c) the base and support center for the Russian military presence in the Pacific region and an economic, engineering and technical base for the Russian Pacific Fleet.

2. Perspective of Local Governments

The local governmental authorities, taking into account the Krai's geographic location and the complex situation evolving in its marketplace and in its social fabric, believe that the local economy must develop in a way that will allow:

(a) the people to buy the consumer goods they want and need;

(b) a source of stable revenues to support local governments;

(c) a well-balanced mix of occupations within a stable labor environment; and

(d) the establishment and maintenance of a clean and healthy environment.

3. Perspective of Business Interests

Local and foreign business with economic development interests are primarily concerned with:

(a) the Krai's rich reserve of raw materials, valuable in both domestic and international markets;

(b) high-tech processing industries in which return on capital investment is most expedient; and

(c) those economic sectors and activities with quick capital turnover that demand minimal investment of time or effort (trade intermediaries, financial operations, hotel and tourism services, computer engineering, etc.).

Although private businesses and investors share many common interests, certain elements which are not strictly economic also play a role in their decision making, for example, patriotism, a sense of responsibility and a commitment to the future of the region, which sometimes exhibit themselves in a readiness to take part in social and ecological programs and in the creation of nonprofit but essential infrastructure construction. Any strategy for local development should seriously consider and encompass the objectives of these enterprises.

4. Future Economic Direction

Different motivations lead to different agendas—consequently, in order to come to agreement on one united program, compromise is essential. Certain factors are absolute—predetermined not only by political history but also by natural, geographic, and geopolitical realities.

For example, the region must preserve its natural resources sector, provide transportation for Russian and foreign goods and support the Pacific Fleet of the Russian Navy. It therefore becomes doubly important to transform these factors into positive attributes through technical development, through changes in natural resources policies and through formulating rational and realistically enforceable government regulations.

Successfully fulfilling the Krai's strategic state functions can be achieved only through mutual economic commitments. As economic decentralization gains strength, new factors will compete for influence in the Krai's economic development. It will be extremely difficult during this transition period to set, and then implement, a list of priorities. Reference to the following guidelines should help to safeguard our priorities as diversionary pressures mount:

(a) The Krai should function as a link for the economies of Russia and the Asia-Pacific region and between the countries of the former Soviet Union and the Asia-Pacific Region.

(b) The Krai should help to create an economic community around the Sea of Japan that will be unique in world history and will serve to integrate several different national and regional economic systems.

(c) The Krai should be a national marine economic sector with special internal and external economic powers.

(d) The Krai should develop a recreational industry suited to its unique natural and ecological assets.

(e) The Krai should work toward agricultural cooperation with its neighboring countries.

D. Tasks Required by Local Governments
1. General Tasks Required

During 1992–1994 it will be necessary to devote all of our efforts to overcoming the current crises confronting Russia, the City and the Krai and in adapting all aspects of our economy, our society and our governments to the new structures demanded by the advent of capitalism and the market economy. During this phase the tasks faced by the City and the Krai include:

(a) mobilization of efforts to stimulate industrial production, protection of priority services, such as political, and maintenance of life-supporting infrastructure;

(b) passage of legislation that facilitates privatization, land reform, conversion of accounting standards to internationally recognized principles, and other issues in the governmental, managerial and commercial areas which the dynamics of perestroika and glasnost and the reform process demand;

(c) stimulation of small and medium-sized businesses, encouragement of economic cooperation between the local authorities of the City and the Krai and large enterprises, support of foreign investment projects, and the creation of a governmental, legal and taxation infrastructure attractive to foreign investors which will assure a profitable return on their investments; and

(d) consistent adherence to the principles of an open-market economy, signaling advantages of the region for priority investment by local and foreign capital, and strategic appeals to the federal government for compensation in order to fulfill the tasks necessary to prevent social and ecological imbalance.

2. Specific Tasks Required

Specific tasks faced by the authorities of the City and the Krai include:

(a) attracting a variety of sources able to make a financial commitment to the region in terms of public sector tasks, business and industry investment, and the banking and insurance sectors;

(b) developing policies conducive to the stimulation of a vigorous and balanced export-import industry;

(c) regulation of investment incentives to facilitate both consumer demand items and infrastructural redevelopment;

(d) establishment of limits to raw materials exploitation as well as legal protection for medium and high-tech businesses and innovation of economic activities;

(e) establishment of rational and innovative foreign trade policies;

(f) establishment of progressive policies for structural economic transition;

(g) support for modern management training as it relates to both business and industry practices, as well as a clear understanding and appreciation for diverse ways of doing business within the free-market system;

(h) strengthening of social guarantees for currently unprotected sectors of the population; and

(i) continuation of the local programs aimed at privatization, conversion of governmental/military facilities and other new economic programs.

3. Phasing of Tasks

The second phase of the Primorie Concept, 1995–2000, should be characterized by stable growth in the federal government's financial resources. That will allow the standard of living to begin to rise and close the gap in social and technological standards with other industrialized countries.

The third phase, 2001–2005, the technological and social reconstruction, should bring the region's standard of living to a level comparable to other industrialized countries.

The second and third phases may be accelerated in the event of substantial, successful domestic and foreign investment dedicated to the Primorie Concept.

IV. Territorial Differences and Priorities in the Krai

A. Economic and Geographic Zones

There are five distinct economic and geographic zones within the Krai:

1. South Primorie: from Posyet along the seacoast to Nakhodka, with Vladivostok situated in the center;

2. the Central Forest, with Arsenyeo at the center;

3. the Khanka Zone, Ussuriysk;

4. the Cavalervo–Dalnegorsk Mining Zone;

5. the Northwest Zone: running northward from Spassk along the Trans-Siberian Railroad.

There are marked differences between these zones which are the result of disparate resource availability and differing levels of economic development. The largest zone—South Primorie—possesses the most favorable combination of assets for economic development. The two major port cities in the Krai and RFE, Vladivostok and Nakhodka, are located in this zone. More than 40 percent of all Krai revenues and approximately 50 percent of the workforce are concentrated in this zone. Moreover, as in most countries, socioeconomic development is more rapid and intense in the coastal areas, such as South Primorie.

B. Positive Factors for Economic Growth in South Primorie

South Primorie has the greatest potential for rapid development due to several factors:

1. a favorable economic and geographic position in relation to both international and domestic markets;

2. a well-developed transportation infrastructure based on four deepwater seaports and three railway lines that terminate at the coast. This transportation network supports one of the heaviest concentrations of freight turnover, as well as a large proportion of the entire transportation services, in the Russian Federation;

3. the opportunity for economic growth as a result of military plant conversion;

4. the availability of large fishing, fish-processing, freight and passenger transport fleets. Far Eastern Shipping Company based in Vladivostok is one of the largest shipping companies in the world;

5. the concentration of the scientific communities in Vladivostok and Nakhodka. In coordination with foreign consultants, the most advanced material handling and production techniques can be developed and implemented;

6. the availability of a well-educated population, many of whom are specialists with international work experience, and a well-developed educational system;

7. five coastal and Taiga (forest) areas which lend themselves to the development of world-class resort facilities.

The coastal economic centers of Vladivostok (including Artyom), Nakhodka (including Port Vostochy), Posyet, Zarubino, Slavyanka, Bolshoi Kamen and possibly several others, could become points of rapid growth incorporating different industrial sectors and thereby set the stage for the stimulation of socioeconomic development in the inner sections of the Krai. Such development would occur through the production of much-needed consumer and technical goods, management services, provision of transportation and storage facilities and services, and provision of information, consulting and other business services, as well as the judicious use of tax revenues. Ussuriysk, Partisanski and some other industrial centers that have close contact with coastal centers can also be regarded as bordering points for South Primorie.

The overall aim of the Primorie Concept is the intensive socioeconomic development of the interdependent industrial and port areas in South Primorie based on both foreign investment and self-help and the construction of close ties in market economies between Russia and the RFE, China, the Koreas, Japan and other Asia-Pacific Rim countries. In order to achieve this aim, social, ecological and economic policies which target the expenditure of tax receipts to local areas in ways designed to increase local living standards while safeguarding the environment must be formulated. Effective market development policies must be pursued, and modern and effective facilities for the transportation, storage and other basic infrastructural services for goods for Far Eastern markets must be constructed. Sufficient tax revenues to help stabilize the budget of the Russian

Federation, as well as to provide an essential transit and market links between the Federation and the Asia-Pacific Rim countries, must be generated.

C. Points and Zones of Rapid Growth

The Vladivostok Region (Vladivostok, Artyom, Nadejdinsky District) is the nucleus of the South Primorie urban system. This subregion has significant economic potential.

The second rapid growth center is the Nakhodka Free Economic Zone ("FEZ"), which is now attracting the anticipated foreign investments. De jure and de facto functioning of the Nakhodka FEZ is developing according to its own schedule, subject to its own autonomous management. It functions in coordination with other South Primorie project subzones on the basis of horizontal cooperation, by permitting coordination activities and by delegating a portion of its authority to the Soviet Coordination Committee of the South Primorie project.

The Khasan District Economic Development Area is centered on three points: Posyet, Zarubino and Slavyanka. Even at the first stage, it is very important to use the now insufficiently developed Khasan (Zarubino) and Posyet seaports. For this purpose, these ports must be completely opened to foreign ships without waiting for the Chinese to complete their project of achieving access to the Sea of Japan through the Tumen River Basin Project. The Greater Vladivostok Project should begin building a binationally beneficial freight railroad from the Russian coast to Kunchung which could serve as the means of delivery of goods from the northeast provinces as well as Chiling. This development could be a viable alternative to the Tumen project, at least for the next decade, and could then serve to supplement an international free trade zone, if one were to be established at the Russian, Chinese and Northern Korean borders.

Slavyanka, as a part of the South Primorie complex, is engaged in ship repair and shipbuilding of both common and specialized ships. Production activities in the Khasan District must be limited to these activities. The rest of the territory should be used for rehabilitation and medical centers and for tourism. In addition, this area can support fur breeding, agriculture, fish farming and various other ecologically sound activities.

Thus the three subzones, Vladivostok, Nakhodka and the Khasan district, are the region's main centers of economic development and as such are the primary targets for both domestic and international capital investment.

Additional ports and industrial centers included in South Primorie are Bolshoi Kamen and Ussuriysk. Bolshoi Kamen specializes in shipbuilding, ship repair and the production of ship machinery. It could continue in these sectors and could also fill orders from various Vladivostok plants

ng the products available to domestic consumers and in-
structural investment. In two to four years the investment
uld grow in direct proportion to defense industry conver-
tization revenues and to an influx of foreign capital secured
rces and from other guarantees and concessional invest-
t time, raw material production should be deemphasized, in
s, and the manufacturing and services sectors should be tar-
phasized.

suffers from an underdeveloped infrastructure and impru-
ale natural resources exploitation. Simply passing revenues
iral resources sector to the targeted sectors in the short term
; about the desired restructuring. A well thought out transi-
m, which serves not just to redistribute existing income but
otential revenues for all enterprises is essential.

Place of Vladivostok in South Primorie
ites and Factors of Development

of an aquaterritorial production complex in South Primorie
he strengthening of the economic interdependence and unifi-
cities and outlying areas into one complex. It should also
en the territorial division of labor and the region's socioeco-
lization. Opening Vladivostok in 1992 allowed it to move for-
nd and enhance a network of interrelationships throughout
m and thereby significantly strengthened its role as the Krai's
tical and economic activities.

k is the nucleus of South Primorie, indeed Primorie (see Ta-
A.2). Forty percent of the volume of industrial production of
ai is found in the City. Vladivostok is also home to a major
ent of the City's revenue comes from its marine economy.
es with a 20 percent rate for the Krai as a whole. The City's
that of the Krai, is typically industrial. Thirty-two percent of
dustrial revenue and 30 percent of its employment are con-
re. In fact, figures show that economically Vladivostok is at
ent more efficient than the Krai as a whole.

biggest banks and its stock exchange are in Vladivostok, as
state and private firms and joint ventures. There is also a high
n of scientific resources in the City. The majority of the Rus-
iy of Science Institutes in the Far East and nine colleges as
us major sectors of scientific research, governmental and
anizations are centered in Vladivostok. The City's economy
ports itself but also interacts closely and positively with eco-
nts throughout South Primorie.

that need to be relocated in order to allow for other kinds of growth within Vladivostok proper.

The Ussuriysk railway junction is the main center in controlling almost 100 percent of the Krai's rail traffic. As such, it will play a very large role in South Primorie's economic development. Economic growth in this zone will stimulate a second tier of components in the territorial structure: agroindustrial zones around Ussuriysk and along the Partisanski River—territories which have longstanding agricultural traditions. They have the best climate and soil conditions in the Krai, are close to the largest group of consumers and possess a relatively well-developed food processing industry. The Ussuriysk and Partisanski agricultural districts and the possible free customs zone at Grodeko are areas that will fall within the influence of the Primorie Concept.

The project of creating a Russian-Chinese free trade zone along the Mudanchang-Suifenhe-Grodeko border deserves special study. Its primary impetus may be the economic opening of the borders between Primorie and Kheilnchang Province. These regions complement each other in several ways. The Chinese province has problems with overproduction and has difficulties in marketing its agricultural and consumer goods. Suifenhe, a city near the border, was recently opened and is now growing rapidly. If it continues in this direction, it will become an important trade and transport center. At the same time, certain Primorski enterprises (especially engineering, mining and construction) have difficulties in marketing themselves in the Asia-Pacific Rim countries. The Chinese market is perhaps more amenable to working with these Primorski industries; their proximity and comparable geographic features would seem to make such an arrangement beneficial to both sides. In the meantime, Mudanchang and Ussuriysk will play a role in this scenario as centers of trade and business contacts for the two territories. Geographically, Suifenhe and Grodenko are natural gateways for Russian-Chinese trade.

The realization of the South Primorie development program must take place in concert with the international FEZ project in the Tumen River Basin. The Tumen River estuary has a unique geographic position: not only is it situated at the junction of three national borders—Russia, China, North Korea—it also has access to the sea. Clearly, this river will be immensely valuable in promoting trade between Russia, China, Mongolia, North Korea and Japan, as well as with other Asian and Asia-Pacific Rim countries. Its geographic and strategic value alone will draw significant traffic and capital. It is in the attraction of traffic and foreign capital that the Tumen and South Primorie projects may be in competition. It would be far better if the two regions complemented one another on the basis of division of labor, as well as specialization in specific types of goods handled and shipped. In addition, it would be far more productive to all parties if they would also complement one another in terms of industrial, technical and consumer goods produced and commercial services offered. Competition between the two will obviously exist in the areas of land and sea transportation, potential markets and potential industrial enterprises.

Coordination of the projects may be based upon drawing the following distinction between the two: South Primorie is a zone of territorial-economic development, while Tumen is a zone of territorial-economic initial formation. In other words, in the Primorski development zone, capital must be attracted to further develop the industrial and port complexes already in place and to redevelop its urban economy. In the Tumen initial formation zone, capital must be attracted to the development of virgin territory and the creation of the basic infrastructure necessary to achieve its realization. Drawing these basic distinctions should help to alleviate the competition between the two projects for capital and may serve to promote cooperative relationships.

If the Tumen Project is allowed to continue in an uncontrolled and uncoordinated manner, its adverse effect on the freight transportation network, industrial opportunities and other development options envisioned in the Primorie Concept will be extensive. If, however, the two economic centers are developed and stimulated in these project frames, both could actively become components of a strong economic structure around the Sea of Japan, thus positively interacting and reinforcing one another.

D. Functional Priorities Common to the Whole Zone
Every rapid growth program contains its own set of local economic priorities. The basic functions to prioritize, however, can be divided into production, service and infrastructure.

1. The Production Function
Priority goals in production activities are as follows:
(a) diversification of port and transport services;
(b) improvement of fish processing techniques which will result in a wider variety of superior products;
(c) creation of efficient fish farms;
(d) creation of new biochemical and pharmaceutical products from the Krai's natural resources;
(e) conversion of defense plants perhaps to ship repair, ship building and instrument-making industries in order to provide products and services for both the domestic and international markets;
(f) increasing the range of consumer goods available; and
(g) storing and processing raw agricultural products.

2. The Service Function
Priority goals in service activities are as
(a) improvement and strengthening o
bring it to international standards, thus p
eign partners and client activities;
(b) sale of the products resulting from s
planning organizations and such other a
well as the creation of applied and experi
and other structures;
(c) development of recreational service
East, as well as hotel services and other d
services;
(d) creation of a system for the trainin
tive and service personnel;
(e) organizing and developing housin
for socially disadvantaged persons; and
(f) formation of a simplified system o
private businesses.

3. Infrastructural Functions
Priority goals in infrastructural functic
(a) development of ecologically comp
reconstruction and improvements of the
(b) modernization of the City's water
(c) large-scale improvement and devel
tem to provide reliable transportation li
other project centers in the territory, incl
tenance of well-designed highways a
routes; and
(d) development and modernizatior
tions system.

Proposals regarding specific costs of
and organizational structures for Sou
stages. To maximize regional growth
should (1) address the basic issues of s
sumer demands and (3) increase dome:

Most of the resources available for e:
in the traditional raw materials sector
sector. For this reason it is essential to f
neously, however, it is necessary to inc
restructuring of the economy by impi

base, i
creasin
potenti
sion, to
by our
ments.
relative
geted ar

The r
dent lar,
from the
will not
tional pr
to increa

V. Role a
A. Prere
The crea
will lead
cation of
serve to c
nomic sp(
ward to e
the Pacifi
center of p

Vladivo
bles A.1 ar
the entire
port; 60 p(
This comp
economy,
the Krai's
centrated
least 10 pe

The Krai
are the larg
concentrati
sian Acade
well as va
planning o
not only su
nomic elem

that need to be relocated in order to allow for other kinds of growth within Vladivostok proper.

The Ussuriysk railway junction is the main center in controlling almost 100 percent of the Krai's rail traffic. As such, it will play a very large role in South Primorie's economic development. Economic growth in this zone will stimulate a second tier of components in the territorial structure: agroindustrial zones around Ussuriysk and along the Partisanski River—territories which have longstanding agricultural traditions. They have the best climate and soil conditions in the Krai, are close to the largest group of consumers and possess a relatively well-developed food processing industry. The Ussuriysk and Partisanski agricultural districts and the possible free customs zone at Grodeko are areas that will fall within the influence of the Primorie Concept.

The project of creating a Russian-Chinese free trade zone along the Mudanchang-Suifenhe-Grodeko border deserves special study. Its primary impetus may be the economic opening of the borders between Primorie and Kheilnchang Province. These regions complement each other in several ways. The Chinese province has problems with overproduction and has difficulties in marketing its agricultural and consumer goods. Suifenhe, a city near the border, was recently opened and is now growing rapidly. If it continues in this direction, it will become an important trade and transport center. At the same time, certain Primorski enterprises (especially engineering, mining and construction) have difficulties in marketing themselves in the Asia-Pacific Rim countries. The Chinese market is perhaps more amenable to working with these Primorski industries; their proximity and comparable geographic features would seem to make such an arrangement beneficial to both sides. In the meantime, Mudanchang and Ussuriysk will play a role in this scenario as centers of trade and business contacts for the two territories. Geographically, Suifenhe and Grodenko are natural gateways for Russian-Chinese trade.

The realization of the South Primorie development program must take place in concert with the international FEZ project in the Tumen River Basin. The Tumen River estuary has a unique geographic position: not only is it situated at the junction of three national borders—Russia, China, North Korea—it also has access to the sea. Clearly, this river will be immensely valuable in promoting trade between Russia, China, Mongolia, North Korea and Japan, as well as with other Asian and Asia-Pacific Rim countries. Its geographic and strategic value alone will draw significant traffic and capital. It is in the attraction of traffic and foreign capital that the Tumen and South Primorie projects may be in competition. It would be far better if the two regions complemented one another on the basis of division of labor, as well as specialization in specific types of goods handled and shipped. In addition, it would be far more productive to all parties if they would also complement one another in terms of industrial, technical and consumer goods produced and commercial services offered. Competition between the two will obviously exist in the areas of land and sea transportation, potential markets and potential industrial enterprises.

Coordination of the projects may be based upon drawing the following distinction between the two: South Primorie is a zone of territorial-economic development, while Tumen is a zone of territorial-economic initial formation. In other words, in the Primorski development zone, capital must be attracted to further develop the industrial and port complexes already in place and to redevelop its urban economy. In the Tumen initial formation zone, capital must be attracted to the development of virgin territory and the creation of the basic infrastructure necessary to achieve its realization. Drawing these basic distinctions should help to alleviate the competition between the two projects for capital and may serve to promote cooperative relationships.

If the Tumen Project is allowed to continue in an uncontrolled and uncoordinated manner, its adverse effect on the freight transportation network, industrial opportunities and other development options envisioned in the Primorie Concept will be extensive. If, however, the two economic centers are developed and stimulated in these project frames, both could actively become components of a strong economic structure around the Sea of Japan, thus positively interacting and reinforcing one another.

D. Functional Priorities Common to the Whole Zone

Every rapid growth program contains its own set of local economic priorities. The basic functions to prioritize, however, can be divided into production, service and infrastructure.

1. The Production Function

Priority goals in production activities are as follows:

(a) diversification of port and transport services;

(b) improvement of fish processing techniques which will result in a wider variety of superior products;

(c) creation of efficient fish farms;

(d) creation of new biochemical and pharmaceutical products from the Krai's natural resources;

(e) conversion of defense plants perhaps to ship repair, ship building and instrument-making industries in order to provide products and services for both the domestic and international markets;

(f) increasing the range of consumer goods available; and

(g) storing and processing raw agricultural products.

2. The Service Function

Priority goals in service activities are as follows:

(a) improvement and strengthening of the market infrastructure to bring it to international standards, thus providing opportunities for foreign partners and client activities;

(b) sale of the products resulting from scientific research organizations, planning organizations and such other assets as patents and licenses, as well as the creation of applied and experimental joint laboratories, centers and other structures;

(c) development of recreational services oriented to Siberia and the Far East, as well as hotel services and other domestic and international tourist services;

(d) creation of a system for the training and certification of administrative and service personnel;

(e) organizing and developing housing and employment opportunities for socially disadvantaged persons; and

(f) formation of a simplified system of registration and regulation for private businesses.

3. Infrastructural Functions

Priority goals in infrastructural functions are as follows:

(a) development of ecologically compatible energy sources, as well as reconstruction and improvements of the current central energy system;

(b) modernization of the City's water supply and sewage systems;

(c) large-scale improvement and development of the transportation system to provide reliable transportation links from the center of the Krai to other project centers in the territory, including the construction and maintenance of well-designed highways along the most heavily traveled routes; and

(d) development and modernization of the region's telecommunications system.

Proposals regarding specific costs of resource usage, financing sources and organizational structures for South Primorie, are in the formative stages. To maximize regional growth it would seem that management should (1) address the basic issues of stimulating exports, (2) satisfy consumer demands and (3) increase domestic investments.

Most of the resources available for export at this time are concentrated in the traditional raw materials sector and in the international transport sector. For this reason it is essential to focus efforts in these areas. Simultaneously, however, it is necessary to increasingly direct export profits to a restructuring of the economy by improving and broadening the export base, increasing the products available to domestic consumers and increasing infrastructural investment. In two to four years the investment potential should grow in direct proportion to defense industry conversion, to privatization revenues and to an influx of foreign capital secured by our resources and from other guarantees and concessional investments. At that time, raw material production should be deemphasized, in relative terms, and the manufacturing and services sectors should be targeted and emphasized.

The region suffers from an underdeveloped infrastructure and imprudent large-scale natural resources exploitation. Simply passing revenues from the natural resources sector to the targeted sectors in the short term will not bring about the desired restructuring. A well thought out transitional program, which serves not just to redistribute existing income but to increase potential revenues for all enterprises is essential.

V. Role and Place of Vladivostok in South Primorie
A. Prerequisites and Factors of Development
The creation of an aquaterritorial production complex in South Primorie will lead to the strengthening of the economic interdependence and unification of its cities and outlying areas into one complex. It should also serve to deepen the territorial division of labor and the region's socioeconomic specialization. Opening Vladivostok in 1992 allowed it to move forward to expand and enhance a network of interrelationships throughout the Pacific Rim and thereby significantly strengthened its role as the Krai's center of political and economic activities.

Vladivostok is the nucleus of South Primorie, indeed Primorie (see Tables A.1 and A.2). Forty percent of the volume of industrial production of the entire Krai is found in the City. Vladivostok is also home to a major port; 60 percent of the City's revenue comes from its marine economy. This compares with a 20 percent rate for the Krai as a whole. The City's economy, like that of the Krai, is typically industrial. Thirty-two percent of the Krai's industrial revenue and 30 percent of its employment are concentrated here. In fact, figures show that economically Vladivostok is at least 10 percent more efficient than the Krai as a whole.

The Krai's biggest banks and its stock exchange are in Vladivostok, as are the large state and private firms and joint ventures. There is also a high concentration of scientific resources in the City. The majority of the Russian Academy of Science Institutes in the Far East and nine colleges as well as various major sectors of scientific research, governmental and planning organizations are centered in Vladivostok. The City's economy not only supports itself but also interacts closely and positively with economic elements throughout South Primorie.

TABLE A.1 Economic Structure of South Primorski Krai (%)

| | Vladivostok | | | |
	Total Zone	And Artyom	Nakhodka	Khasan
Industry	41.0	41.3	38.0	32.9
Agriculture	6.2	2.2	—	30.0
Transport	33.6	34.8	47.1	13.2
(including sea)	(28.5)	(28.1)	(46.9)	(13.2)
Communication	1.3	1.6	—	—
Construction	4.8	4.4	9.5	0.1
Trade, logistics, market, intermediaries	9.83	11.7	7.0	—
Communal living orgs.	1.7	1.97	0.7	2.6
Services	0.3	0.3	0.1	0.2
Banking	0.02	0.03	—	—
Other	1.35	1.7	—	0.4

Note: Fund values as of 1/1/92.

TABLE A.2 Financial-Economic Indicators of Vladivostok, 1991

	Net Profit or Loss	Level of Profitability to Funds	Level of Profitability to Costs
Industry	45.4	24.1	24.9
Agriculture	3.2	31.8	41.3
Transportation, incl. sea	15.5	9.7	17.9
Communication	1.0	13.5	17.2
Construction	7.6	37.1	20.2
Trade, logistics, market intermediaries	16.4	30.8	25.6
Communal living orgs.	-0.7	-7.9	—
Services	0.1	11.2	—
Banking	9.5	254.1	161.7
Others	2.0	25.5	15.5
Total	100.0	21.9	20.3

Note: Includes Artyom.

B. Negative and Positive Factors for Vladivostok's Economic Growth
1. The factors which are negative to the City's economic growth are as follows:

(a) the lack of available, undeveloped territory on the Muravjiny Amurski Peninsula;

(b) the fact that its peninsular geography limits transportation access to only one land outlet;

(c) the hazardous ecological situation in its marine and coastal zone and in the atmosphere; and

(d) the relatively low social, educational and economic level of the City's general population.

2. The factors which are positive to the City's economic growth are as follows:

(a) world prominence and political significance;

(b) a unique strategic, geographic, economic and political position which allows unique access to the Asia-Pacific Rim countries;

(c) a high level of educational and intellectual potential (scientific, professional, administrative, technical and cultural) within the City's managerial, governmental and academic population; and

(d) a rapidly growing commercial potential and economy which is propelling Vladivostok into consumer markets and into the Asia-Pacific market complex.

All these factors serve to reinforce Vladivostok as a primary political, business, scientific, cultural and educational center, not only in South Primorie but also in the entire RFE. It has become a point of contact and integration for Russia and the other newly independent states of the former Soviet Union with the Asia-Pacific countries. Vladivostok, as the administrative center of Primorie, already plays the role of a distributive center of international cooperation with a focus on consumer market development.

3. Specialization and Development Directions

Vladivostok's economic specialization should develop with the following activities:

(a) oceanic resources, including fisheries, offshore living and nonliving resources and merchant fleet;

(b) sea, air, port and complementary transportation services;

(c) commercial, financial, diplomatic, scientific, educational, informational, cultural and tourism facilities and services for both domestic and international markets;

(d) support, technical and logisitcal activities and services connected with the Russian Navy Fleet and other RFE military forces (administration, scientific, personnel training, social, material and technical necessities); and

(e) both scientifically generated products and consumer products, basically marine-related.

4. Principles for Structural and Functional Respecialization

Structural and functional respecialization should be based on the following principles:

(a) placing a halt on the haphazard construction of new middle and large-scale industrial enterprises;

(b) locating low-tech, ecologically less desirable and/or material- and land-consuming enterprises outside of the borders of the City;

(c) reducing military authority in local planning and control, as it relates to both land, water and air usage and to freight and passenger transportation;

(d) converting the military-industrial complex to the production of technical and consumer goods and toward the establishment of industrial cooperation with foreign firms;

(e) development and improvement of the City's infrastructure;

(f) technological reconstruction of the rest of the industries of South Primorie, introduction of efficient production methods, increased variety and quality of products and coordination of production with local market demand; and

(g) administrative and economic assistance to the service and consumer product sectors of the economy.

The City's investment and development policies should be based upon the principles of openness, trust and mutual benefit. Vladivostok needs strong business infrastructural development—banks, financial exchanges, insurance companies, project planning and scientific organizations, educational institutions, hotels, tourist and entertainment centers, as well as transport and telecommunications networks. In order for these essential components to develop, the formerly restricted military-marine sector must be converted to allow for the free and open stimulation of international business. At the same time, the City's international policies should implement its citizens' desire for true market economy growth. To do so the City should support the priorities specified in the Primorie Concept.

5. City Development during the Primorie Concept

During the period envisioned in the Primorie Concept, the City's development must proceed in the following directions:

(a) The City's own resources and any foreign investments generated should primarily be used for the reconstruction of industrial infrastructure—utilities, transportation, communications, and so on. This is the foundation for the effective functioning of the City and the Krai.

(b) New enterprises and institutions based on science applications, education, and high-tech production should be created. Operation of the existing entities should be coordinated with the overall efforts of a Vladivostok technopark.

(c) The environmental, sanitary and ecological conditions of the region must be improved.

(d) Local administrative power should be directed to the improvement of social conditions and infrastructure. The City will continue to be dependent on the Krai for the condition of the fuel/power industry, a situation that will be improved only by eliminating the region's chronic fuel shortages and focusing intensive efforts on developing and increasing the reliability of the City's electric power generation.

(e) The City's transportation system should be developed so as to fully respond to the needs of its citizens and the business sector in providing safe, convenient, prompt and dependable service.

(f) Reconstruction and implementation of the existing transportation system and utility infrastructure are essential if the City's economic and political development is to proceed; social tensions in these areas must be alleviated.

6. Territorial Planning Structure

During the period contemplated for the implementation of the Primorie Concept, it will be important to develop most rapidly the exterior perimeter of Greater Vladivostok, which, including the Amur and Ussuriysk coasts, would be the largest economic region in the RFE. As development proceeds, Vladivostok as the nucleus will undergo significant changes. One of the most important will be a strengthening of its intellectual, scientific, informational and other high-tech sectors, while its industrial production will, to a certain extent, be reduced. This industrial production capacity should be relocated from the City itself to the region's east and north perimeters. A comprehensive general plan for future development needs to be drawn to consider and establish careful standards for zoning, building, parks, consumer, cultural and recreational facilities, transportation and public utilities within the City. Geographically, City planners may decide that land currently occupied by the military (Second River, Egersheld, Uliss, etc.) suitable for redevelopment by the private sector should be designated for such redevelopment for the region's best interest. Planners will also want to consider the imposition of restrictive zoning for light and heavy industry and private housing and the establishment of business and recreational districts in selected parts of the region. For example, creating an uninterrupted recreational zone along the Amur Bay coast that would establish and maintain ecological balances may have value. The need for intensive land use within the City may also require the redevelopment and reconstruction of entire areas. Intelligent land use planning in the City would delimit residential, office and industrial areas, preserve and require the reconstruction of its unique historical district and establish a public and international district, including sophisticated commercial and financial infrastructure.

In summary, the ultimate goal of the Primorie Concept and its implementation is to encourage the development of a region in which movement from work to home to recreation is logical and rational—a region, in short, that encourages its citizens to live productively and comfortably and which has been thoughtfully developed according to plans that take maximum advantage of the natural beauty and serenity inherent in our unique geographic area.

VI. Mechanism and Funding for the Realization of the Primorie Concept
A. Alternative Mechanisms
The regulating mechanisms of the Primorie Concept will depend to a great extent on the organizational-economic form it assumes. Taking the Chinese experience as well as some of our Russian models into account, in the beginning the Greater Vladivostok project was visualized as a free economic zone, as proposed in the UNIDO report of December 1991. The FEZ model is attractive in certain respects:

1. The national status of the FEZ allows for initial state financing of necessary infrastructure which may not be viable commercially and is beyond the means of local and regional budgets.

2. A FEZ provides the mechanism for the application of concessional rates of taxation, the use of hard currency, credit, customs insurance and administrative and border control operations.

The FEZ model is, however, effective only to the extent that the federal government can meet its fiscal responsibilities with respect to it. If the federal government supports the concept only on paper, it is discredited and cannot work. The present reality is such that the feasibility and desirability of setting up a FEZ for South Primorie is very low and it is not recommended. A different form of federal government support for the Greater Vladivostok Project is in order, a program original to the region. A regional program in coordination with the financial participation of the federal government could be superior to a FEZ in the development of South Primorie.

The key to the acceptance and subsequent success of the program will be its financial viability. Potential sources of financing include (1) federal, territorial and city budgets; (2) federal, territorial and city revenue from other sources; (3) resources from state and municipal organizations; (4) public investment; (5) private capital; (6) bank and insurance company capital; (7) resources from regional funds such as trust funds, revenue and general obligation bonds; and (8) foreign capital through private companies, banks or other sources.

B. Participation of the Federal Government in the Primorie Concept

Participation of the federal government in regional development is of prime importance. It would not only provide badly needed capital but serve to elevate the status of the entire program as well. The federal government could participate in the Primorie Concept in one of several ways:

1. direct investment from the federal budget in areas that are of overall importance to the region but lack immediate commercial viability;

2. indirect financing of certain programs or projects by allowing duty-free imports, relaxation of import and export rules, accelerated depreciation, interest-free or low-interest credits, and tax exemptions and credits;

3. administrative, economic and tax protection with respect to the creation of banks, funds, consortia, companies, movement of people, goods and capital; and

4. progressive legislation in such areas as natural resources, securities, investment tax credits, and conversion of military industries, and structurally sound and internationally accepted taxation and export systems.

This last area is especially important if the economic authority of the territory in the distribution of natural and other resources is to be strengthened and the tools for regional economic development are to be improved. If regional economies are nurtured and allowed to grow and prosper as a result of progressive legislation and a certain amount of state financial participation, the result can only increase the viability of both the regional and the federal governments. All would benefit from the consequent increased generation of revenues, stronger employment levels, more rational use of natural and social resources and the ability of persons at each administrative level to strategically manage and implement those programs with which they are most closely and directly involved.

C. Responsibility in Distribution/Use of Natural Resources

The sphere of responsibility in the distribution and use of natural resources should be delineated in an agreement between the Russian Federation and the Krai. It must include:

1. a detailed inventory of exactly which natural resources are under the jurisdiction and control, respectively, of the Federation and the Krai, based upon scientific and objective criteria. There should be a detailed and express agreement of the sharing of revenues from the development of such resources between the Federation, the Krai and the City under the 1992 Natural Resources Law.

2. establishment of a definite limit on the use and exploitation of essential natural resources; and

3. provisions for leases or other concessions.

Similar agreements between the Krai, the City and the Krai's other administrative subunits will also need to be negotiated. If the Primorie Concept succeeds in winning support, a project directorate to control state resources and coordinate nonstate resources in South Primorie should be considered.

D. Future Considerations of the Primorie Concept

Future considerations of the Primorie Concept would include:

1. the definition of the duties and authority of a program directorate or economic development corporation;

2. an agreement between federal and territorial authorities on the division of natural resources and federal property;

3. an outline of the status of the regional banks to assist in the coordination of the Primorie Concept;

4. an agreed Federal/Krai/City order on the formation and use of a regional trust fund;

5. developing a strategy for creating a technical park in Vladivostok;

6. defining districts for Port Franko of Vladivostok, Posyet and Khasan; and

7. developing a legislative proposal for endorsement or agreement by the federal government regarding the free transit zone for Posyet (Zarubino)–Khunchung.

E. General Conditions for Attracting Foreign Capital

At the same time that the proposal for federal support for the Project is being developed, work should be underway on encouraging the participation of foreign and domestic financing. A foreign company considering investing in the Project would look for the following conditions:

1. reasonable guarantees of market stability and the long-term protection of investments;

2. a strong and growing economic activity in the region; and

3. predictable and positive federal, regional and local taxation and monetary policies.

The guarantee of market stability and protection of long-term investments are factors of the overall economic and legislative environment of the Russian Federation. The investment laws of Russia contain standard guarantees for foreign capital, such as the illegality of confiscation, setting provisions for adequate compensation in the case of nationalization, guaranteeing free repatriation of profits and other property in case of liquidation. At this time, however, there is no mechanism for actually implementing these laws or any real certainty of investment as would be viewed by a prudent foreign investor. Obviously, this and some cases of unsatisfactory results from foreign investment in Russia make a potential foreign investor cautious. On the Krai level, territorial authorities must be able to reassure the foreign investor that the natural resources and real estate under their control are administered in a stable and rational manner and that the investor will have secure title in them.

A strong and growing economy consists of the material base for supporting positive economic activity (infrastructure) and the functional base. According to a report prepared by the Engineering Consulting Firms Association of Japan, the following infrastructural components are essential:

1. working standards, documentation procedures and other business practices that correspond to international norms;

2. widespread, high-quality commercial services in the fields of communications, insurance, accounting and scientific and legal support;

3. developed and codified banking laws and regulations;

4. established and applied international arbitration rules;

5. internationally acceptable exchange and broker regulations;

6. a well-trained, motivated labor force; and

7. established and fair mechanisms for resolving labor disputes.

The federal government and territorial authorities must bring their legislative processes and legal standards into line with internationally recognized parameters. Formulating the strategy for developing this business infrastructure and then actually bringing it into effect will undoubtedly be one of the more complicated tasks faced by the Russian governments at every level. This task is a priority and is essential to the work of the Primorie Task Force.

In addition, a set of incentives typical of projects with intensive international capital participation should be formulated and adopted by the federal and territorial governments. They include:

1. relatively low tax rates on profits;

2. tax exemptions on profits for the first two to five years;

3. custom duty exemptions on import-export operations;

4. the right to buy land or to execute a long-term lease; and

5. a guarantee of repatriation of profits.

VII. Budget and Other Forms of Resource Mobilization

The Krai receives financial support from all levels of government under its control, including the City. These resources are, however, extremely limited. From 60 to 80 percent of the budget is spent on social programs and on program administration. The remainder is used to subsidize necessary services. Consequently, the role of local units of government in influencing production is almost nonexistent. Increasing the size of the budget by increasing taxes does not solve any material problems, for two reasons: (1) the base is so small that even a large increase in the tax rates does not generate a significant amount of revenue; and (2) such collections as a rule are designed to cover future expenses and distributions. Therefore, using such limited additional tax revenues to compensate the budget for losses due to those tax and tariff concessions given as incentives to financial structures participating in the Greater Vladivostok Project is a much more rational use of this revenue source. Subject to the approval of the Krai, every administrative-territorial unit (city, district, village) in the Krai currently makes its own taxation and tariff decisions. Accordingly, each must take into account (1) the responsibilities of various enterprises as they relate to local infrastructural problems; (2) the level and type of labor organization, qualification and safety standards in the various enterprises; (3) the level of each enterprise's production assessed in terms of the technology employed and in its environmental impacts; and (4) the compatibility of the organization to the structural-economic profile of the City or district.

The price structure of raw materials will be important in strengthening the financial base of the Krai. This type of income stays in the territory and thus creates a base for current as well as projected budgets. Serious thought ought to be given to creating a regional trust fund for the receipt of revenue generated from this source. A trust fund for economic development would be a depository in which revenues generated from bonus, royalty and rental payments from the granting of raw material rights and leases, or other payments connected with the use of territorial resources, are accumulated. This revenue could then be used to promote conservation activities, resource-saving technologies, the replication or reproduction of resource reserves and the economic regulation of resource production. Revenues generated by our natural resources will flow primarily to the north and northeast regions of the Krai, areas which are not included in the primary investment zone. This fact should help alleviate the need for cities and districts in South Primorie to continue contributing a portion of their budgets to subsidize those areas.

Because budget resources are concentrated at different administrative levels, an important task will be to organize them into more logical units. Additionally, a special strategy will have to be designed to resolve the question of means and methods of generating nonbudget capital for the Project, which would include the consideration of the proposals described in Part VI hereof. The natural resources of the Krai, especially minerals which are not likely to be exploited in the near future, could be used today at their present value based upon economic potential as security for economic investment through an investment fund or regional project bank.

The sum total of the Krai's natural resources are a significant economic asset. A small part of that asset might be profitable if sold at auction or by tenders and the capital thus generated deposited in a fund and used as investment capital. It is essential to the integrity of the fund that money generated in this way be used strictly for long-term capital expenditures and never for operating or short-term expenses. There will, of course, be strong opposition from certain sectors of the public and some elected officials concerning the sale, or even the granting of limited leases or concessions, of the natural resources of Russia. Under the threat of real economic collapse, however, it is useful to prepare innovative financing alternatives regardless of the potential controversy they may generate.

A much larger amount of our natural resources producing or capable of present production could be used as a security for attracting foreign capital in priority areas of the Primorie economy. The market value of these assets would have to be carefully assessed in order for bonds, loans or certificates to be issued against them.

Administration functions of an investment fund would be handled by officials of the fund itself or by a bank or local executive council. The guarantees and security provided by these assets would be as high as their corresponding real value. Failure to make timely payment on loans secured by these assets result in their foreclosure by the creditors in question. Actually transferring ownership of the natural resources to the creditor would take place only when the fund had used the loan proceeds in losing ventures. This situation would have to be guarded against at all costs. A special council of experts to monitor projects undertaken by the investment fund would be essential in all such programs.

Obviously this is a complicated and difficult financing mechanism. It could, however, be an effective way to convert natural resources into capital relatively quickly. It would require authorization from the legislative bodies of the federal government, the Krai and the districts—all of which greatly reduces the probability that it will ever be put into effect. Resources at the sole disposal of the Krai or the districts are, however, exceptions to this requirement, which makes this alternative viable in a limited context.

Granting concessions is one way to attract capital from abroad. Concessions will focus on localized natural resources (forests, hard minerals, furs, fishing, etc.). An analysis of the Russian experience with concessions in the 1920s shows that this form of foreign investment contains high industrial-economic potential, yields socially oriented development and is preferable to hard currency loans. As such, designing a concessional strategy should be a priority task as the program for capitalizing the Greater Vladivostok Project begins to be implemented. At the same time, the possibility of creating an investment fund or bank for coordinating the Project with mixed capital (federal, regional, local and/or private) deserves special attention.

VIII. Conclusion

The mechanism and means of realizing the Greater Vladivostok Project must remain flexible and adaptable to ever evolving political and economic environments. Under the best of circumstances the federal government will support the Project, foreign firms and agencies including USAID will conduct positive preinvestment studies for regional projects, and federal, regional and local authorities will agree upon a single course of action for reform, the creation of free-market conditions and coordination of activities, and the Greater Vladivostok Project will move forward in a logical and rational manner.

However, whether or not Vladivostok and the region receive such domestic or foreign funding, the Project will proceed. It will simply require more Russian will and determination, but the people and resources are there to support it fully.

Notes

1. Messrs. Krueger and Polott represented the City of Vladivostok and the Primorski Krai in their efforts to obtain international technical assistance for the implementation of the Primorie Concept.

2. Anders Aslund, "Russia's Success Story," *Foreign Affairs* 73 (Sept./Oct. 1994), 58.

3. Leading experts and institutions contributed their efforts to the Primorie Concept. The Land Use Policy Committee was chaired by Professor P. Y. Baklanov, Director of the Pacific Institute of Geography, Far Eastern Branch of the Academy of Sciences. The Financial Resources Policy Development Committee was chaired by V. V. Savaley, Director of the Pacific Center of Economic Development and Cooperation of the Institute for Economic Studies Far Eastern Branch of the Academy of Sciences. The Energy Supply Policy Development Committee was chaired by L. D. Filatov and V. S. Turetsky of the Far Eastern Energy Systems Planning Institute. The Social Support Policy Development Committee was chaired by S. E. Yachin, Department of Philosophy, Far Eastern State Technical University. The Automation and Information Policy Development Committee was headed by S. F. Mitrofanov, Physio-Mathematical Sciences of the Far Eastern Technological Institute. The Island Territories Development Committee was headed by V. I. Prelovsky, Biological Sciences. The Transportation and Industry Policy Development Committee was chaired by J. N. Semenikhin, President of the Far Eastern Marine Research Design and Technology Institute, Far Eastern Scientific-Research Institute of Sea Fleet (DNIMFA). The City Planning and Construction Policy Development Committee was chaired by V. V. Anikeev and E. M. Melnikov of the Primorski Citizens Planning Project. The Ecological Policy Development Commit-

tee was chaired by V. V. Preobrazhenski, Pacific Institute of Geography, Far Eastern Branch of the Academy of Sciences.

4. Richard M. Nixon, *Beyond Peace* (New York: Random House, 1994), pp. 60–61.

5. The Primorie Concept was prepared and presented prior to the armed confrontation in the streets of Moscow in October 1993, which led to the dissolution of local Soviets, and prior to the ratification of the new Russian Constitution. Consequently, this work does not address the shifts in power and changes in intergovernmental dynamics resulting from these developments.

Appendix 3: Selected Energy and Mineral Cooperative Projects

James P. Dorian

Project and Partners	Description and Projected Investment (US$)
Khabarovsk and Komsomolsk-na-Amure refineries, Russia C. Itoh (Japan); Russian government/private enterprise	Russian-Japanese cooperation includes reconstruction and expansion of the two refineries. C. Itoh will double the capacity of the Komsomolsk refinery to 120,000 b/d and equip the plant with modern equipment. The general cost of the work will be $300–400 million. Reconstruction of the Khabarovsk refinery began in 1991 and will continue for 4 or 5 years. It will be completely modernized at a cost of about $100 million.
Gas pipelines from Yakutia to Japan Tokyo Boeki (Japan); Far East Energy (US); Russian government	Agreement to study a proposal to lay two pipelines from the Yakut oil and gas fields to Hokkaido and Kyushu. The companies have also won rights to take part in a natural gas exploitation project in Yakut on a priority basis. All the pipelines are expected to be completed by the second half of 1996. Total investment, $7.5–11.4 billion.
Port of Nakhodka Sumitomo (Japan); Port of Nakhodka (Russia); Oblkemerovougal (Russia)	Proposed joint venture to study expansion of coal export capacity.
Yakutia natural gas, Russia Korea Petroleum Development Corp., Korea Gas, Daewoo, Yukong (all S. Korean); Russian consortium	Korean and Russian consortia for developing natural gas in Yakutsk signed an agreement on a preliminary feasibility study in December 1992.

(continues)

Project and Partners	Description and Projected Investment (US$)
Gazprom, Russia Nippon Steel, Sumitomo Metal Industries, NKK, Kawasaki Steel (all Japanese companies)	Gazprom reached a basic agreement with four Japanese steelmakers and nine trading companies to purchase $400 million of natural gas steel pipes and related construction machinery on deferred basis. This agreement is part of a $700 million overall deal.
Oil Terminal, Nakhodka C. Itoh (Japan); Nakhodka Russia Port Authorities; Urengoy Gas-Condensate Producer (Russia)	Plans are to build a terminal to store gas condensate on way to Japan from Urengoy.
Petrochemical plant, Russia Nichiman (Japan); Toblosh Petrochemical Plant (Russia)	Nichiman will build a production control system for a plant in Western Siberia. Total investment, $28.5 million.
Urgal coal mine, Russia Hyundai Resources Development (S. Korea); Daewoo (S. Korea); Russian government/private enterprise	Urgal coal mine has reserves of 150 million tons. Hyundai and Daewoo want to expand the project to produce 2–3 million tons of coal yearly. Total investment, $100–200 million.
Prouvou Urmi metal mine, Khabarovsk, Russia Hyundai Resources Development, Lucky-Goldstar, Sam Sung, Daewoo (all S. Korea); Russian government/private enterprise	Prouvou Urmi metal mine is rich in tin, copper, and tungsten and covers a 5,000 km^2 with reserves of 35 million tons. South Korean companies are to form a consortium to set up a 50:50 joint venture with their Russian counterparts. Yearly production will reach 1 million tons by 1993. Total investment, $100–200 million.
Mirnyi diamond deposit, Sakha Republic Japan-Soviet Trade Association (Japan); Sakha Republic	Russian and Japanese specialists will cooperate in developing the Mirnyi diamond deposit in Sakha. 70% of the diamonds mined will be sold on the Japanese market and 30% in Russia. In addition to diamond mining, the protocol envisages feasibility studies for the joint development of some rare metal deposits.
Pravourminskoe tin deposit, Russia Hyundai Business Group (51%), Sam Sung Group, Daewoo Group, Samwhan, Dongbu Industrial (all S. Korea); Russian government/private enterprise	Five South Korean firms will form a consortium to develop the tin deposit. In the consortium Hyundai Business Group will have 51% and the other partners will share the rest. The mining joint venture will be a 50:50 project with a Russian partner.

Project and Partners	Description and Projected Investment (US$)
Tyumen, Russia Kogalymnneftegas (Russia); Mitsui (Japan)	Mitsui selling $700 million worth of oil pumps, steel tubes, drilling and, measuring equipment.
Yantai-Mitsubishi Cement Company, Russia Yantai City Building Materials (Japan); Mitsubishi (Japan)	Advanced technology developed by Mitsubishi will be used to produce high grade cement. Japanese investment amounts to 70% of the total funds in the project, $16 million. The contract is valid for 33 years.
Natural gas project, Sakha Republic Daewoo; Lucky-Goldstar Intl.; Korean Petroleum Development Corp.; Korea Gas; Sam Sung; Yokong; Pohang Iron and Steel (all S. Korean companies)	Consortium of South Korean companies hopes to win proposed $15 billion natural gas development project in Sakha Republic. A feasibility study for the project could take 2–3 years and production is not likely until the 21st century.
Sakha-Japan diamond joint venture Arda (Japan); Toimada Diamond Company (Sakha Republic diamond producer)	Sakha-Japan Diamond joint venture has begun operations. It expects to ship 200,000 carats of polished diamonds to Japan in 1993 and aims for an eventual 300,000 carats, or 10% of the Japanese market. Arda has invested Y1 billion ($8.06 million) to build 3 factories in Sakha and plans to build 12 more, each employing 200 workers. FR Corp. (Tokyo) has exclusive right to import the diamonds and will train Sakha workers at its cutting center.
Oil and gas development, Sakhalin Island Marathon Oil (US); McDermott International (US); Mitsui (Japan); Royal Dutch/Shell (Holland); Mitsubishi (Japan)	After six years of negotiations, the Russia–MMMSM consortium is set to develop reserves in the Piltun-Astokhskoye and Lunskoye fields. The areas combined are estimated to hold 750 million gallons of oil and 14 trillion cubic feet of gas. Production is slated to commence by the year 2000. Total investment, $10 billion.
Sakhalin offshore oil development China Offshore Oil Logging; Russian Okha Offshore Logging	Joint venture formed in 1992 to provide services for Western and Russian oil companies.
Gas pipeline, Sakhalin to Hokkaido Russian government and private consortium; Sakhalin Oil Development Corp. and other private interests	In 1970 the Soviets proposed constructing a one-meter diameter gas pipeline tying Sakhalin and Hokkaido. The line would run Yakutsk-Khabarovsk-Sakhalin-Hokkaido and provide Japan an alternative to large volumes of LNG imported by tanker.

(continues)

Project and Partners	Description and Projected Investment (US$)
Oil fields, Siberia Chinese Petroleum Corp. (Taiwan); Yuganskneftegaz Production Assoc. (Russia)	CPC is considering developing oil resources in Russia by forming a joint venture there.
Petrochemical plant, Tianjin, China Tianjin Petrochemical (China); Mitsui Petrochemical (Japan)	The project, one of the largest Sino-foreign petrochemical joint projects since the 1950s in China, is designed to produce 250,000 tons of pure terephthalic acid (PTA) annually after it is completed in 1995. The project is a major part of the Tianjin 200,000-ton polyester project. Investment in the PTA project accounts for about one-fifth of total investment in the 200,000-ton polyester project. Total investment, $258.6 million.
Nuclear power plant, Liaoning Russian Atomic Energy Ministry; Chinese govt.	Russia will design and help China build a 1,000-MW nuclear power station and a uranium enrichment plant.
Zhuhai Refinery, Guangdong Province, China Yukong (S. Korea); Chinese govt.	China has proposed a 50:50 joint venture refinery to process 150,000–200,000 barrels of crude a day with Yukong, a subsidiary of the Sunkyong Group. The Zhuhai Special Economic Zone is not far from oil fields in the South China Sea. Total investment, $200 million.
Turkmenistan pipeline to Europe Marubeni, Mitsubishi (Japan)	Feasibility study under way for a 5,200-km gas pipeline to Europe. Total investment, $7 billion.
Turkmenistan pipeline to Tientsin, China Turkmenistan government; All-Russian Construction Corp. for Oil and Gas Projects; Chinese govt.	Study under way for a 5,500-km gas pipeline from Turkmenistan to Tientsin, where gas liquefaction plant and terminal would enable transport to Japan. Pipeline would travel via Uzbekistan, Kazakhstan, and the Mongolian border. Pipeline investment, $9.8 billion; plant and terminal investment, $6.3 billion.
Shanghai tinplate factory, China Pohang Iron and Steel (S. Korea)	POSCO has applied to establish a joint-venture factory for tin plate in Shanghai. Ground for the steel mill will be broken in April for full operation from 1996, starting at 8,500 tons of tin plate and reaching 120,000 tons a year five years after. Total investment, $36 million.
Heilongjiang Province, China Zeya Hydropower Station (Russia); Chinese govt.	Russia will provide up to 200 million kw-hours of electricity to Heilongjiang Province after 88 km of power transmission lines are built.

Project and Partners	Description and Projected Investment (US$)
Oil fields, Kazakhstan and Uzbekistan Chinese government; Japanese private sector	China would provide the technology and manpower for the endeavor, and Japan would provide the necessary funds. The oil could be made available for consumption in China, while a commensurate amount taken from China's northeastern oil fields could be exported to Japan.
Galuhe gold mine, China Russian "Gold Company"; Heilongjiang Gold Company (China)	Russian and Chinese companies agreed on joint investment to develop the deep alluvial Galuhe gold mine in Huma County, Heilongjiang Province.
Hungnam oil fields, North Korea N. Korea presently searching for Western investors, including Japan and Britain	Since North Korea lacks its own oil field development technology, it has proposed to oil development companies in Western countries, including Japan and Britain, to jointly develop its oil fields.
Tumen River Basin development UNDP; North Korean, South Korean, Chinese, Mongolian, and Russian governments	Long-term plan for tranforming the Tumen River delta into an economic and industrial hub. A special economic zone would be created on the river to facilitate growth. Development interests vary by participating country, ranging from enhancing trade prospects to improving infrastructure to facilitating enery and mineral development. Total investment, $30 billion over 15–20 years.
Niigata natural gas storage port, Japan Ministry of Transport (Japan)	Japan is drafting plans to build a port in Niigata to promote the import of natural gas from the RFE in the next century. The plan calls for building Japan's largest liquified natural gas storage facilities at the site. The new energy port will serve as a key link between Japan and Russia, China and the two Koreas. Total investment, $8 billion over 10 years.

Sources: Created by James Dorian from personal files and the following publications: *Interflo: A Soviet Trade News Monitor*, various issues, Maplewood, N.J., September 1992–March 1993; FBIS, "Daily Report: East Asia," and "Daily Report: China," various issues, January–April 1993; Center for the Soviet Union in the Pacific and Asian Region, "SUPAR Report," nos. 12 and 13, University of Hawaii, Honolulu, January and July 1992; Center for Russia in Asia, "CeRA Report," no. 14, University of Hawaii, Honolulu, January 1993.

About the Book and Editor

Russia, and especially the Russian Far East, has reached a political and economic crossroads as the trans-Pacific economic axis—so prominent in the Cold-War era—gradually expands to include broader intra-Asian relationships. Multilateral economic interaction across ideological and political boundaries is creating a "soft" regionalism in Northeast Asia that offers the Russian Far East unprecedented scope for collaboration with its neighbors.

Indeed, the contributors—leading scholars and experts from private industry—argue that the future of the Russian Far East will be molded by its economic and political relations with the rest of Northeast Asia. Long known to be a rich storehouse of natural resources, the Russian Far East now faces the challenge of utilizing those resources in a manner that is sustainable and that is empowering to its people. Exploring the opportunities for and obstacles to multilateral ties within the region, the contributors analyze the prospects for economic cooperation in labor supply, minerals and energy resources, transportation, and fisheries.

Mark J. Valencia is a senior fellow in the Program on International Economics and Politics at the East-West Center.

Index